50 WALKS IN
Devon

50 Walks in Devon

Published by AA Publishing (a trading name of AA Media Limited, whose registered office is Grove House, Lutyens Close, Lychpit, Basingstoke, Hampshire RG24 8AG; registered number 06112600)

© AA Media Limited 2024
Fourth edition
First published 2001

Mapping in this book is derived from the following products:
OS Landranger 180 (walks 46–50)
OS Landranger 181 (walks 7–10, 12–13)
OS Landranger 190 (walks 43–45)
OS Landranger 191 (walks 11, 17–20, 34–39, 42)
OS Landranger 192 (walks 1–6, 14–16)
OS Landranger 201 (walks 31–32, 40, 41)
OS Landranger 202 (walks 21–30, 33)
OS Explorer 20 (walks 23, 24)
OS Explorer 28 (walks 38, 39)
OS Explorer 112 (walks 41)

© Crown copyright and database rights 2024 Ordnance Survey. 100021153.

Maps contain data available from openstreetmap.org © under the Open Database License found at opendatacommons.org

ISBN: 978-0-7495-8371-2
ISBN: 978-0-7495-8381-1 (SS)

A CIP catalogue record for this book is available from the British Library.

AA Media would like to thank the following contributors in the preparation of this guide:
Clare Ashton, Tracey Freestone, Lauren Havelock, Nicky Hillenbrand, Lin Hutton, Graham Jones, Ian Little, Richard Marchi, Nigel Phillips, Victoria Samways.

Cover design by
berkshire design company.

Printed and bound in the UK by
Oriental Press, Dubai.

A05851

We would like to thank the following photographers, companies and picture libraries for their assistance in the preparation of this book. Abbreviations for the picture credits are as follows:
Alamy = Alamy Stock Photo
Trade Cover, Shaun Mccaughan - Coastal/Alamy
Special Cover, Douglas Lander/Alamy
Back Cover Advert, SolStock/istockphoto; 9, Sebastian Wasek/Alamy; 12/13, travellinglight/Alamy; 39, Alex Hinds/Alamy; 64/65, tony mills/Alamy; 75, Stuart Black/Alamy; 94/95, Alan Gardiner/Alamy; 165, Tommy (Louth)/Alamy; 176, SolStock/istockphoto;

The contents of this book are believed correct at the time of printing. Nevertheless, the publishers cannot be held responsible for any errors or omissions or for changes in the details given in this book or for the consequences of any reliance on the information it provides. This does not affect your statutory rights. We have tried to ensure accuracy in this book, but things do change and we would be grateful if readers would advise us of any inaccuracies they may encounter by emailing walks@aamediagroup.co.uk

We have done our best to make sure that these walks are safe and achievable by walkers with a basic level of fitness. However, we can accept no responsibility for any loss or injury incurred while following the walks. Advice on walking safely can be found on pages 10–11.

Some of the walks may appear in other AA books and publications.

Discover and book AA-rated places to stay at www.RatedTrips.com.

AA

50 WALKS IN
Devon

CONTENTS

How to use this book	6
Exploring the area	8
Walking in safety	10

The walks

WALK		GRADIENT	DISTANCE	PAGE
①	The River Coly	▲	5 miles (8km)	14
②	Cliffs of East Devon	▲▲	7.75 miles (12.5km)	17
③	Sidmouth	Negligible	5 miles (8km)	20
④	River Otter	▲	5.5 miles (8.9km)	23
⑤	Ottery St Mary	▲	3.5 miles (5.7km)	26
⑥	Broadhembury	▲▲	6.25 miles (10.1km)	29
⑦	Culmstock	▲▲	9.25 miles (14.9km)	33
⑧	Grand Western Canal	Negligible	6 miles (9.7km)	36
⑨	Knightshayes	▲	2 miles (3.2km)	40
⑩	Withleigh	▲▲	3.75 miles (6km)	43
⑪	Upton Hellions	▲▲	6.25 miles (10.1km)	46
⑫	Bampton	▲▲	5.5 miles (8.8km)	49
⑬	Molland Common	▲▲▲	3 miles (4.8km)	52
⑭	Killerton Park	▲	4.5 miles (7.2km)	55
⑮	Brampford Speke	Negligible	4 miles (6.4km)	58
⑯	Exeter to Topsham	Negligible	5.7 miles (9.1km)	61
⑰	Steps Bridge	▲▲▲	5.5 miles (8.8km)	66
⑱	Trenchford	Negligible	3.75 miles (6km)	69
⑲	Lustleigh Cleave	▲▲▲	5.5 miles (8.8km)	72
⑳	The Bovey Valley	▲	4.25 miles (6.8km)	76
㉑	Dartington Hall	▲	6.5 miles (10.4km)	79
㉒	The Dart Valley Trail	▲	6 miles (9.7km)	82

WALK		GRADIENT	DISTANCE	PAGE
23	Coleton Fishacre	▲▲▲	5.5 miles (8.8km)	85
24	Dartmouth Castle	▲▲	4 miles (6.4km)	88
25	Start Point	▲▲	6 miles (9.7km)	91
26	Prawle Point	▲▲▲	4.25 miles (6.8km)	96
27	East Portlemouth	▲▲	4.5 miles (7.2km)	99
28	Kingsbridge	▲▲	3 miles (4.8km)	102
29	Bigbury-on-Sea	▲▲	4 miles (6.4km)	105
30	Kingston	▲▲▲	6 miles (9.7km)	108
31	Wembury Beach	▲▲	4 miles (6.4km)	111
32	Tamar and Tavy	▲▲	3.5 miles (5.7km)	114
33	Cadover Bridge	▲▲▲	3.75 miles (6km)	117
34	Princetown	▲	7.5 miles (12.1km)	120
35	Postbridge	▲	4.5 miles (7.2km)	123
36	Grimspound	▲▲	6.5 miles (10.4km)	126
37	The Teign Gorge	Negligible	4 miles (6.4km)	130
38	Belstone Cleave	▲▲▲	4 miles (6.4km)	133
39	Meldon Reservoir	▲▲	6 miles (9.8km)	136
40	Brent Tor	▲▲	5 miles (8km)	140
41	Lifton to Stowford	▲	8 miles (12.9km)	143
42	Hatherleigh	▲	8.5 miles (13.7km)	146
43	Morwenstow	▲▲▲	6 miles (9.7km)	149
44	Hartland Point	▲▲▲	10 miles (16.1km)	152
45	Clovelly	▲▲▲	6 miles (9.7km)	156
46	Northam Burrows	Negligible	3.25 miles (5.3km)	159
47	North Devon Coast	▲▲▲	8 miles (12.9km)	162
48	Hele Bay and Comyn	▲▲	3.5 miles (5.7km)	166
49	Heddon Valley	▲▲▲	6 miles (9.7km)	169
50	Watersmeet	▲	4 miles (6.4km)	173

HOW TO USE THIS BOOK

Each walk starts with an information panel giving all the information you will need about the walk at a glance, including its relative difficulty, distance and total amount of ascent. Difficulty levels and gradients are as follows:

Difficulty of walk	**Gradient**
🟢 Easy	▲ Some slopes
🟠 Intermediate	▲▲ Some steep slopes
🔴 Hard	▲▲▲ Several very steep slopes

Maps
Every walk has its own route map. We also suggest a relevant Ordnance Survey map to take with you, allowing you to view the area in more detail. The time suggested is the minimum for reasonably fit walkers and doesn't allow for stops.

Route map legend

--→--	Walk route	▨	Built-up area
❶	Route waypoint	▨	Woodland area
- - - -	Adjoining path	🚻	Toilet
●	Place of interest	🅿	Car park
⌂	Steep section	⌸	Picnic area
☼	Viewpoint	)(	Bridge
⸺	Embankment		

Start points
The start of each walk is given as a six-figure grid reference prefixed by two letters referring to a 100km square of the National Grid. More information on grid references can be found on most OS Walker's Maps.

Dogs
We have tried to give dog owners useful advice about how dog friendly each walk is. Please respect other countryside users. Keep your dog under control, especially around livestock, and obey local by-laws and other dog control notices.

Car parking

Many of the car parks suggested are public, but occasionally you may have to park on the roadside or in a lay-by. Please be considerate about where you leave your car, ensuring that you are not on private property or access roads, and that gates are not blocked and other vehicles can pass safely.

Walks locator map

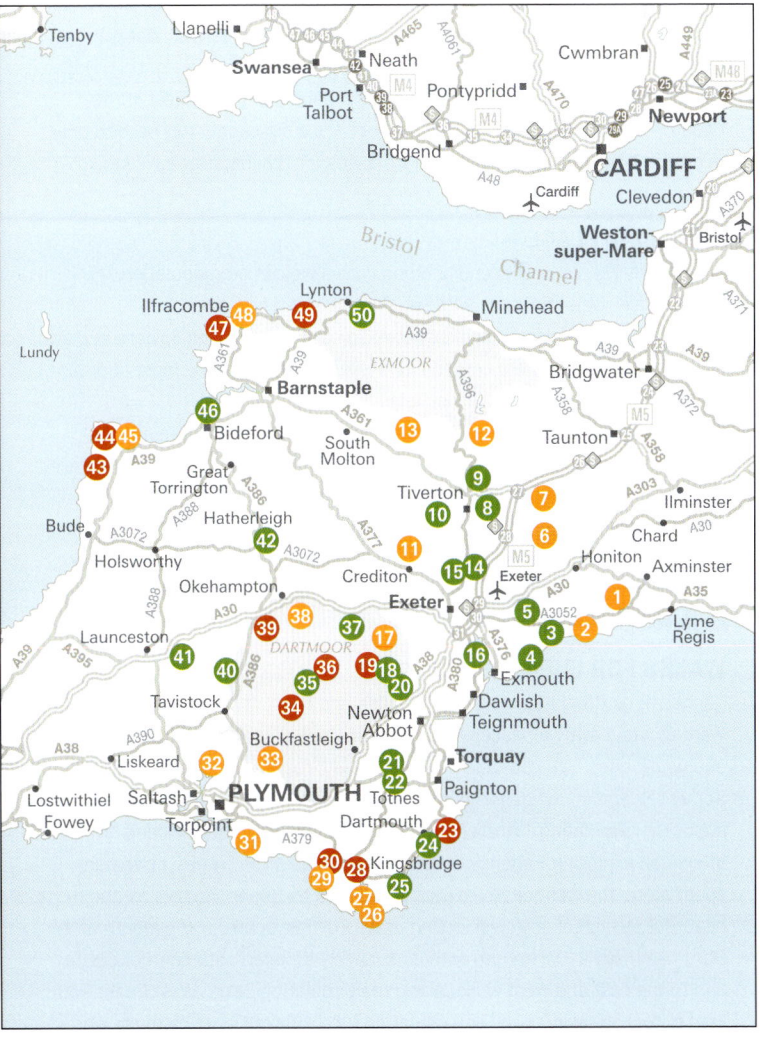

EXPLORING THE AREA

Devon's got it all. Surely no other county in the country has such a variety of landscapes waiting to be explored, from the comfortable, rolling, red-earth farmland of east Devon, and the deeply wooded river valleys and granite-studded wilds of Dartmoor, to the rocky coast and safe sandy coves of the South Hams. Then there's the huge expanse of relatively unexplored undulating countryside north of Dartmoor, the land of the Taw and Torridge rivers, culminating in the unforgiving cliffs – some of the highest in the country – overlooking the Bristol Channel. It's a big county too, second only in size to North Yorkshire, so there's masses for the inquisitive walker to investigate.

A SPECIAL PLACE

This satisfying range of scenery, along with a welcoming population, picturesque cob-and-thatch villages, ancient stone-built churches, characterful pubs, deeply banked lanes smothered with wild flowers and an equable maritime climate combine to make Devon one of the most popular holiday destinations in the British Isles.

'Devon' is thought to derive from a Celtic tribal name, meaning 'the people of the land', and it is certainly true that those born in Devonshire are extremely proud of their roots. Those who move away tend to gravitate back to their birthplace sooner rather than later. Devon has a way of getting under the skin, and the range of walks described in this book, designed to suit every requirement from an easy farmland stroll to a tough coastal tramp, aim to show you just what a special county it is.

WALKS FOR EVERYONE

There are gentle ambles along riversides and canal tow paths for those who want to while away a peaceful summer afternoon among the dragonflies and water lilies. You can take a long, yet easy, route across the border into Somerset, and investigate the lovely Blackdown Hills of east Devon, learning about the fascinating 19th-century whetstone industry there. Spend an afternoon exploring Regency Sidmouth, or Elizabethan Totnes, or wander south along the tranquil River Dart (described by Queen Victoria as 'the most beautiful stretch of any river in England'). Further south, at the mouth of the Dart, lies historic Dartmouth with its superbly situated 15th-century castle, and to the east and west walks along the undulating South West Coast Path lead to tucked-away coves and estuaries rarely visited even by those who live in the county.

And then there's Dartmoor, southern England's greatest wilderness, rising to 2,037ft (621m) and home to all manner of spine-chilling legends, not to mention holding the best evidence of Bronze Age habitation in Europe.

But even the highest parts of Dartmoor are relatively accessible, providing you keep an eye on the weather and don't walk if there is any danger of mist. There are routes here that will introduce you to the very heart of the moor and give you an insight into its social and industrial history. By contrast there are explorations of the beautiful rocky, wooded stream-filled valleys that fringe the moor, of chocolate-box villages such as Lustleigh, and of mysterious granite formations such as the Dewerstone with its infamous links to the Devil. Turning north you can follow part of the Tarka Trail through the little-visited heartland north of the moor, and then try some tough routes along the cliffs of the north Devon coast, culminating in the hardest walk in the book, which takes in rugged Hartland Point with its glorious views across the water to Lundy Island.

PUBLIC TRANSPORT

Regular public transport isn't one of the county's strongpoints, and in the more remote areas you can wait for a bus for a couple of days! None of the walks described therefore relies upon public transport, and the linear ones are 'there-and-back' walks, though a straightforward alternative return route has been described where possible. For information on train, coach and bus travel both to and within Devon visit Traveline at www.traveline.info

Walk 44

WALKING IN SAFETY

All these walks are suitable for any reasonably fit person, but less experienced walkers should try the easier walks first. Route-finding is usually straightforward, but you will find that an Ordnance Survey walking map is a useful addition to the route maps and descriptions; recommendations can be found in the information panels.

Risks

Although each walk here has been researched with a view to minimising the risks to the walkers who follow its route, no walk in the countryside can be considered to be completely free from risk. Walking in the outdoors will always require a degree of common sense and judgement to ensure that it is as safe as possible.

- Be particularly careful on cliff paths and in upland terrain, where the consequences of a slip can be very serious.
- Remember to check tidal conditions before walking on the seashore.
- Some sections of route are by, or cross, busy roads. Take care, and remember that traffic is a danger even on minor country lanes.
- Be careful around farmyard machinery and livestock, especially if you have children with you.
- Be aware of the consequences of changes in the weather, and check the forecast before you set out. Carry spare clothing and a torch if you are walking in the winter months. Remember that the weather can change very quickly at any time of the year, and in moorland and heathland areas, mist and fog can make route-finding much harder. Don't set out in these conditions unless you are confident of your navigation skills in poor visibility.
- In summer remember to take account of the heat and sun; wear a hat and carry water.
- On walks away from centres of population you should carry a whistle and survival bag. If you do have an accident that means you require help from the emergency services, make a note of your position as accurately as possible and dial 999.

Countryside Code
Respect other people:

- Consider the local community and other people enjoying the outdoors.
- Co-operate with people at work in the countryside. For example, keep out of the way when farm animals are being gathered or moved, and follow directions from the farmer.

- Don't block gateways, driveways or other paths with your vehicle.
- Leave gates and property as you find them, and follow paths unless wider access is available, such as on open country or registered common land (known as 'open access land').
- Leave machinery and farm animals alone – don't interfere with animals, even if you think they're in distress. Try to alert the farmer instead.
- Use gates, stiles or gaps in field boundaries if you can – climbing over walls, hedges and fences can damage them and increase the risk of farm animals escaping.
- Our heritage matters to all of us – be careful not to disturb ruins and historic sites.

Protect the natural environment:
- Take your litter home. Litter and leftover food don't just spoil the beauty of the countryside; they can be dangerous to wildlife and farm animals. Dropping litter and dumping rubbish are criminal offences.
- Leave no trace of your visit, and take special care not to damage, destroy or remove features such as rocks, plants and trees.
- Keep dogs under effective control, making sure they are not a danger or nuisance to farm animals, horses, wildlife or other people.
- If cattle or horses chase you and your dog, it is safer to let your dog off the lead – don't risk getting hurt by trying to protect it. Your dog will be much safer if you let it run away from a farm animal in these circumstances, and so will you.
- Everyone knows how unpleasant dog mess is and it can cause infections, so always clean up after your dog and get rid of the mess responsibly – bag it and bin it.
- Fires can be as devastating to wildlife and habitats as they are to people and property – so be careful with naked flames and cigarettes at any time of the year.

Enjoy the outdoors:
- Plan ahead and be prepared for natural hazards, changes in weather and other events.
- Wild animals, farm animals and horses can behave unpredictably if you get too close, especially if they're with their young – so give them plenty of space.
- Follow advice and local signs.

For more information visit www.gov.uk/government/publications/the-countryside-code

THE RIVER COLY AND THE UMBORNE BROOK

DISTANCE/TIME	5 miles (8km) / 2hrs 30min
ASCENT/GRADIENT	197ft (60m) / ▲
PATHS	Fields and lanes, some parts boggy after wet weather, several stiles
LANDSCAPE	Level river meadows and rolling farmland
SUGGESTED MAP	OS Explorer 116 Lyme Regis & Bridport
START/FINISH	Grid reference: SY246940
DOG FRIENDLINESS	Keep on lead in fields with livestock
PARKING	Car park in centre of Colyton (Dolphin Street)
PUBLIC TOILETS	At car park

In some ways the pretty east Devon town of Colyton is a rather misleading place. Situated in rolling countryside on the banks of the River Coly, the town has more than once won 'the prettiest village in Devonshire' accolade. The narrow, winding streets, attractive cottages, with hanging baskets and colourful gardens, give no clues as to why Colyton was once dubbed 'most rebellious town in Devon'. For this we must go back to the 1600s. The town supported Parliament in the Civil War in 1643, and was the scene of many skirmishes against Royalists based at Axminster. It also played a part in the Monmouth Rebellion of 1685, when more than 100 Colyton men – more than anywhere else in Devon – joined the Duke of Monmouth's army. Monmouth landed at Lyme Regis with 80 followers and managed to raise an army of 3,000, but was defeated by James II's army at Sedgemoor near Bridgwater in Somerset. In the trials that followed, the 'Bloody Assizes', 17 Colyton men were hanged, and 18 were transported to the West Indies. Only two of the latter made it back to Devon.

But Colyton's history hasn't always been so colourful. There is evidence of prehistoric occupation – a Pleistocene flint axe as well as Bronze and Iron Age remains have been found locally. The Romans were here from around AD 70, but Colyton is essentially a Saxon town. Egbert, King of Wessex, held a parliament here in AD 827 and a fine restored 9th-century cross can be seen in the church. The town developed into one of Devon's major commercial centres, its wealth based on weaving cloth, silk and serge, and lacemaking. Many of the farms you'll pass on this walk have the suffix hayne, meaning 'enclosure'.

The parish church is prominent in the view of Colyton towards the end of the walk and its most unusual feature is the distinctive and rare octagonal lantern, set on the square Norman tower. This is thought to have been inspired by similar towers seen in Flanders by the town's wool merchants. There is a merchant's mark (representing a 'stapler' or wool merchant) on the floor slate marking the grave of Hugh Buckland in the chancel.

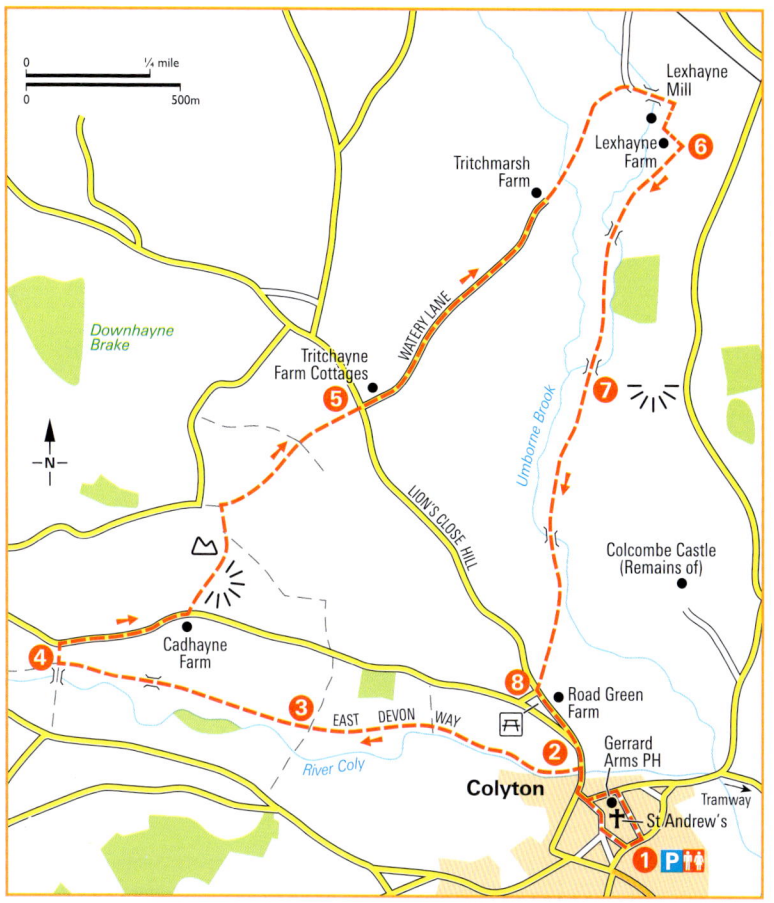

1. From the car park turn right downhill, then left into Lower Church Street. Turn left at the Gerrard Arms into St Andrews Square, then right into Vicarage Street. Go right, towards the river, and cross the bridge.

2. Turn left through a kissing gate and along the river bank on the East Devon Way (EDW). Follow the path through two kissing gates. Ignore the next footpath sign right, but keep ahead over a footbridge and through a small gate.

3. Keep ahead to a footpath junction at the field end; go through the kissing gate ahead on to a concrete riverside path. Go through a kissing gate and cross the field, aiming for a kissing gate/footbridge under three big oaks. Keep ahead to cross another footbridge to reach a footpath junction by a bridge over the river.

4. Turn right (leaving EDW), to reach a gate on to a lane and turn right. Opposite Cadhayne Farm turn left through a gate. Walk steadily up the left field edge, through the gate at the top and straight on. This green lane soon bears sharp left; bear right along a narrow, muddy track, ending at a tarmac road.

5. Cross over, pass Tritchayne Farm Cottages and walk downhill along Watery Lane. Just after Tritchmarsh Farm follow the footpath sign right across a stream. Go sharp left to a gate and keep along the left field edge. Take the small gate/bridge/gate and cross the paddock and the Umborne Brook via a stile and concrete walkway to Lexhayne Mill. The path runs between the house and yard to a kissing gate; cross the stile in the wire fence (the main line railway is ahead). Cross over the next stile, then head diagonally right for the drive to Lexhayne Farm. Cross a stile, and keep ahead through a hedge gap.

6. Cross the field diagonally right to a bridge in the bottom corner. Marshy ground leads to a big footbridge over the brook. Turn left; cross a stile, then follow the brook to another footbridge.

7. Aim for a stile in the fence ahead right. Bear diagonally left and cross the brook on a footbridge. Follow the fenced path left; bear right over a stile into a field. Turn left along the hedge; pass through a gate, and keep ahead to a stile. Bear diagonally right up a huge field, aiming to the right of Road Green Farm to find a stile onto a lane.

8. Turn left; pass the picnic area/ playground at Road Green, then over the bridge. Take the first left (Vicarage Street) and go straight on to pass the church (left), through the town centre and down Silver Street to the car park.

Where to eat and drink
The Gerrard Arms at the start of the walk is a free house with an attractive garden, a skittle alley and bar food. Liddon's Dairy is an excellent place for a cream tea, with outside seating and animals including llamas. There is the Tramstop Café at Colyton Station and several other pubs and cafés in the village.

What to see
Take a trip in an open-top tramcar beside the River Axe on the Seaton Tramway, which runs for 3 miles (4.8km) from Colyton to Seaton via Colyford. You should see a wide range of birds, including grey herons, kingfishers, oystercatchers, curlews and egrets. More than 50 different species have been spotted from the tram in one day. The tram line, the first section of which opened in 1970, utilises part of the old Seaton branch railway, which closed in 1966. The extension to Colyton opened in 1980. Trams depart every 20 minutes (mid-March to the end of October; and at other selected times outside this period).

While you're there
It's worth going to have a look at Blackberry Camp Iron Age hill fort, an English Heritage site signposted from the A3052 Colyton to Sidford road. Probably occupied by a cattle farming community between the 1st and 2nd centuries AD, this D-shaped enclosure is a peaceful spot for a picnic.

THE CLIFFS OF EAST DEVON

DISTANCE/TIME	7.75 miles (12.5km) / 3hrs 30min
ASCENT/GRADIENT	492ft (150m) / ▲▲
PATHS	Coast path (one steep ascent), country lanes, several stiles
LANDSCAPE	Exposed cliffs, farmland and woodland
SUGGESTED MAP	OS Explorer 115 Exmouth & Sidmouth
START/FINISH	Grid reference: SY166889
DOG FRIENDLINESS	Keep on lead around livestock and near unfenced cliffs
PARKING	Grammar Lane car park, Weston
PUBLIC TOILETS	Behind Branscombe village hall, also in car park at Branscombe Mouth

Picturesque Branscombe, where three deep, wooded valleys converge, is one of the most secluded villages in this unspoiled corner within the East Devon National Landscapes (AONB). Pretty flower-decked cottages sit either side of a long narrow lane that runs gradually down the valley from Street, giving rise to the claim that Branscombe is one of the longest villages in the county.

This walk takes you to the village along the coast path from Weston. There are extensive views all along the path, and on a clear day Portland Bill can be seen to the east. The sloping grassy area on the cliff above Littlecombe Shoot is a popular spot for paragliders, and if the weather conditions are favourable you can spend hours sitting on the cliff top watching them. At the footpath marker post here, a sign leading right appears to direct you straight over the edge of the cliff. This steep, narrow, zig-zag path will take you on to the pebbly beach below.

St Winifred's Church nestles halfway down the valley from Street, and is one of Branscombe's treasures. Dedicated to an obscure Welsh saint, it dates from the 11th century and is significant in Devon in that it reveals evidence of continuous development up to the 16th century. The squat tower dates from Norman times. Inside, there are remnants of medieval paintings that once adorned the walls, an Elizabethan gallery and an unusual 18th-century three-decker pulpit. Near the village 'centre', by the village hall, many buildings are owned by the National Trust: The Old Bakery (the last traditional working bakery in Devon until 1987) is now a tea room, Manor Mill (a restored water-powered mill), and The Forge, complete with a working blacksmith. Branscombe Mouth beach is busy in summer, although it is pebbly and the seabed shelves away quickly. This is the halfway point of the walk and you can always wander a little way to east or west to escape the crowds.

Branscombe hit the national headlines in January 2007 when modern-day 'wreckers' invaded the beach in search of cargo washed up from the MSC *Napoli* which had foundered offshore.

1. From the car park take the flinty track through the gate and onto the footpath signposted 'Weston Mouth'. As the track descends and the sea comes into view bear left on a permissive path under trees, and follow this to meet the coast path on Weston Cliff.

2. Turn left on the coast path. Pass Point 8 and go through two kissing gates on Coxe's Cliff; after the second kissing gate the path runs inland via a deep combe towards a kissing gate in the top left corner of the field. Keep round the right edge of the next field and through a kissing gate on to grassland above Littlecombe Shoot.

3. At the footpath turn half left to Berry Barton. Aim for a broad gap in the bank ahead, keep ahead to a gate and kissing gate in the top corner of the next field, then turn left down the track to join the lane at Berry Barton.

4. Turn right down the lane to The Fountain Head pub. Turn right again down the valley, passing groups of thatched cottages and St Winifred's Church (right). Continue downhill past The Forge to the village hall and St Branoc's Well on the left.

5. Turn right opposite Bucknall Close down the lane signposted 'Branscombe Mouth'. After 200yds (183m) at a path junction keep ahead through a small gate and follow the path to a footbridge (go left here for The Masons Arms). Follow the fenced path down the valley to reach the beach at Branscombe Mouth, with the Sea Shanty Beach Café on your left.

6. Turn immediately right through a kissing gate to join coast path signs uphill beneath the coastguard cottages (now a private house). Go through an open gateway and left uphill to a kissing gate. Keep left up steps, then ignore all paths to left and right until, after two kissing gates and 0.5 miles (800m), a signpost points left between old quarry workings towards the cliffs.

7. Follow the coastal footpath signs to rejoin the cliff edge via a gate, going through two more gates to reach Littlecombe Shoot. Retrace your steps through fields and kissing gates to regain Weston Cliff via another kissing gate.

8. Turn immediately right through a kissing gate into a wildflower meadow. Pass the cottage and outbuildings (on the right) over two stiles and on to a track leading to a tarmac lane. Go left and in a short while you'll reach Weston and the car park.

Where to eat and drink

The 14th-century Fountain Head at Street, has great food and a local feel. The Masons Arms (hotel and restaurant) at the bottom of the valley is more upmarket but both pubs welcome families. The National Trust Old Bakery Tearoom can be found opposite The Forge, and the Sea Shanty Beach Café and Shop is at the beach at Branscombe Mouth.

While you're there

The Donkey Sanctuary at Slade House Farm (signposted off the A3052) is a charity devoted to caring for donkeys that have been neglected or badly treated, or are unwanted. It's the largest donkey sanctuary in the world and is open 365 days a year from 9am until dusk, admission free.

SIDMOUTH

DISTANCE/TIME	5 miles (8km) / 2hrs
ASCENT/GRADIENT	Negligible
PATHS	Good level paths or pavements
LANDSCAPE	Meadows, town park and seafront
SUGGESTED MAP	OS Explorer 115 Exmouth & Sidmouth
START/FINISH	Grid reference: SY136898
DOG FRIENDLINESS	Dogs should be kept under control at all times
PARKING	By Sidford Social Hall, Byes Lane
PUBLIC TOILETS	The Esplanade and The Triangle

Originally a small market and fishing town, Sidmouth became a popular holiday venue in the late 18th century due to its pleasant scenery and mild climate. With the growth of Torquay in the mid-19th century as a result of the coming of the South Devon Railway (which reached Torquay in 1848, and was amalgamated with the Great Western Railway in 1876) Sidmouth was somewhat bypassed and its rate of development slowed. Early plans for a branch line to Sidmouth were abandoned, and the town was not linked to the main line until 1874, by which time Torquay had become Devon's premier seaside resort and holiday destination. But in some ways this delay was very much to Sidmouth's advantage, in that today much of the beautiful Georgian architecture remains, unaffected by later Victorian building work.

Considering the civilised nature of the town, it seems fitting that this walk should provide a peaceful, gentle way in along the River Sid, at just over 6 miles (9.7km) in length said to be the shortest in Devon. Surfaced easy-access walk- and cycleways now thread the Sid Valley between Sidford and the coast.

Sidmouth is full of lovely buildings, and the town is justifiably proud of its architectural heritage. The Toll House, passed on Point 4, was built for the Honiton & Sidmouth Turnpike Trust in 1817, and controlled the eastern approach to the town. The original crossing point of the Sid was the ford, just downstream. On the promenade look out for Beach House, the first house to be built on the seafront in 1790; the thatched open-fronted building attached to it at that time – the Shed – became a popular meeting place. The latter is now much changed and occupied by The Mocha Restaurant. Connaught Gardens was originally part of a private estate, known as Sea View, and given to the public by The Duke of Connaught in 1934.

Sidmouth takes on a different persona for one week at the start of August, when it hosts the world-famous Sidmouth Folk Festival but in recent years it has been scaled back due to financial uncertainty and has reverted to its original name. Today, it is a full week of traditional music, dance and song.

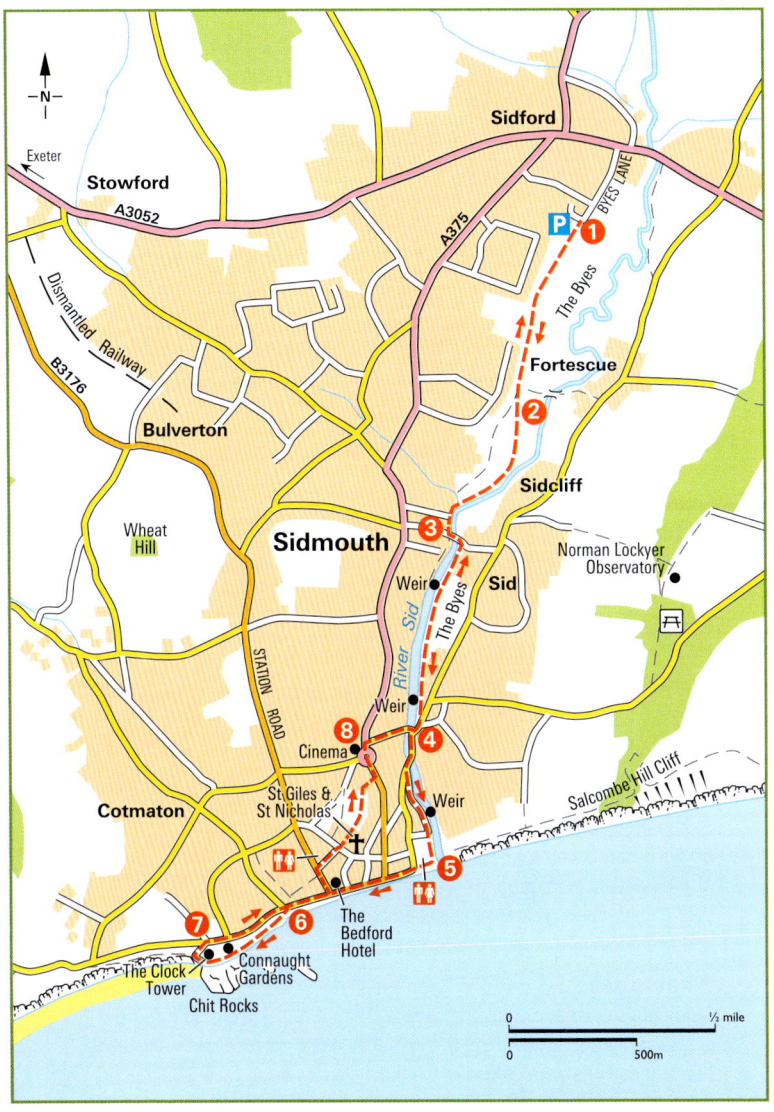

1. From the car park pass through the gate and follow the walk- and cycleway past the sports field.

2. Reach a crossroads of tarmac paths (Fortescue left) and keep ahead. Escape the cycles by turning left through a gate into Gilchrist Field; turn right along its edge. At the field end follow the field-edge left (passing a gate) towards the River Sid. At the end turn right through the hedge into Margaret's Meadow. Keep along the left edge, passing The Golden Copse (planted in celebration of Her Majesty Queen Elizabeth's Golden Jubilee) to regain the walkway.

3. Turn left to cross a footbridge and follow the river. At the wooden footbridge turn left across the river, then right to enter The Byes, parkland with splendid mature trees – lime, holm oak, sweet chestnut, sycamore, willow and copper beech. Keep straight on, passing two footbridges.

4. Just after the next weir leave The Byes by a white metal gate to meet the road by the early 19th-century Greek revival style Byes Toll House. Cross over and down Milford Road, over the river via a wooden footbridge at a ford, and down Mill Street. Turn first left (Riverside Road); when that turns sharp right keep straight on past the playground to the seafront.

5. Turn right along Sidmouth's seafront past delightful Regency terraces. The tourist information centre is signed right (at the swimming pool). The long boulder banks offshore were constructed in the early 1990s to prevent beach erosion. Pass The Bedford Hotel, on the right, and carry on to the end of the promenade.

6. Follow signs for Connaught Gardens along The Clifton Walkway at the back of the beach. (Note: In heavy sea conditions leave the seafront and continue uphill to reach Connaught Gardens on the left.) The walkway leads under the marl cliff to overlook the beach at Jacob's Ladder. Climb the white-painted steps up the cliff. Bear left, then right into Connaught Gardens under an arch (The Clock Tower).

7. From the gardens emerge on to the road, turning right downhill to rejoin the promenade. At The Bedford Hotel turn left along Station Road; turn first right towards the Church of St Giles & St Nicholas. Pass through the graveyard, left of the church, and keep ahead past the bowling green. Turn right into Blackmore Gardens, and follow the path left. Leave the gardens and keep ahead to the High Street; turn left.

8. Opposite the cinema turn right down Salcombe Road to the Toll House (Point 4) and turn left to retrace your steps to Sidford.

Where to eat and drink

Sidmouth is bursting with pubs, cafés, restaurants and takeaways. The Bedford Hotel overlooks the sea and the views are terrific all year round. At the halfway point stop for tea at the Clock Tower (open 364 days of the year, 10am–5pm). There's a refreshment kiosk at Jacob's Ladder beach, and great fish and chips from Prospect Plaice near the seafront.

What to see

Sidmouth's dramatic cliffs are under constant attack from both the sea and the weather. If warnings are in place do not venture on to the beach below these unstable cliffs. During the Triassic period (250–200 million years ago) this part of the country experienced hot, desert-like conditions, and the red colour of the rock results from the weathering of iron minerals.

While you're there

The Norman Lockyer Observatory on Sidmouth Hill, to the east of the town, was founded by Sir Norman Lockyer as an astrophysical research centre in 1912. Since the 1980s it has been run on a voluntary basis. You can go there to learn more about the solar system, carry out research, or simply watch the stars – on a clear night, of course.

RIVER OTTER AND JURASSIC COAST

DISTANCE/TIME	5.5miles (8.9km) / 2hrs 30mins
ASCENT/GRADIENT	663ft (202m) / ▲
PATHS	Good level paths, coastal section and lanes
LANDSCAPE	River meadow, cliffs and undulating farmland
SUGGESTED MAP	OS Explorer 115 Exmouth & Sidmouth
START/FINISH	Grid reference: SY076831
DOG FRIENDLINESS	Keep on lead near livestock and unfenced cliffs
PARKING	By side of broad, quiet lane near entrance to South Farm
PUBLIC TOILETS	Behind Otterton Mill

Peaceful, tranquil, lush, idyllic – these are all words that could easily be applied to this stroll along the banks of the River Otter. The river wends its way to meet the sea just east of Budleigh Salterton, its lower reaches a haven for a wealth of birdlife. In contrast to this, the walk continues along the top of the red sandstone cliffs typical of this area – but the coast path here is not in any way heart-thumpingly strenuous. The combination of the serene river meadows and the glorious coastal scenery – and then, perhaps, tea at Otterton Mill – make this an ideal family walk.

The Nature Reserve, south of White Bridge, is a SSSI and nationally important wildlife habitat, one of the smallest in the South West. The estuary was much more extensive in the past, and 500 years ago cargo ships could travel upriver as far as Otterton. Today, the estuary provides a haven for all kinds of birdlife, best seen between October and March. Oystercatchers, dunlins and other wading birds come to feed here; large flocks of waders and ducks, such as wigeons and teal, attract peregrine falcons, sparrowhawks and mink. Three-quarters of the estuary has been colonised by saltmarsh, which is also home to warblers in the summer months, linnets and greenfinches all year round, and kingfishers in winter. To catch the action, about 0.25 miles (400m) from the start of the main walk take a small path right towards the river to a birding hide.

The coastal section runs along part of the 95-mile (153km) Jurassic Coast, England's first natural UNESCO World Heritage Site, designated in 2001. Quartzite pebbles on the beach at Budleigh Salterton date from Triassic times. Point 4 crosses Brandy Head, named on account of historic smuggling activity, and home to a World War II range observation post; from 1940 to 1946 Exeter airport was the most important RAF station in the West Country.

The mid-section of the walk brings us within sight of Otterton, a large, pleasant village, with many traditional cob and thatch buildings. St Michael and All Angels church is most impressive. There was a Saxon church here before the Norman Conquest, rebuilt by Benedictine monks when they established a priory in the 12th century. The main monastery building lay on the north side of the church, and part of it – probably the guests' hall – remains today. After Henry VIII's Dissolution of the Monasteries, in 1539, the church gradually fell into disrepair until it was totally rebuilt in the 1870s. The west tower is constructed of the Old Red Sandstone seen in the cliffs earlier in the walk.

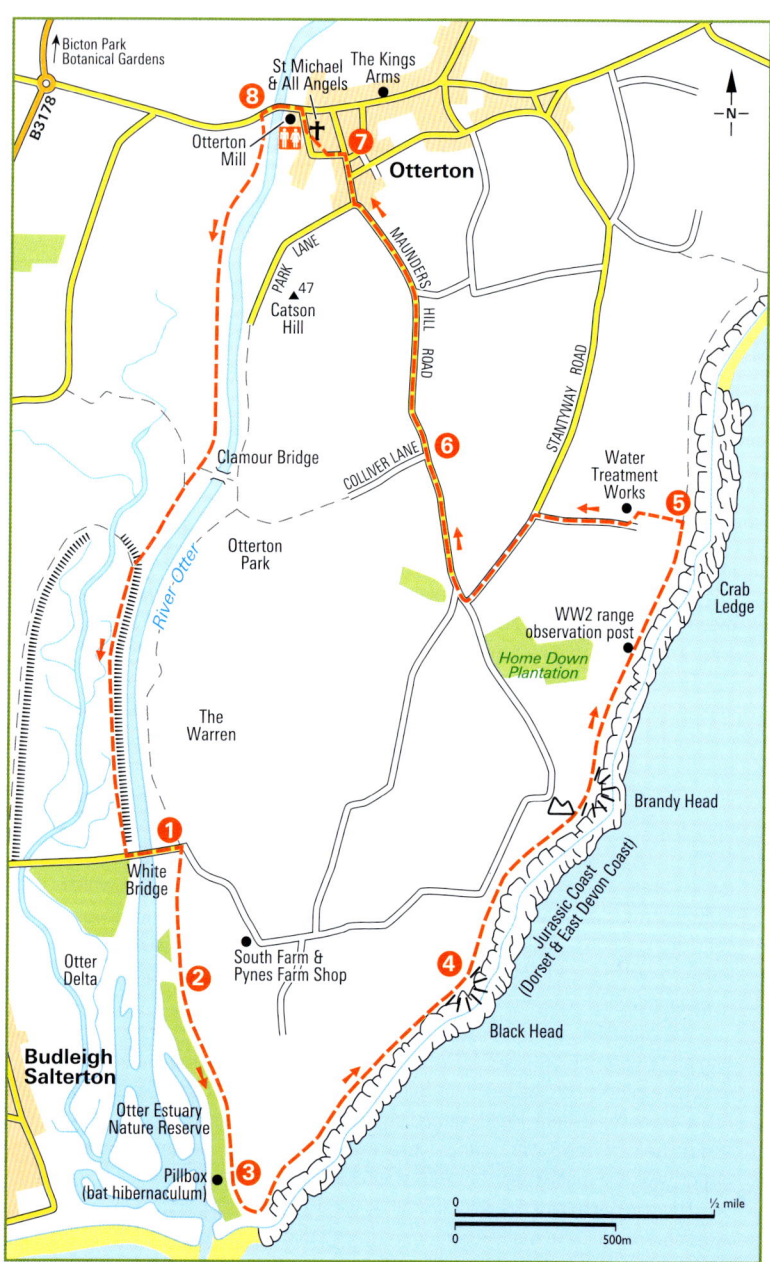

1. Walk away from the river and through the kissing gate by the gate to South Farm. Turn right following signs for 'Coast Path Ladram Bay'. The path runs along the field-edge, with lovely views right over the saltmarshes of the Otter Estuary Nature Reserve.

2. At the end of that field a shallow flight of wooden steps leads to a boardwalk and up into the next field. There are good views downriver to the shingle bank at Budleigh Salterton and across the estuary to the town itself.

3. Continue gently downhill; by a disused pillbox (now 'bat hibernaculum') follow the coast path sharp left (panoramic views right across the Otter delta).

4. After just over a mile (1.6km) the path rises and a view of Lyme Bay opens up ahead, including High Peak (564ft/157m – one of the highest points on the South Devon coast). Follow the coast path: the red sandstone cliffs are extremely friable and unstable, so do not go near the edge. Pass through a small gate by the disused wartime observation post (covered bench), and continue downhill.

5. Turn left to leave the coast path on the 'Permissive path Otterton'; follow this grassy path inland then left through a kissing gate, then right around the water treatment works, and up the gravelly lane to meet Stantyway Road at a path junction. Turn left up the track, which soon bears right, signed to the River Otter, and gives way to a tarmac lane.

6. After 400yds (366m) Clamour Bridge is signed to the left, however, keep straight ahead on the tarmac lane following the Public Right of Way signs along Maunders Hill Road. This pretty lane climbs gently up before dropping down to reach the edge of Otterton.

7. Turn left along Green Close, and through the lychgate into the churchyard of St Michael and All Angels. Leave the church via its main door and turn right down Church Hill to join the road through the village. Turn left for Otterton Mill and cross over the river.

8. Walk alongside the river for just over 0.5 miles (800m) from the mill you reach the Clamour Bridge through a kissing gate. Continue ahead with the river on your left until meeting the White Bridge, turn left and find your car.

Where to eat and drink

Pynes Farm Shop at South Farm near the walk start sells snacks and ice cream. The Otterton Mill Restaurant is open daily from 9.30am to 5pm and serves a great range of delicious home-made dishes. The Kings Arms (dog-friendly) has a large beer garden and children's play area.

What to see

The smallest of the grebe family, the little grebe, although rare in Devon, has been spotted at White Bridge. Often called a 'dab chick', it is a busy little bird, diving and bobbing up again in search for food. Otters can be seen regularly on the River Dart.

While you're there

Visit Bicton Park Botanical Gardens. Open daily (10am – 4pm). It has more than 60 acres (24ha) of landscaped gardens, with an arboretum, lake, secret garden and woodland railway.

AROUND OTTERY ST MARY

DISTANCE/TIME	3.5 miles (5.7km) / 1hr 30min
ASCENT/GRADIENT	131ft (40m) / ▲
PATHS	Field tracks and paths
LANDSCAPE	Farmland and town paths
SUGGESTED MAP	OS Explorer 115 Exmouth & Sidmouth
START/FINISH	Grid reference: SY099956
DOG FRIENDLINESS	Lead required through farmland
PARKING	Canaan Way car park off Fairmile Lane (pay-and-display)
PUBLIC TOILETS	The Flexton; Sainsbury's (Hind Street)

Scratch the surface of the attractive little east Devon town of Ottery St Mary and you'll be amazed – for literary connections and historic interest, it's hard to beat. For a start there's the impressive Church of St Mary of Ottery – the original building here was extended between 1337 and 1342 as a collegiate church along similar lines (though less than half the size) of St Peter's Cathedral in Exeter. Many of the original buildings, such as the cloisters, chorister's house and choirboys' school have now gone; in 1545, at the Dissolution under Henry VIII, St Mary's became a rather grand parish church. In the 18th century Ottery was a prosperous wool town, as evidenced by the large number of fine Georgian buildings, especially near the church. The Flexton, where the walk starts, was site of the town market and fair, granted by Royal Charter under Henry II in 1226.

Ottery is immensely proud of the fact that the poet and philosopher Samuel Taylor Coleridge was born here in 1772. Fascinating documents on display in the church record the handing over of the nine-year-old boy to Christ's Hospital on the death of his father, Revd John Coleridge (Master of the King's School), 'there to be educated and brought up among other poor children'. Both John and Samuel's mother Ann are buried in the church. The poet was born in the School House near the church steps, which was demolished in 1884. A plaque on the wall records the event.

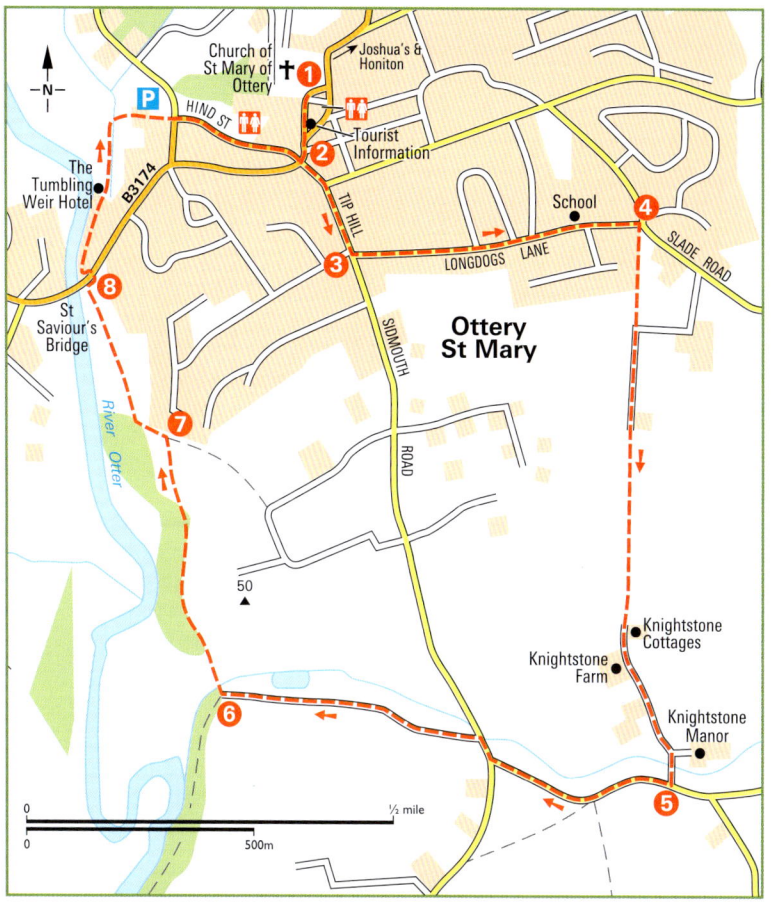

1. From the church steps walk down Silver Street. Follow the lane to reach The Square, off which lanes run in several directions.

2. Cross the road, turn left and then bear right up Tip Hill (Sidmouth Road), passing through a cutting at the top (there is a pavement on the left).

3. At the brow of the hill turn left along Longdogs Lane, passing houses and eventually the primary school. The lane drops downhill to a crossroads.

4. Turn right on a signed bridleway between high hedges. Pass through two bridlegates; the path broadens to a track, passing through a bridlegate by Knightstone Cottages. Keep left at a rounded fork, soon dropping down a track to meet a drive at Knightstone Manor. Keep ahead, with a wall left, across a stream and through iron gates onto a lane.

5. Turn right and follow the lane to a T-junction. Cross with care, bearing right, and pass through a kissing gate on a footpath. Follow the track along the lower right edge of a field. Eventually pass through a metal gate and drop to a footpath junction.

6. Bear right and go through a wide gateway (yellow arrow). Keep along the right field-edge to go through a gate and up steps into woodland. The River Otter can be seen left. Follow the narrow path, later climbing steps into a field via a small gate, and turn left.

7. At the next gate turn left, and descend overgrown steps along the left edge of a rough field, towards a gate/footbridge. Cross over and follow a narrow path through Indian balsam and willow, eventually on to an embankment. Turn right along the bank, which curves left to a kissing gate onto the B3174, opposite the derelict mill.

8. Cross with care and turn left. Just before St Saviour's Bridge turn right on a tarmac footpath along the riverbank, to the drive of The Tumbling Weir Hotel. Cross over to pass the weir and information panel, then follow the tarmac path along the leat. Turn right on the first bridge. Keep ahead, bearing left past the playground and right at the next junction to meet Canaan Way, opposite Hind Street. Cross over, and where Hind Street bears right towards The Square, turn left along Saddlers Lane. Turn left to return to the church.

Where to eat and drink
Within the heart of town there are several pubs and cafés to choose from. Just out of town (signed off the road to Honiton) is Joshua's, a treasure trove of local food, drink and crafts – perfect for a light lunch or tea.

What to see
Allow time for a good look round the church. This glorious building has a carved Beer stone gallery in the Lady Chapel, and beautiful painted and decorated ribs and roof bosses. Don't miss the astronomical clock, thought to date from the 14th century, and the damaged weather cock, used for target practice by Cromwell's soldiers in 1645.

While you're there
For an unexpected taste of 'wild country' in peaceful east Devon go for a walk on Woodbury Common, a large area of woodland and heath to the southwest of Ottery St Mary, criss-crossed by a network of paths and tracks. The highest point (600ft/183m) is crowned by Woodbury Castle, an Iron Age hill fort.

PICTURESQUE BROADHEMBURY

DISTANCE/TIME	6.25 miles (10.1km) / 3hrs 45min
ASCENT/GRADIENT	360ft (110m) / ▲▲
PATHS	Country lanes, pastures and woodland paths, several stiles
LANDSCAPE	Rolling farmland and beech woods
SUGGESTED MAP	OS Explorer 115 Exmouth & Sidmouth
START/FINISH	Grid reference: ST096069
DOG FRIENDLINESS	Dogs on lead in fields and on airfield
PARKING	Unsurfaced car park at Rhododendron Wood
PUBLIC TOILETS	None on route

Broadhembury is one of those unspoiled showpiece Devon villages that gives you the impression that nothing has changed for centuries and that you've entered some sort of time warp. The picturesque main street is lined with well-preserved cob and thatched cottages and pretty flower-filled gardens, and there appears to be a constant cycle of repair and renovation. Much of Broadhembury as you see it now developed as an estate village under the patronage of the Drewe family in the early 17th century, and you still get the feeling that this is not a village struggling for survival.

St Andrew's Church holds many memorials to members of the family, who have been influential in the development of the village. In 1603 Edward Drewe, Sergeant-at-Law to Queen Elizabeth I, bought Abbey Farm from Dunkeswell Abbey, and created a new mansion, The Grange, the family seat for nearly 300 years. Edward Drewe was a successful lawyer, who already owned Sharpham and Killerton. The house is not open to the public, but you can get a view of it from the southeast approach road to the village. The church was consecrated in 1259, but the building dates mainly from the 15th century. It's set at the end of a cul-de-sac of chestnut trees and has been much restored over the last couple of centuries. The tower (from about 1480) is almost 100ft (30m) high. The timbers of the roof were painted in the late 15th century and were only discovered in 1930 when repair work was being carried out. There is also an unusual 15th-century font which is somewhat damaged (probably during the Civil War) and decorated with primitive figures of apostles and clergy, and an 18th-century memorial to Augustus Toplady, who wrote the hymn *Rock of Ages*.

Just a mile (1.6km) to the southeast of the village lies Hembury hill fort, on a spur of the Blackdown Hills at 883ft (269m) above sea level. There was a causewayed camp here around 2500 BC, and in about 150 BC Iron Age dwellers built the defensive earthworks that can be seen today. The site was inhabited until around AD 75. The best time to explore the hill fort is in May, when the ramparts are smothered with bluebells.

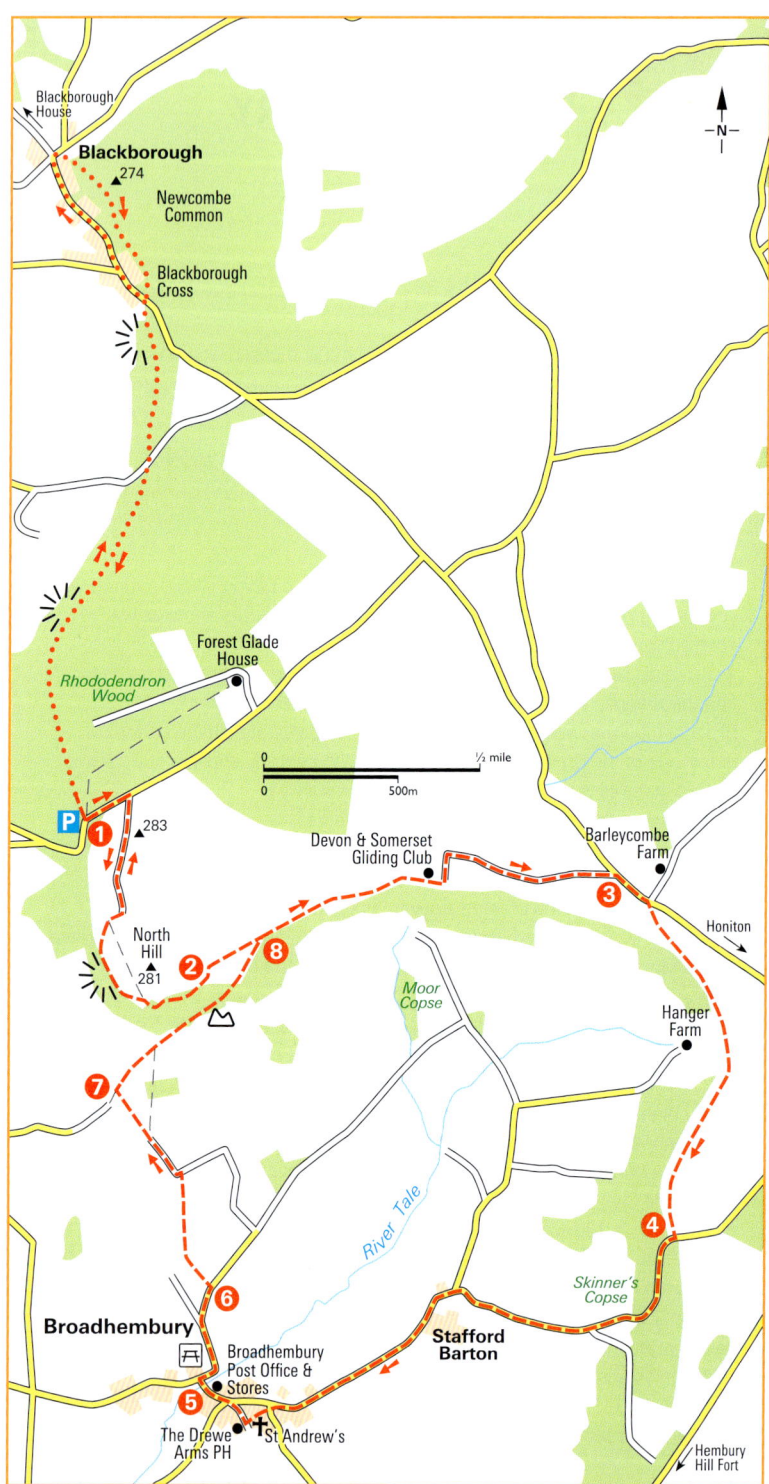

1. Turn left up the road, steeply uphill. As it levels, turn right on a bridleway through a small parking area. Follow this path – with wonderful views west – along the perimeter of the airfield. Keep left at a fork and ascend to a wooden gate.

2. Turn right along the edge of the airfield, eventually keeping to the right of the clubhouse. Follow the tarmac drive right over a cattle grid and keep ahead to join a road.

3. Turn right; pass Barleycombe Farm (left), then follow bridleway signs right through a gate, downhill on a fenced path, then left through another into a field. Walk along the bottom edge. The path curves right through a stand of beech trees and a metal gate, then runs straight across the next field towards the top edge of woodland. Keeping the fence on the right walk through a gate onto a fenced path, with a conifer plantation right.

4. The path ends at a lane, turn right downhill towards Broadhembury. At St Andrew's Church cross the road and go through the churchyard (no dogs allowed), then under the lychgate and downhill to find The Drewe Arms (left) for a welcome break.

5. To continue the walk, from the pub, turn left down the main street to reach the bridge and ford. Turn right up the lane, past the playground and up the hill, eventually bearing right.

6. Just past two thatched cottages (right) go left over the stile in the hedge and up the field, aiming for a stile in the top left corner. Go over that and straight ahead, crossing a stile by a gate to the left of the farmhouse. Keep ahead up the left field edge and cross another stile; then right, round the edge of the field, and over two a stile into a small copse. Pass a stile into the next field; bear slightly right to locate the next stile in the beech hedge opposite which takes you into a green lane.

7. Turn right and walk uphill with conifers left and fields right, until a metal gate leads to another and back onto the airfield.

8. Turn left along the edge of the field. Follow the bridleway left through the first gate, and continue back to the road. Turn left downhill to find your car.

Extending the walk If you feel like a more relaxing (3.5-mile) alternative, which will teach you something about local industry in the rural heart of Devon, have a look at the nearby village of Blackborough.

Leave the car park through the gate opposite the entrance and walk along a broad bridle path, lined with rhododendrons, through Woodland Trust land. This lovely, well-surfaced track, with views west over the rolling mid-Devon landscape, leads to a junction of tracks. Keep straight on to meet a lane under beech trees. Turn left downhill past pretty cottages. Go straight ahead at Blackborough Cross to reach the northern end of the village. This whole area feels forgotten but a notice board tells you that this remote village was the centre of a flourishing whetstone industry in the 18th and 19th centuries. Whetstones (or 'batts') were used to sharpen scythes and sickles for cereal harvesting, and were exported to London and even abroad. The locals spoke their own distinct dialect, but the invention of carborundum killed their industry, and by 1900 only three mines remained. This is a fascinating place – ahead you will see old iron gates leading to the old churchyard (a haven for wildlife and great for picnics).

The church, which had fallen into disrepair, was closed in 1994 and subsequently demolished. To the northwest lies the Italianate Blackborough House (built in 1838), which was never completed, and which has gained a reputation as something of a folly. Take a slightly different route back to your car by turning right by the notice board and following the footpath sign uphill towards the woods, then almost immediately right again. This lovely path climbs above the houses and winds through woodland, passes two stiles, and leads back to the lane near the bridle path which you follow back to your car.

Where to eat and drink
The Drewe Arms in Broadhembury dates from the early Tudor period. It has an excellent reputation and a very attractive garden. Broadhembury Village Stores, incorporates a Post Office and tea room, and the café at the Gliding Club is open to non-members.

What to see
The Devon & Somerset Gliding Club is near the start of the walk at North Hill, over 900ft (280m) above sea level – a popular spot with skylarks too. The walk skirts the edge of the airfield; the gliders are launched using a steel cable, so stick to the right of way. There's something quite magical – and tempting – about watching the gliders drift silently through the air above you, often reaching heights of over 2,000ft (600m).

FROM CULMSTOCK TO THE WELLINGTON MONUMENT

DISTANCE/TIME	9.25 miles (14.9km) / 4hrs
ASCENT/GRADIENT	590ft (180m) / ▲▲
PATHS	Damp pasture, green lanes and woodland tracks, several stiles
LANDSCAPE	Rolling farmland and heathery ridge on Blackdown Hills
SUGGESTED MAP	OS Explorer 128 Taunton & Blackdown Hills
START/FINISH	Grid reference: ST102135
DOG FRIENDLINESS	Keep on lead in fields
PARKING	Fore Street, Culmstock, near entrance to All Saints Church
PUBLIC TOILETS	None on route

One of the landmarks that heralds your approach to Devon as you travel south on the M5 is the Wellington Monument, a strange, triangular obelisk standing 175ft (53.8m) high on the edge of the Blackdown Hills, and particularly impressive when illuminated at night. It's also a great focus for this walk, which starts off through the water-meadows at Culmstock. Once a small market town with a woollen industry, today it lies off the main tourist trail among rolling fields and peaceful beech woods, a couple of miles from the Somerset border. Several farms, such as beautiful Culm Pyne Barton (passed at Point 8), were recorded in the Domesday Book.

The extravagant Wellington monument was erected by local gentry to celebrate the Duke of Wellington's victory at Waterloo in 1815. Earlier military success brought Arthur Wellesley the right to a title: since his family originated from Somerset, he chose the place most closely resembling the family name. He only visited the estate once, in 1819, but local pride was such that his triumphs were publicly celebrated – and in a big way! The foundation stone of the obelisk, on the highest point of the Blackdown Hills (on the Duke's own land), was laid in 1817, but work was spasmodic, and it didn't reach its final form until the late 19th century. The trustees gave the estate to the National Trust in 1934.

The AA distance board here shows how far you can see in all directions. On a clear day you can pick out the Black Mountains in South Wales, 70 miles (113km) north. Prominent at the start and finish of the walk is All Saints Church dating from the 14th century. Beautifully light and airy, it's constructed of local flint, the characteristic pinkish colour of Blackdown chert. The tower is adorned by two ferocious gargoyles and four pinnacles, each topped with a weathervane, erected when the original spire was taken down in 1776. Culmstock's famous yew tree, seen on top of the tower, probably took root at that time – it now has a substantial trunk and, during the drought of 1976, was painstakingly watered by volunteers; perhaps another example of the pride of these Devon/Somerset borderers.

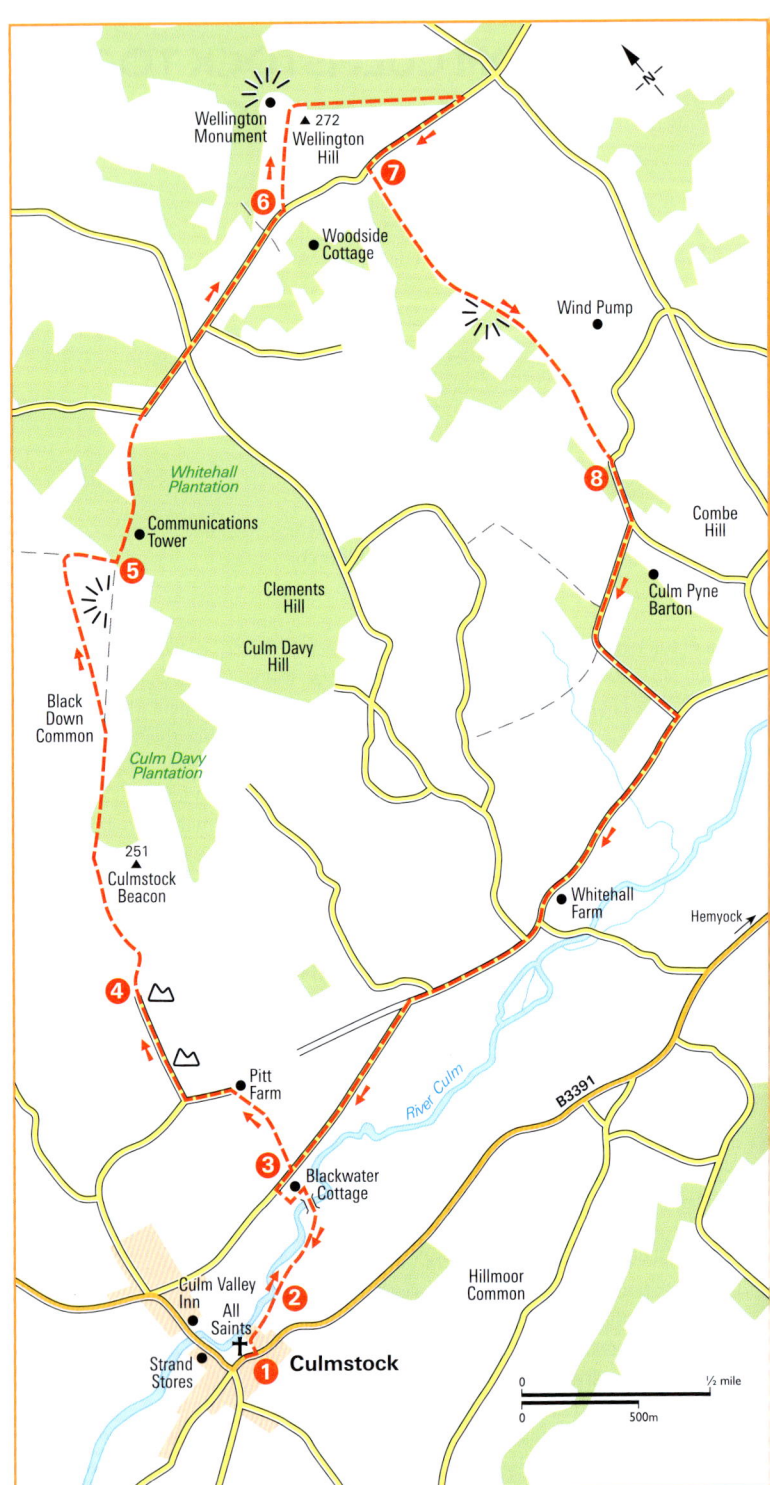

1. Walk along Fore Street with the church to the left. As it bends right, take the small lane ahead around the church wall. At Cleeve Cottage turn right towards a small gate. Make for the bottom left corner of the field, dropping towards the river, and through a kissing gate.

2. Turn right and follow the river to cross a stream by a single oak, then go forward to pass through a gate by double ash trees. A wooden footbridge takes you across the river. Bear left, cross the field to a gate, then cross the next field to a gate by stables, and on to a lane. Turn right.

3. Just past Blackwater Cottage (right), turn left through a gate. Walk straight up the field with the hedge left. When the hedge bears left, aim for the top right corner of the field and a stile. Continue uphill across the next field, aiming to the left of red-brick Pitt Farm. Pass through a white iron gate and walk on to the farm drive. Turn left; where the drive meets a lane, turn right uphill.

4. The lane becomes a rough track and eventually bears left; a few steps round the corner turn right through a small gate and climb up to the trig point on Culmstock Beacon. Follow the left edge of the ridge on a track. Your destination is the communications tower ahead; the track eventually leads into a broad grassy ride, which curves sharp right. When almost level with the tower (left) bear left across heather towards woods.

5. Pass through a metal gate into beech woods, and take the broad track ahead. The path eventually leaves the trees and runs downhill to join a tarmac road; carry straight on to meet a larger road on a sharp bend, and continue straight ahead.

6. When the road curves right turn left over a stile as signed and up the field; pass over two stiles, then a third in the top corner to gain the monument. Turn right down the approach track to meet the road and turn right again.

7. Where the road bends right take the footpath signed left over a stile. Cross the field and the next stile on to a broad grassy ride (often muddy). Cross the next two stiles and a field to enter a woodland by a stile. Emerge over another stile, carry straight on and over two more stiles to meet the lane. Turn right.

8. After 250yds (229m) turn right downhill, then right at the first junction. Go straight ahead passing Whitehall Farm on the left and follow the lane to the house at Point 3. Turn left past the house and retrace your steps home.

Where to eat and drink
Culmstock has the Culm Valley Inn (free house) by the River Culm, and the wonderful Strand Stores (has a café and deli within it).

What to see
Ascent of the steep, muddy path to Culmstock Beacon on the edge of Black Down Common is rewarded by fantastic views. This restored beacon hut was part of the network of beacons across England providing an early warning system at the time of the Spanish Armada in the summer of 1588.

THE GRAND WESTERN CANAL COUNTRY PARK

DISTANCE/TIME	6 miles (9.7km) / 2hrs 30min
ASCENT/GRADIENT	Negligible
PATHS	Canal tow path
LANDSCAPE	Farmland, by the canal on edge of Tiverton
SUGGESTED MAP	OS Explorer 114 Exeter & the Exe Valley
START/FINISH	Grid reference: SS999131
DOG FRIENDLINESS	Keep dogs under control while in country park
PARKING	Parking and picnic area at Tiverton Road Bridge
PUBLIC TOILETS	Grand Western Canal Basin

Just a few miles west of Junction 27 on the busy M5 can be found another world. This section of the Grand Western Canal was built between 1810 and 1814, and now provides the opportunity for a lovely, easy afternoon stroll. Now run as a country park, the reed-fringed tow path along this stretch of canal invites you to walk to the canal basin in Tiverton. Note that the tow path between the walk start and Manley Bridge is shared with National Cycle Route 3 (Land's End to Bristol) so keep an eye out for cyclists on this stretch.

The original plan, formulated by James Brindley in 1768, was for a canal system that would link Bristol to Exeter. In 1796 an Act of Parliament was obtained for the construction of the Grand Western Canal, to run from Topsham to Taunton, with three branches – to Cullompton, Tiverton and Wellington. But due to the Napoleonic Wars, the scheme was dropped until 1810, when the route was re-surveyed, and work began near Burlescombe. The section from Lowdwells to Tiverton opened in 1814, at a cost of over £220,000, a vast sum in those days. The section from Taunton to Lowdwells opened in 1838, but was never profitable and closed in 1869.

The development of the railway system in the area in the mid-19th century heralded an end to the commercial use of the canal, which was used primarily by barges conveying limestone from the quarries at Westleigh. These travelled to the Tiverton Basin where the limestone was processed in lime kilns, which can still be seen today. Operations finally stopped in 1924. Wharves and lime kilns can also be seen south of Waytown Tunnel at Lowdwells to the north. The car park at the Tiverton Road Bridge, where the walks starts, was also the site of a wharf where stone was unloaded and crushed for use in road-making.

Many of the bridges display mason's marks: the stonemasons marked their work so that poor examples could be traced to the right culprit! Look to the left of the path before you pass under the road bridge at the start of the walk to find a milestone, its three bars telling you that there are 3 miles to go to the canal basin.

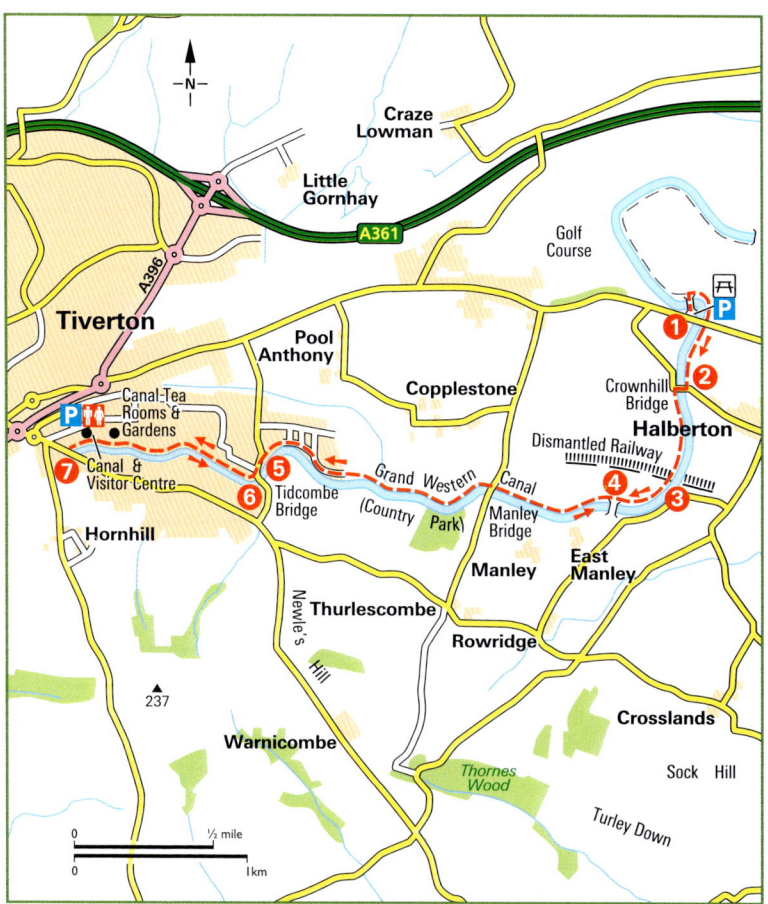

1. Cross the white bridge (the Dudley Weatherley Jubilee Bridge, opened in 2002 in memory of a local artist and long-term supporter of the canal) and turn right along the canal, soon passing under the road bridge.

2. Follow the tow path to cross the canal at Crownhill (or Change Path) Bridge, where horses were once lead over to pick up the tow path on the opposite bank; there's another picnic area on the west bank. Turn left and continue along the tow path.

3. The canal runs over the now dismantled Tiverton branch line of the Bristol & Exeter Railway, which closed to traffic in 1964. Here it is in an aqueduct, built in 1847 and 40ft (12m) above the railway line, an information board gives more details. Just past the aqueduct there are glorious views left across farmland towards the Blackdown Hills. You may well see a brightly painted horse-drawn barge at some point between here and the canal basin; the Tiverton Canal Company operates trips along the canal from late April to end of September.

4. The path continues to East Manley Bridge, Manley Bridge (note the memorial to two members of the RAF who died here when their plane crashed in 1961) and Warnicombe Bridge, where there are glorious willows, oak, ash and beech trees.

5. There is a milestone just before the next bridge, Tidcombe Bridge: 1 mile (1.6km) to go. The loop in the canal here came about as a result of the then Bishop of Exeter's refusal to let the canal run within 100 yds of his home, Tidcombe Hall.

6. As the edge of Tiverton's residential area is reached, neat gardens front the water's edge. The tow path passes under a modern footbridge, then an old stone bridge pier on the opposite bank, still showing the grooves for a stop-gate. This would have been used to seal off part of the canal in times of emergency or when repairs were needed to this section.

7. The canal basin is reached after 3 miles (4.8km) of pleasant, gentle walking. Take a look at the Visitor Centre, which gives details of the canal's history and current status. Once you've had a look around just retrace your steps back to the car park at Tiverton Road Bridge.

Where to eat and drink
The Canal Tea Rooms and Gardens, a 16th-century cottage (the only thatched building left in Tiverton), is situated below the canal basin and open every day, 10.30am–5pm, April to September. Refreshments are also available at the Ducks' Ditty Floating Café Bar in the basin. Halberton Court Farm Shop and the Swans Neck Café is 0.5 miles (0.8km) away from the canal down a footpath near Tiverton Road Bridge.

What to see
The Country Park is home to a host of flora and fauna. Much of the canal is edged with white water lilies – once gathered for sale and sent by train to markets in London and Birmingham – and you will see coots, moorhens and mallards, and perhaps heron and kingfisher. Typical flowers include hemp agrimony, arrowhead, cuckoo flower and yellow iris.

While you're there
The Devon Railway Centre, at Bickleigh a few miles down the Exe Valley from Tiverton, is a must for all railway enthusiasts. Based in the old Cadeleigh GWR station, there are train rides, model railways (in an old railway carriage), a miniature village and all kinds of railway memorabilia.

KNIGHTSHAYES: A WOODLAND WALK

DISTANCE/TIME	2 miles (3.2km) / 1hr
ASCENT/GRADIENT	197ft (60m) / ▲
PATHS	Woodland paths (may be muddy after wet weather) and pathless grassland
LANDSCAPE	Woodland and parkland
SUGGESTED MAP	OS Explorer 114 Exeter & the Exe Valley
START/FINISH	Grid reference: SS962153
DOG FRIENDLINESS	On lead in parkland, can run free in woods
PARKING	Knightshayes car park
PUBLIC TOILETS	At The Stables, Knightshayes
NOTES	The park is open all year round

A wander round the rolling expanse of the 200-acre (81ha) Knightshayes estate is a step back in time to the days when wealthy Victorians commissioned the construction of grand country houses in idyllic surroundings. The estate has been under the ownership of the National Trust since 1972, and somehow manages to swallow up the huge number of visitors each year. An information board at Point 1 displays a useful map with a number of different walking route options.

Knightshayes was built for the lace millionaire and MP Sir John Heathcoat-Amory, and designed by the eccentric architect William Burges. It's an imposing and rather romantic building, sited to give views of the family factory on the banks of the River Exe in the valley below.

The building was commissioned in 1867, and the foundation stone laid two years later. Work was completed in 1874, by which time Burges had fallen out with his employer and been replaced by J D Crace. The beautiful gardens were designed by Edward Kemp, and include a wonderful topiary of a fox and hounds, as well as many specimen trees, rare shrubs, amazing seasonal colours, and a huge walled kitchen garden that is now in full working order.

Knightshayes also has a rare stické court – there are only two known in the UK – dating from 1907. Stické is a racket-and-ball, court-based game invented by the military in the late 19th century.

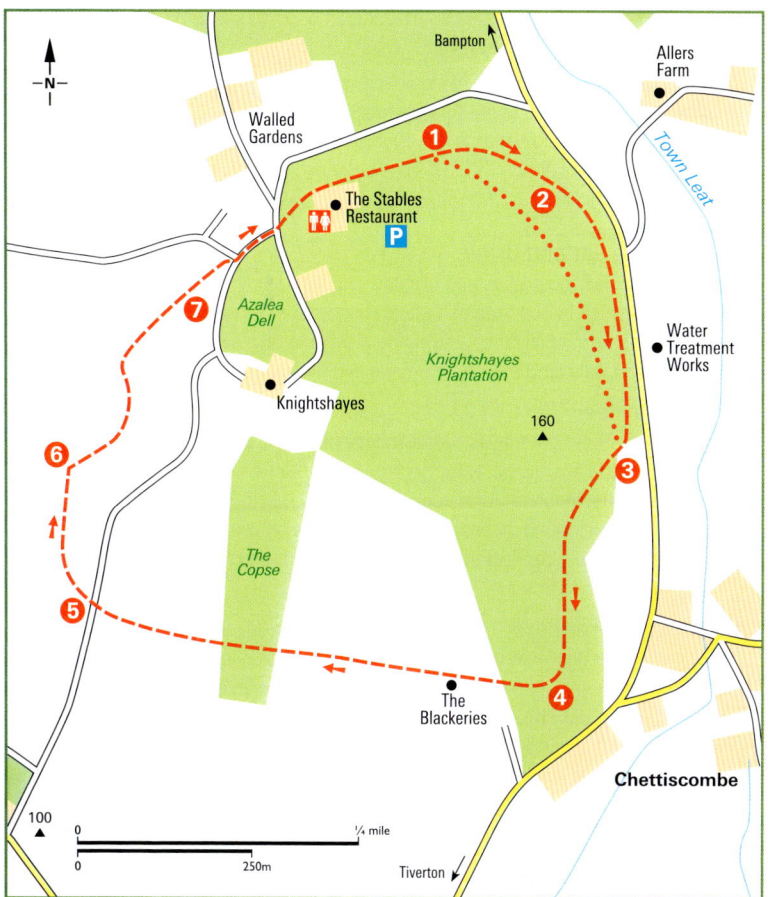

1. The walk starts at the sign for the Impey Walk, opposite the disabled parking area just below the public parking area behind The Stables. Follow the broad woodland path into Knightshayes Plantation.

2. The path soon drops to run parallel to a lane. Follow it through the plantation to a path junction.

3. To shorten the walk to 0.5 miles (800m) turn sharp right to return to the car park. For the parkland stretch on the main route keep ahead as signed, descending gently through beechwoods.

4. At the next footpath sign turn right through an iron gate into The Blackeries. Follow park railings, with a wire fence on the right. Pass through iron gates into and out of The Copse, and into parkland. Keep straight ahead, and look right for a wonderful view of the front of the house. Head towards the park railings, aiming for a big gate a few paces to the right of a smaller one.

5. Cross the main drive and go through a gate to reach a waymarker post. Follow the arrow to pass beneath huge horse chestnut and oak trees across rough grassland. As the land drops steeply, with a wooden seat left, bear right downhill past a fenced plantation to your left, heading for a five-bar gate. Pass through and keep ahead, then bear left to cross a small stream.

6. Turn right to walk past a fenced-off pond among trees, then keep ahead, gently uphill, parallel to the stream.

7. Pass through a gate in iron railings and keep straight on, passing to the left of Azalea Dell. Continue uphill to a signpost pointing back, downhill, to 'Parkland'. Keep ahead towards The Stables and car park, passing the restored Victorian walled garden.

Where to eat and drink
As well as delicious cakes and biscuits you can sample produce from the kitchen garden in The Stables Café at Knighthayes – not only fresh, but also in the form of jams, chutneys and pickles to take away. Local wines are also for sale, and even home-made dog treats.

What to see
In springtime Knightshayes' woodland garden is carpeted with delicate flowers: wood anemones, wood sorrel, lesser celandine, pink purslane and bluebells. In late autumn look out for fungi – Britain has 12,000 species – often found on dead wood or the base of tree trunks. You may spot the oak milk cep (reputed to smell like bed bugs) or the penny bun, a curiously shaped boletus.

While you're there
For further insight into the social history of this area visit Coldharbour Mill at Uffculme, just off the M5 east of Tiverton. It's an old woollen and worsted mill, built by Thomas Fox in 1799. The mill closed in 1981, but the original machinery is still in place; the textile museum opened in 1982, with guided tours and 'steam up' days. Refreshments are available in the Grist Mill Café Bar.

THE DART VALLEY, WITHLEIGH

DISTANCE/TIME	3.75 miles (6km) / 2hrs
ASCENT/GRADIENT	150ft (45m) / ▲▲
PATHS	Waymarked paths, tracks (some muddy) and quiet lanes
LANDSCAPE	Wooded valley and riverside meadows
SUGGESTED MAP	OS Explorer 114 Exeter & the Exe Valley
START/FINISH	Grid reference: SS905121
DOG FRIENDLINESS	Keep on lead in fields
PARKING	NT Buzzards Woodland car park just west of Withleigh
PUBLIC TOILETS	None on route

There are three, little-known but wonderful, areas of National Trust woodland – Cross's Wood, Thongsleigh Wood and Huntland Wood – tucked away in the secluded, undulating mid-Devon countryside to the west of Tiverton. This walk, very much off the beaten track, explores these lovely woodlands draping over the steep hillsides above the valley of the tiny River Dart, which runs into the River Exe at nearby Bickleigh.

There are several excellent riverside picnic spots along the route, and intermittent open areas where you can gaze across the valley and spend some quality time admiring that magnificent bird of prey so typical of this kind of landscape – the buzzard.

Watching a pair of common buzzards gliding through the sky has to be one of the most magnificent sights above the hills and valleys of the West Country. Using updraughts to soar overhead, their broad wings held forward and wing feathers extended, these most common of the larger raptors scan the ground below for their prey – small mammals, and rabbits in particular. Their characteristic 'whee-eur' call is frequently heard in hilly country, and if you're lucky enough to see one perched upright on a fence post you will notice it has a heavily barred tail, a small head and a black, hooked bill. With the decline in persecution by gamekeepers, and with a plentiful supply of rabbits, the buzzard population now runs to tens of thousands.

By contrast the scarce honey buzzard is one of the country's rarest breeders. It lives on a diet of wild bees and their honey, as well as on other insects. This rather refined food source may be supplemented occasionally by small mammals. The honey buzzard is only a summer visitor to southern England, and fewer than a dozen pairs attempt to nest each year. They are very unusual in this part of Devon but have been spotted over the Haldon Hills to the southwest of Exeter.

The woods, fields and banks encountered on this walk are full of interest all year round. As well as a glorious range of wild flowers, there is a fantastic chatter of birdsong here in spring and summer, and a chance of seeing roe deer, and in the early evening perhaps a badger trundling along the path. You should also see dragonflies skimming over the sparkling waters of the Dart. The walk follows waymarked paths and tracks, parts of which (especially the bridlepaths) can be muddy at any time of year.

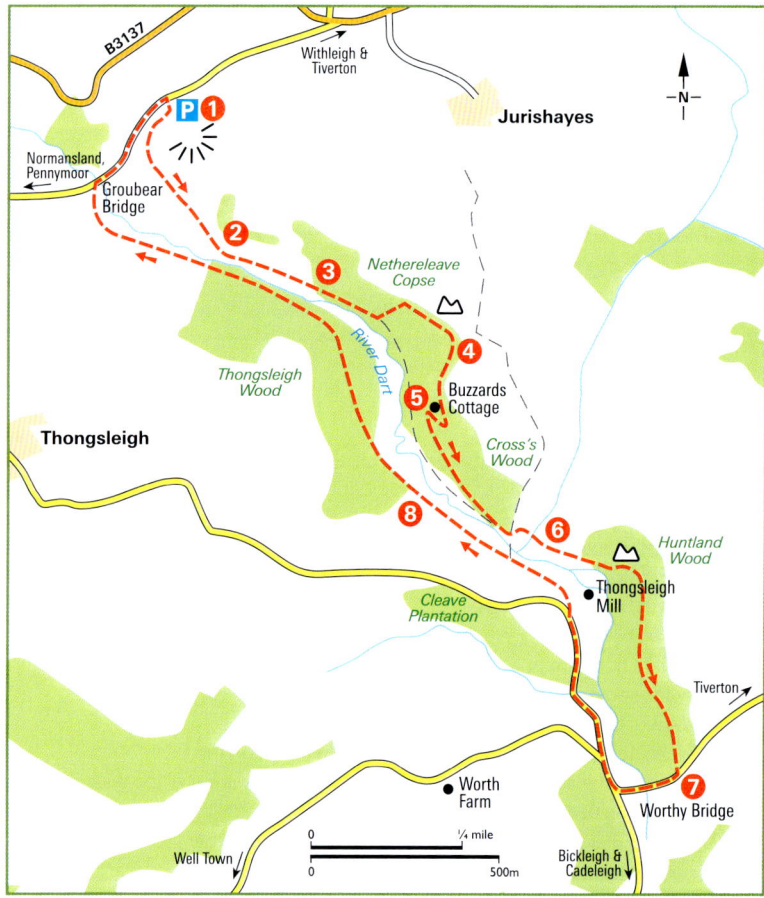

1. From the car park cross the stile/gate into a field, and turn right along the field edge. Go left with the hedge and keep ahead. Descend steeply at the wood edge, heading for the gate and a stone water trough.

2. Go through the gate and straight ahead, keeping the hedge left. Go through a gate and continue alongside the little River Dart. Before the bridge turn left at the waymarker, through a small gate into a field. Turn right along the hedge.

3. Leave the field through the next gate onto a broad track which rises through Cross's Wood. Soon after passing a bench a waymarker directs you left, off the track up a fairly steep path, which can be muddy in places. Continue to climb until the path reaches a wide track at the top of the woods, with a house, left.

4. Turn right to follow the track gently downhill, through a gate into an open area to zig-zag more steeply downhill between gorse, broom and bracken.

5. Pass Buzzards Cottage and follow the track left to join the riverside track at a gate, and keep ahead. Before the bridge over the river (right), turn left on a broad track. After a few paces turn right over a stile and plank bridge to enter a field.

6. Keep the high hedge on your left and walk through the field for about 250yds (229m) to reach a small gate into Huntland Wood. Follow the path steeply uphill. Eventually it joins a track; bear right. The track levels off through the beautiful upper wood before descending gradually to a lane.

7. Turn right downhill, cross the Dart at Worthy Bridge, and turn right at the junction (signed 'Cruwys Morchard'). Continue ahead, passing over a stream and then a couple of properties on the right. Soon after that the road starts to climb and where the road again bends left go straight ahead through a gate on to a track. At a fork take the raised left path, eventually passing through a gate and into Thongsleigh Wood.

8. Continue along the track, with the river, right. At a big gate leave the wood and enter some meadows; keep along the right edge. In the field corner two metal gates lead to a lane. Turn right over Groubear Bridge and climb back up the ancient rocky lane to the car park.

Where to eat and drink
There is nothing very close by, but the Mount Pleasant Inn at Nomansland is open all day, except Mondays, and serves good food. The Fisherman's Cot in Bickleigh enjoys a great setting on the banks of the River Exe and serves freshly prepared dishes and good traditional grub.

What to see
Deciduous woodlands such as these support a great variety of wild flowers. Shade-loving plants abound, but many early flowers bloom in spring before the leaf canopy shuts out too much light. Look out for primroses and delicate wood anemones in early spring; then in May there's a carpet of bluebells so typical of this sort of habitat.

While you're there
Take a trip to Knightshayes, signposted off the A396 at Bolham, 2 miles (3.2km) north of Tiverton. The family home of the Heathcoat Amorys, this splendid house looks down on Tiverton and on the site of the lace-making factory set up by industrialist John Heathcoat in 1815, which once employed 1,500 people, and from which the family gained their wealth. The house was begun in 1869 under John Heathcoat's grandson, and designed by William Burges. You really do get an impression of grand 19th-century country house life here. The gardens, which merge into woodland, are superb. The National Trust has an excellent restaurant, shop and plant centre in the old stables.

UPTON HELLIONS AND THE HELLIONS RIDGE

DISTANCE/TIME	6.25 miles (10.1km) / 2hrs 30min
ASCENT/GRADIENT	328ft (100m) / ▲▲
PATHS	Farm tracks (some muddy), fields and country lanes
LANDSCAPE	Rolling farmland and woodland
SUGGESTED MAP	OS Explorer 114 Exeter & the Exe Valley
START/FINISH	Grid reference: SS830025
DOG FRIENDLINESS	Keep on lead in fields
PARKING	Sandford Parish Hall car park
PUBLIC TOILETS	At Sandford AFC, on southern edge of village

Sandford is a quintessential Devon village: thatched cottages, 14th-century church, excellent pub and wonderful community shop and post office. This walk makes the most of the parish's network of footpaths and green lanes that weave through rolling pasture fields and woodland around the valley of the River Creedy. It's a walk that – unusually for Devon – enjoys sweeping large-scale arable landscapes. The name Sandford (from 'sandy ford') predates the Norman Conquest, and the village is thought to have Saxon origins. In a charter dated AD 930 King Athelstan granted land at Sandford to Bishop Eadulf and the clergy of the minster church at Crediton (see below). There are a number of fine houses in the parish: the original house at Creedy Park dated from about 1600, and Sandford's primary school is housed in a large classical building erected in 1825 by Sir Humphrey Phineas Davie, also of Creedy Park.

The walk visits the little hamlet of Upton Hellions, where the simple church of St Mary's overlooks the Creedy Valley. Now only used at the great festivals, the church, which has a flagstone floor and box pews and a wonderfully unsophisticated feel, dates from the 12th century. The name 'Hellions' is unique, and derives from the name of a Norman settler. The nearby town of Crediton has played an important role in Devon's ecclesiastical history, being the birthplace of the missionary Wynfrith (later St Boniface) in AD 680. He went on to found the Christian church in parts of Europe (now the Netherlands and Germany). His connections with Crediton probably led to the selection of the town as the seat of the first bishop for Devon and Cornwall, and the building of a cathedral in AD 909. The see moved to St Peter's Cathedral in Exeter in AD 1050. Work began on a Norman collegiate church in Crediton in 1150; much of the Perpendicular Gothic work seen today in the Church of the Holy Cross dates from 15th-century rebuilding. Interestingly, Boniface is credited with the invention of the Christmas tree when he claimed that a fir tree growing in the roots of a felled pagan oak symbolised Christ and new beginnings.

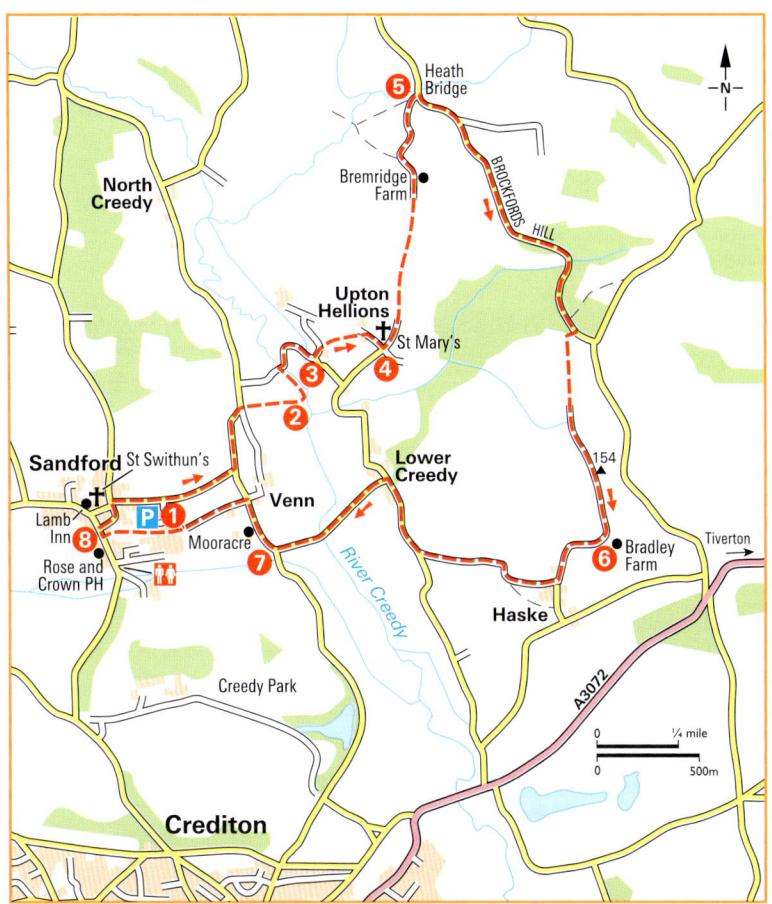

1. From the car park turn right along the lane. At the T-junction turn left; the lane soon descends. Just before a left bend turn right through a gate into fields. The permitted path runs left along the field edge to a gate in the far corner (boggy). Keep ahead to another onto a riverside path and turn left.

2. The path bears right over a footbridge then follows the River Creedy. Pass through a gate and cross a muddy track, then Shaky Bridge over the river. Meet the track again and turn right through a gate into a field; keep straight on, aiming to the right of The Old Mill. Pass through a small gate before the mill and bear right to the lane.

3. Turn left; after 90yds (100m) turn right through a gate into a field and keep uphill, alongside a fence. Go through a small gate in the fence and continue uphill; bear right by a wall below a big house. Pass through a gate and down the drive to reach the church; keep ahead to a track junction.

4. Bear left on a track (footpath) that rises steadily between hedges. Stay on it as it undulates through huge fields and gateways with far-reaching views, eventually descending past buildings at Bremridge Farm (dating from around 1450). Follow the drive downhill to the lane near Heath Bridge.

5. Turn right; a long, steep climb follows but at last the lane levels past Broxford Cottage. About 160yds (146m) later turn right on a bridleway track, with woodland right. Follow the track left and along the left edge of huge rolling fields, with sweeping views towards Dartmoor. The final climb and descent gains the entrance to Bradley Farm (left).

6. Turn right across fields to reach a track junction at Haske Farm. Keep straight on along a hedged green lane (muddy in places) to reach a tarmac lane. Turn right to reach a junction at Lower Creedy. Turn left downhill to cross the river and meet a T-junction at Thornhedges Cross.

7. Turn right, slightly uphill. Pass thatched Mooracre (left); opposite farm buildings turn left on a footpath down a narrow lane which leads onto a track across a field. Keep straight on through a small gate onto a path, then through another back into fields. Pass through a bank and then a gate onto a fenced path to meet the road on Rose and Crown Hill.

8. Cross over and through The Square (Lamb Inn ahead, Sandford Community Stores right). At the corner turn right uphill past St Swithun's Church; turn left, then first right to the car park.

Where to eat and drink
The Lamb Inn is a 16th-century posting house with accommodation, good food, a lovely garden and a skittle alley. The Rose and Crown is found on the road to Crediton. For delicious home-made cakes and a touch of railway nostalgia visit Crediton Station Tea Rooms.

What to see
Parts of Devon are known for their red sandstone soils, and – as you will see from the state of your boots – Sandford is located in the Devonshire 'redlands'. The Devonshire Heartland Way, a 43-mile (26.7km) waymarked route, enjoys gentle pastoral landscapes from Okehampton to the Exe Valley, and passes through Crediton.

While you're there
Take a ride from Crediton station on the Tarka Line, along the route of the old Exeter and Crediton Railway, which opened in 1851 and was extended to Barnstaple by the North Devon Railway three years later. You'll get a real feel of Devon's rural heartland, plus opportunities for circular walks from stations along the line, or from one station to the next.

BAMPTON

DISTANCE/TIME	5.5 miles (8.8km) / 2hrs 30min
ASCENT/GRADIENT	425ft (130m) / ▲▲
PATHS	Fields, tracks and lanes, many stiles
LANDSCAPE	Rolling farmland and wooded combes
SUGGESTED MAP	OS Explorer 114 Exeter & the Exe Valley
START/FINISH	Grid reference: SS955221
DOG FRIENDLINESS	Keep on lead in fields
PARKING	Station Road car park opposite church
PUBLIC TOILETS	By car park

Bampton is one of those places that isn't really on the way to anywhere. As you drive north towards Exmoor from Tiverton you might sweep past the turning to Bampton, making for Dulverton up the Barle Valley. But it would be a mistake not to go and have a look at this quiet, ancient town, situated at a natural crossing place on the River Batherm, and whose Saxon origins are still evident in the layout of its building plots, streets and almost circular churchyard. In 1258, a royal charter established St Luke's Fair, which survives today as a funfair and street market.

Bampton held important cattle and wool sheep markets from the 14th century, and the various fine buildings in the town to be seen today are evidence of wealthier times in the 17th and 18th centuries, when the cloth industry was at its most prosperous. The town was famous for the Bampton Notts, said to be the finest breed of sheep in Devon, but which died out in the late 19th century. Before the coming of the railway in 1884, the sheep were herded on foot to Bristol, 60 miles (97km) away, for sale.

It's worth deviating from your route a little to have a look at the church of St Michael and All Angels in Bampton, dating in part from the 12th century, though an earlier one occupied the site. A late Saxon or early Norman window arch can be seen high in the south wall. An interesting feature here is the stone casing around two enormous yew trees in the churchyard, to prevent the sheep that used to graze here from being poisoned. The roots of these huge trees may be responsible for the cracks that have appeared in the south wall.

As the walk penetrates deeper into the Devon countryside, it reaches the tiny village of Morebath, essentially a farming community, as it has been since Saxon times. There are warm springs of chalybeate water here in a marshy basin, from which the name Morebath derives. The simple tower of St George's Church probably dates from the 11th century but its most unusual feature is the saddleback roof, part of the 19th-century restoration, which is unlike anything seen elsewhere in the county.

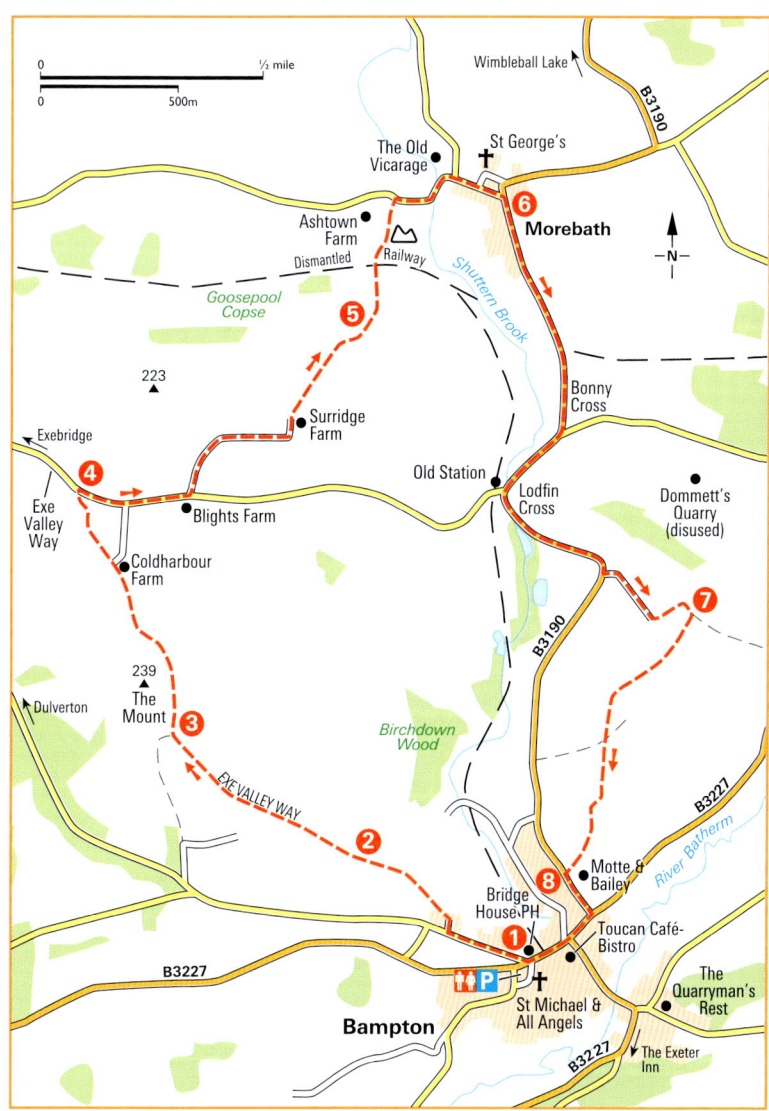

1. Leave the car park by the toilets, cross the road and turn left up the steep, narrow lane signposted 'Dulverton'. After a few minutes follow Exe Valley Way (EVW) signs right up a drive, left through a gate and up the field keeping right. Cross over the stile and go left down the track to cross a double stile in the top corner of the field. Turn immediately right over another then turn left through a tree-studded bank and right, uphill (with bank right).

2. Follow EVW signs over the next stile, straight across the field to a gate (top left) and cross the next field to an open gateway. Turn left, then immediately right, keeping the hedge left, to reach a metal gate just over the brow of the hill, with views towards Exmoor.

3. Continue downhill along the right field edge to pass through a gate before Coldharbour Farm. Bear half left towards a gate; follow the signed path through fields, eventually through a big gate and along the left field edge. A gate leads onto the lane.

4. The EVW goes left, but turn right up the lane to reach Blights Farm. Turn left up the drive towards Surridge Farm. Just past a bungalow turn left through a gate in the fence, then half right up the field to pass through another gate (barns right). Keep ahead through another gate, and follow the right field edge through a gate onto a green lane (muddy in winter). There are views of Morebath ahead.

5. Keep ahead downhill and over the dismantled railway towards Ashtown Farm, then right down the drive. Turn right and follow the deep lane uphill past The Old Vicarage to the centre of Morebath village. Keep ahead to meet the B3190.

6. Turn right down the road, taking care. At Bonny Cross keep right (signed 'Bampton') to pass Lodfin Cross and the old station. When the road bends sharply right take the unsigned stony track ahead, slightly uphill.

7. At the hilltop a footpath sign leads right through a kissing gate. Keep along the right edge of the field, through a gate and over a stile, then straight on through a gate, over another stile. Go through a gate at the top of the next field, and turn immediately left through a gate. Cross the field diagonally right towards the left of two gates. Pass through the next field to a stile at the top, then down a narrow fenced path towards Bampton. Cross over the next stile and field to gain the road via a gate.

8. Cross over, turn left, then bear right down the old road into the town. Turn right towards the church and your car.

Where to eat and drink
Bampton has several pubs and cafés. Try The Bridge House by the car park or The Quarryman's Rest on Briton Street; pop into the Toucan Café-Bistro on Brook Street for tea or coffee and snacks.

What to see
Beyond Point 7 of the walk you get your first sight of the Norman motte and bailey of Bampton Castle which was built on Saxon foundations in 1067. Traces of the original enclosure are still visible within the bailey.

While you're there
Drive into Somerset to Wimbleball Lake, straight up the B3190 and over Haddon Hill beyond Morebath. Wimbleball – 374 acres (151ha) of water and 500 acres (202ha) of surrounding meadow and woodland – lies just inside the Exmoor National Park and there are plenty of recreational opportunities here: sailing and rowing clubs, a gift shop and café, a camping field and miles of waymarked trails, as well as a nature reserve.

A CIRCUIT TO MOLLAND COMMON

DISTANCE/TIME	3 miles (4.8km) / 1hr 45min
ASCENT/GRADIENT	328ft (100m) / ▲▲▲
PATHS	Field paths and moorland tracks (some muddy after wet weather); several stiles
LANDSCAPE	Farmland and moorland
SUGGESTED MAP	OS Explorer OL9 Exmoor
START/FINISH	Grid reference: SS808284
DOG FRIENDLINESS	On lead in nesting season (1 March–15 July), and in churchyard
PARKING	Near St Mary's Church, Molland
PUBLIC TOILETS	None on route

If you approach South Molton via the Chulmleigh road, which heads north through rolling farmland, the town known as 'the gateway to Exmoor' suddenly appears against a wonderful backdrop of Exmoor's southernmost hills. Granted a market charter and the right to hold an annual fair (still celebrated in June) in 1357, it still has an active pannier market and main weekly market. The undulating farmland around the town is some of the least walked in the county, yet home to a wealth of small villages, hamlets and scattered farmsteads, linked by a labyrinth of narrow lanes. One particularly interesting settlement is Molland, nestled in unspoiled countryside between the A361 and Exmoor, 7.5 miles (12.1km) east of South Molton.

This tiny village shelters beneath the swell of Molland Common, surrounded by hilly farmland and wooded combes. Molland is home to a good pub, a village shop, and the most perfect example of a Georgian church found in Devon. St Mary's Church escaped the attentions of Victorian restorers. Step through the enormously heavy wooden door (the weight in itself implies you have arrived somewhere special) and you are met by dark, high box pews, flagstone floors, ornate 17th- and 18th-century monuments to the Courtenay family who lived at West Molland, leaning arcades and an impressive three-decker canopied pulpit. During conservation work in 2009, a section of the original seating dating from 1500 was found partially supporting the pulpit – the existing box pews are later, and date from the early 18th century.

In the church you will also find information relating to the Molland lily, rare in the country and thought to have been introduced to north Devon by monks from Spain in medieval times.

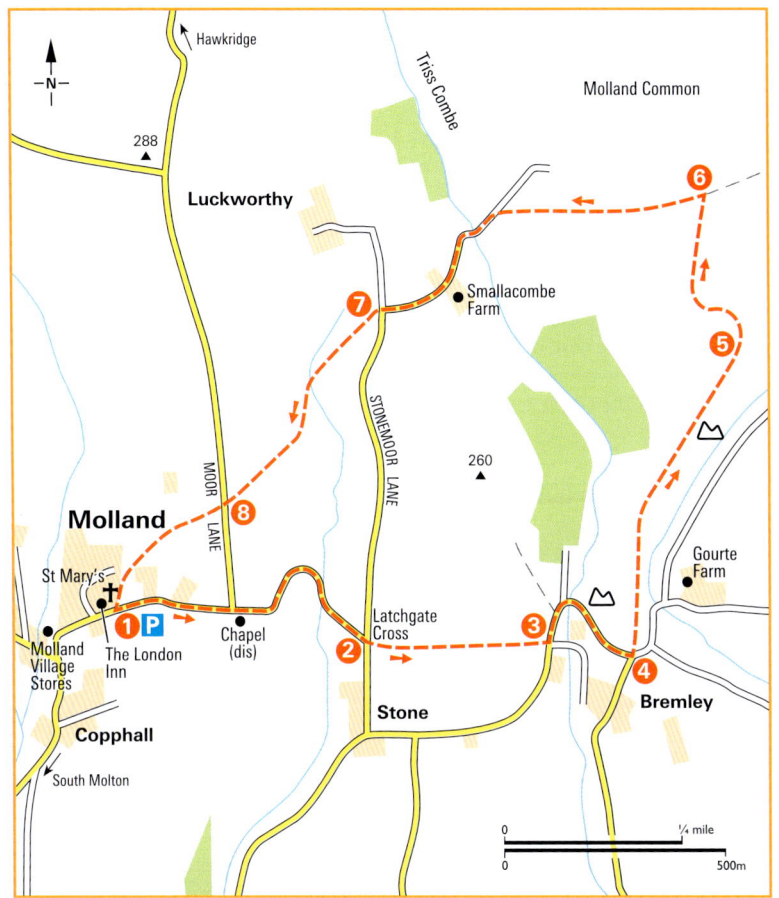

1. With the church on your left, follow the lane away from The London Inn. Where it bears sharp left (Moor Lane) by a disused chapel, keep straight on, dropping steeply into and out of a combe to reach Latchgate Cross. The lane bears sharp right.

2. Keep ahead, turning right through a gate. Turn left along the top edge of two fields via gates. At the end of a third, cross a stile – the ground ahead drops steeply. Keeping right of a gully, descend carefully to a footpath post, and bear left down to a stile leading onto a lane.

3. Turn left on the lane, cross a stream and ascend steeply to Bremley Cross.

4. Ignore bridleway signs ahead, but immediately turn left towards a signed gate. Follow the track up the west side of a combe, with Gourte Farm on your right. The track bears right, away from the hedge bank, and climbs steeply (good views to Dartmoor behind). The wide-open spaces of Molland Common appear invitingly ahead. Eventually follow the track left through a gate.

5. Keep along the left edge of the field. Turn right at the corner, and about 100yds (91m) before the field end pass through the right of two gates onto Molland Common.

6. Turn left along the lower edge, soon descending, with a hedge bank left. The track becomes more defined and drops steadily to cross a small ford and footbridge over a stream. Pass through a gate, and follow the hedged track uphill past Smallacombe Farm.

7. At a T-junction keep ahead through a gate into a field. Cross diagonally, passing to the right of a fence corner, then through a gate in the field corner. Keep straight ahead, dropping steeply over a disused leat to a footbridge/stile/footbridge, then ascend steps onto a grassy track. Turn left. Where the track forks, keep ahead, uphill, passing a line of beech trees. Cross the field in the same direction, and go through a gate onto Moor Lane.

8. Cross over and go through a gate. Cross the field to pass through a gate. Head across the next, dropping through a gate onto a track. Keep ahead downhill, to the left of farm buildings. After a few paces turn left into the churchyard, then right, left and left again to find your car.

Where to eat and drink
The London Inn is a 16th-century coaching inn and traditional country pub. On South Molton's South Street you will find The Corn Dolly, one of the best tea rooms in Devon and patronised by devotees from many miles around.

What to see
You'll see Exmoor ponies on Molland Common, and you're also quite likely to see some of Exmoor's red deer. Exmoor was once a Royal Forest, and the red deer population was hunted for venison. Today, there are around 3,000 of these creatures – the largest wild animal found in England – living on the moor.

While you're there
Just north of West Anstey Common is the beautiful valley of the River Barle, and the isolated village of Hawkridge. Tarr Steps, the largest clapper bridge on Exmoor and an iconic 15th-century landmark, crosses the Barle just north of Hawkridge – all but one span was washed away in the floods of August 1952.

AROUND KILLERTON PARK

DISTANCE/TIME	4.5 miles (7.2km) / 2hrs
ASCENT/GRADIENT	131ft (40m) / ▲
PATHS	Good footpaths, bridleways and farm tracks
LANDSCAPE	Gently undulating woodland and parkland
SUGGESTED MAP	OS Explorer 114 Exeter & the Exe Valley
START/FINISH	Grid reference: SS976001
DOG FRIENDLINESS	Keep on lead
PARKING	National Trust car park
PUBLIC TOILETS	Between car park and stable courtyard

This gentle exploration of the countryside around the National Trust estate at Killerton, just north of Exeter and given to the Trust by Sir Richard Acland in 1944, uses a variety of public footpaths and bridleways, but does not give access to the gardens; if you wish to visit them you must pay an entrance fee (NT members free). Killerton was formed by the Acland family and their original house (only the gatehouse and chapel remain) was at Columbjohn, and was used by the King's troops during the siege of Exeter in the Civil War.

Killerton is well worth a visit: quite apart from the house – rebuilt in 1778 to the design of John Johnson – and delightful gardens (with colour-coded waymarked walks) there is a National Trust shop, tea room and plant centre in the old stable block and courtyard, as well as a playground, orchard and picnic area. The whole estate covers 6,400 acres (2,591ha) and includes Ashclyst Forest, 2 miles (3.2km) to the east (with waymarked walks), the Red Lion Inn in Broadclyst, to the south, and the disused paper mill by Ellerhayes Bridge.

The park and gardens at Killerton were created in the late 18th century, making full use of the contours of the natural landscape, and are characterised by a wide variety of exotic tree species, including tall Wellingtonias (named after the Duke of Wellington). The gardens feature magnolias, azaleas and rhododendrons on the wooded slopes above the house, and superb herbaceous borders on the lower levels. As you enter the parkland at Point 2 you pass some splendid examples of cedar of Lebanon and holm oak, and a beautiful weeping willow on an island in a pond (on the left).

Just past the house the walk leads uphill near the memorial to Sir Thomas Dyke Acland, and you can enjoy good views west towards the Exe Valley and beyond to Cosdon Hill on Dartmoor. In Columbjohn Wood badger tracks abound, and in spring the air is heavy with the scent of wild garlic and bluebells. You may glimpse roe deer; you will certainly hear the deep croak of ravens, and the mewing cry of a buzzard soaring overhead. But look out for the dragon which travels by underground tunnel between the twin Iron Age hill forts of Dolbury Hill, which lies just north of the house in the centre of the estate (not visited) and Cadbury Castle, 6 miles (9.7km) to the northwest.

1. From the car park return to the road and turn right to reach the gate and cattle grid at the entrance to Killerton house. Follow the public footpath across the park, parallel to the drive, passing the stable courtyard from where ticket holders approach the house.

2. Continue across the park to pass to the left of the house and keep straight on, past formal gardens. Towards the end of the park bear half left to pass through a kissing gate in the hedge ahead, into a large sloping field.

3. Turn right uphill, keeping by the hedge and then an iron fence on your right. At the top of the field ignore the public footpath sign and 'Bluebell Gate', and turn left down across the field to enter Columbjohn Wood through a small gate.

4. Turn left, and immediately branch left again on the higher path round a wooden barrier, which leads gradually downhill. Leave the wood by another kissing gate, and keep straight on to meet Point 6 and follow a farm track. After 250yds (229m) go right as signed through a gate onto a fenced path. Pass a cottage to arrive at the peaceful 16th-century Columbjohn Chapel.

5. Go through a kissing gate to gain the grassy drive on the other side of the chapel, and take a look left at the old arched gatehouse. Retrace your steps through the field back to the track junction.

6. Keep ahead and follow this delightful track through woods and fields around the edge of the estate, above the River Culm. (A cycle track bears off right through a gate where indicated on the map: a good alternative if the main track is too wet.) The track reaches the road by Ellerhayes Bridge.

7. Do not go on to the road; turn right to follow the edge of gently ascending parkland, keeping the road on your left. You will pass through several gates on a NT bridlepath, which eventually goes through two gates to join a gravel track. Turn left downhill to find the entrance to the Chapel of the Holy Evangelists, built in the Norman style in 1842 for the Aclands, their tenants and employees, and to replace the one at Columbjohn.

8. Continue on down the road. Turn right at the junction, and right again into the car park.

Where to eat and drink
Killerton has the Kitchen Café and the Stables Café and there is a good pub – the Red Lion Inn – attractively situated by the church in Broadclyst, 2.5 miles (4km) south on the B3181.

What to see
Columbjohn Chapel burial ground is dominated by the graves of the Acland family – look out for the tombstone of the Silverton stationmaster. Unfortunately, the chapel is used as a storeroom and kept locked, but the stone doorway and simple bell tower are quite charming. It's an ideal spot to pause and enjoy a quiet moment of reflection.

While you're there
Go and have a look at Killerton itself, which is open from mid-March to early November (gardens open all year; NT members free). For foodies there's a monthly farmers' market and an annual apple-and-cider weekend, and local produce on sale in the shop; for the active there's a 3-mile (5km) parkrun around the estate every Saturday at 9am.

ALONG THE EXE AT BRAMPFORD SPEKE

DISTANCE/TIME	4 miles (6.4km) / 1hr 45min
ASCENT/GRADIENT	Negligible
PATHS	Grassy field paths, tracks and country lanes; several stiles
LANDSCAPE	Watermeadows and farmland
SUGGESTED MAP	OS Explorer 114 Exeter & the Exe Valley
START/FINISH	Grid reference: SX927982
DOG FRIENDLINESS	Keep on lead in fields
PARKING	On main road through the village to the west of St Peter's Church
PUBLIC TOILETS	None on route
NOTES	Do not park in the private drive called Church Drive leading to the church and house

There is a secluded piece of Devonshire countryside lying just north of Exeter. Few would think of turning off the A377 Exeter to Crediton road to have a look around – but here is a beautiful area of undulating woods and farmland in the Exe Valley. Brampford Speke is just one of the pleasant cob and thatch villages that lies tucked away here, situated on a low cliff of red sandstone overhanging the River Exe as it meanders lazily through its flood plain. Victorian writer George Gissing described the village:

'I have discovered a village called Brampford Speke on the Exe, which I seriously think is one of the most perfect I ever saw. One imagines that some lord of the manor must exert himself to keep it in a picturesque state.'

That impression still holds true today – you almost feel as if the river is relieved to reach Brampford Speke and is taking a rest after a long journey from its source. This is high on Exmoor to the north, from where it tumbles down through deeply wooded combes, past the Norman castle at Tiverton, under the bridge at Bickleigh and on to the flood plain. As you stroll along the banks of the Exe you may notice a number of places where it appears that the river has changed – or is going to change – its course. This is a common flood plain feature. The erosive power of the water alters as the river swings through the level plain, and starts to cut deeply into the outer bends of its course. At the same time silt and alluvial debris carried in its waters are deposited on the inner bends where the current is less strong. As time goes on the process intensifies until eventually the river cuts across the bend and carves a new course, leaving behind a curved 'oxbow' lake, separate from the river.

The fertile red soils of the Exe Valley, derived from Permian sandstones, provide good arable farmland and meadows, the best agricultural land in Devon. The area has been thickly populated and farmed for centuries.

At Upton Pyne a group of Bronze Age burial barrows has been dated to around 2000 BC. It was recorded in the Domesday Book (1086) that of 99 mills in Devon, three-quarters were located in or east of the Exe Valley. This was an important cloth-making area in the 14th century, with a large number of fulling ('tucking') mills (where woven cloth was flattened to improve its appearance). A tax return of 1332 recorded that 38 'tuckers' were sufficiently well off to pay tax, and that a large percentage came from this area.

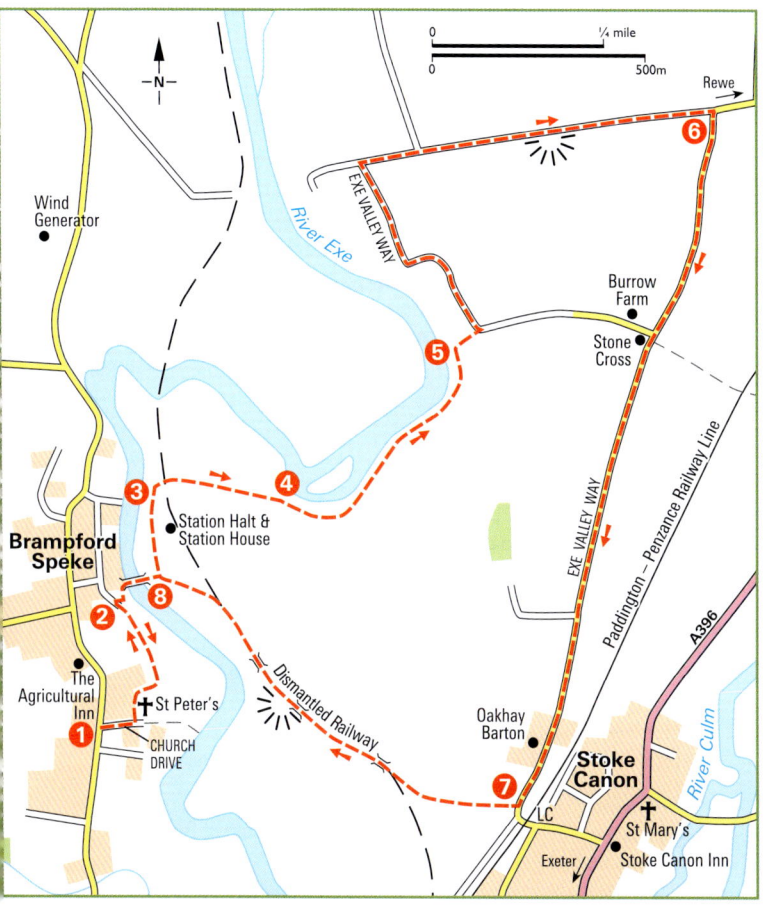

1. Follow Exe Valley Way (EVW) signs down Church Drive (private road) towards the church, then left past its west end and through a metal gate. The hedged path leads to a kissing gate under the lychgate and onto a lane.

2. Turn right and descend towards the river, crossing the Exe on a large footbridge. Bear left along a path. Note the old station and stationmaster's house across the meadow to the right.

3. Follow the footpath sign; before reaching a five-bar gate take the path forking right, passing through a copse to a kissing gate. Keep along the right hedge of two fields to reach the river again and pass through a double kissing gate.

4. Bear right along the riverbank, soon crossing a stile into a huge and level riverside field. Continue alongside the river.

5. Eventually the path bears right away from the river down a hedged track and through a kissing gate. Turn immediately left along a green lane, keeping ahead where the EVW path goes sharp left (unsigned). The green lane leads across arable farmland to reach a lane corner by bungalows on the road to Rewe.

6. Turn right along the lane towards Stoke Canon to pass the old cross at Burrow Farm. Carry straight on to pass Oakhay Barton. Note: the Stoke Canon level crossing on the Exeter–Tiverton line ahead.

7. Just before the level crossing turn right through a kissing gate and along a fenced path. Pass through two more kissing gates to reach the line of the old railway trackbed. Just before a bridge pass through another kissing gate. The River Exe loops in on the left and Brampford Speke church is seen ahead above the river – it's a beautifully serene spot. A kissing gate leads over a small bridge and through a copse. Another kissing gate leads back into marshy meadows: follow the path ahead to regain the footbridge over the river. (Note: in times of very wet weather bear right after the kissing gate to find a stepped footbridge which avoids the boggiest ground.)

8. Retrace your steps over the bridge and up the path, turning left at the lychgate and then back through the churchyard to your car.

Where to eat and drink
The Agricultural Inn in Brampford Speke, serves good food, has a wide range of ales, and afternoon teas are also on offer. A brief detour across the railway line at Point 7 will take you to the Stoke Canon Inn, a successful community-run pub.

What to see
You're quite likely to get a sight of a grey heron during this walk. This large but graceful long-legged wader is unmistakable, but always exciting to see. In early summer keep an eye out for nesting sand martins in the riverbank at Point 7.

While you're there
Have a day out in historic Exeter, 3 miles (4.8km) south of Brampford Speke. Although heavily damaged by bombing in May 1942, the city has much to recommend it. At the lowest crossing point of the River Exe, the Romans established a settlement here – Isca – around AD 50, and traces of the original Roman walls (c. AD 200) can be seen today. The Norman period is represented by Rougemont Castle (1068), and the superb cathedral and close (1114–33), with its intricately carved West Front and unique ribbed, vaulted ceiling above the nave. The restored quay provides an attractive setting for cafés and craft shops.

EXETER TO TOPSHAM ALONG THE CANAL

DISTANCE/TIME	5.7miles (9.1km) / 2hrs 20mins
ASCENT/GRADIENT	Negligible
PATHS	Level tow paths
LANDSCAPE	River estuary and salt marsh; extensive mudflats at low tide
SUGGESTED MAP	OS Explorer OL44 Torquay & Dawlish
START/FINISH	Grid reference: SX972844
DOG FRIENDLINESS	Keep on lead near wildfowl and livestock; be aware of bicycles
PARKING	By St Clement's Church, Powderham
PUBLIC TOILETS	None on route

This easy walk along the picturesque estuary of the River Exe has a huge amount to offer. You can visit nearby medieval Powderham Castle, which is open to visitors from late March–October (excluding Saturdays) and you can see the oldest ship canal in the country. There are usually boat trips to watch rare avocets here in February, and a ferry ride at Point 6 takes you to the historic port of Topsham. An important port since Roman times, it prospered greatly when shipping could no longer reach Exeter, and its eventful history has been based largely on shipbuilding and smuggling. Today, conversely, the estuary is used mainly by commercial and pleasure craft, and by thousands of birds who return each year to feed on the mudflats.

The original canal was begun in 1566, and ran from Exeter to Matford Brook. It was extended to Topsham in 1675, and then to The Turf, enabling trade vessels of over 300 tons to reach Exeter again (the estuary had silted up during the 14th century). In 1827 the Exeter to Topsham Canal was deepened and extended a further 2 miles (3.2km) to the Turf Lock, giving it a total length of 5.25 miles (8.4km). The original wooden lock gates can be seen beside the canal. Weighing 15 tons, these were opened and closed by hand-operated winches, requiring enormous strength; they needed constant repair, and were replaced every 50 years. The gates currently in use are made of steel and electronically operated. Commercial use of the canal started to decrease after the arrival of the railway to Exeter in 1844.

St Clement's Church, the largely 13th-century red sandstone building at the walk's start (note that on Sunday mornings parking is reserved for churchgoers, so you will need to park on the laneside), is situated on the Powderham estate, the historic family home of the Earls of Devon. The original house dates back to the late 14th century when it was the home of Sir Philip Courtenay. Extensive damage caused during the Civil War was followed by a comprehensive programme of restoration in the 18th and 19th centuries. Both house and park are open to the public, and Powderham Farm Shop, on the A379 near the main entrance, has a café, food shop, garden shop and gifts.

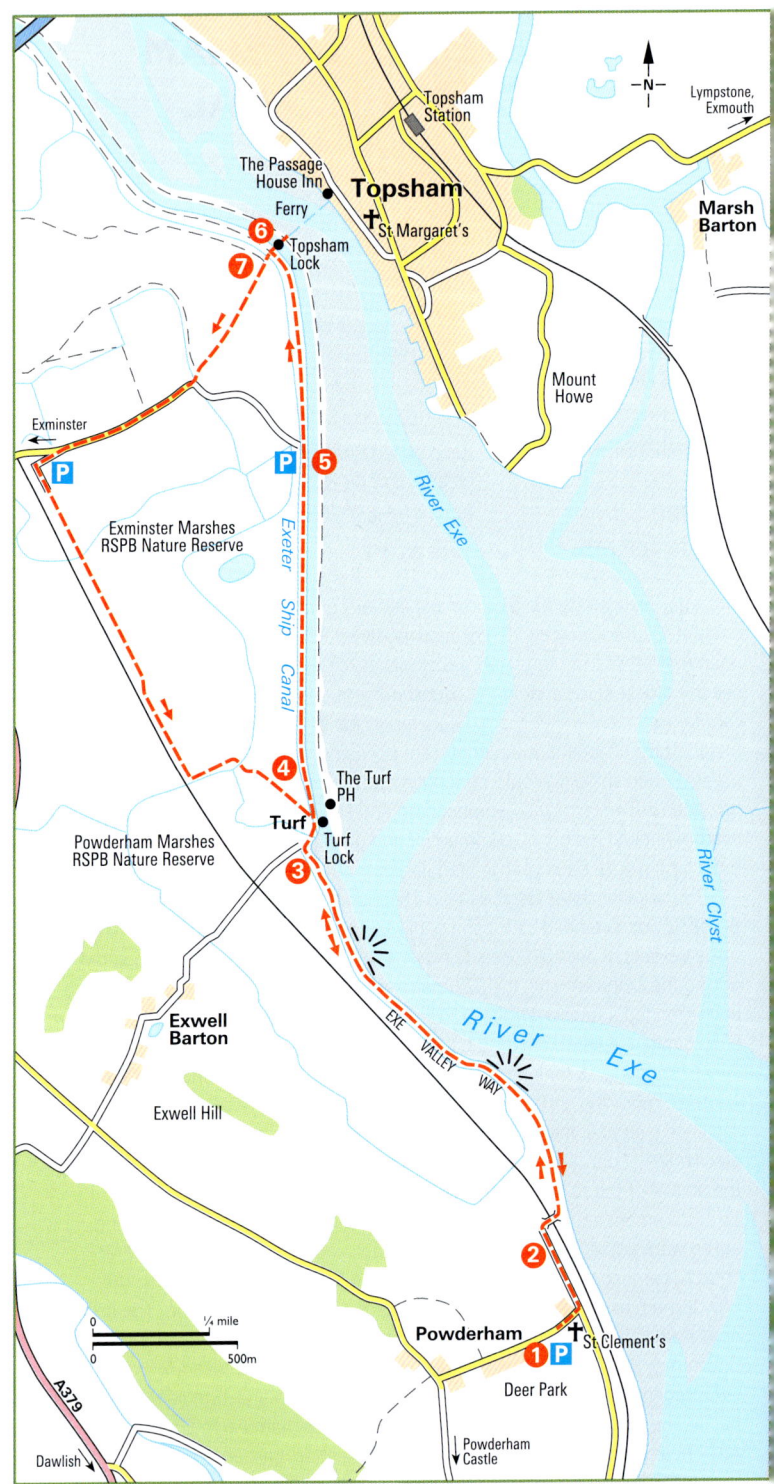

1. Walk down the lane past the church towards the river. After a few paces turn left to join the Exe Valley Way/Exe Estuary Trail (the latter a 26-mile/42km walking/cycling route around the estuary). Follow the path and cross over the Exeter–Newton Abbot railway line.

2. Turn left to walk upriver; there are superb views across the broad estuary to (from left to right) Topsham, Exton, the Royal Marine Commandos Training Centre, Lympstone and Exmouth.

3. Continue and, within 20 minutes, pass through a gate to reach the outlet of the Exeter Ship Canal at the Turf Lock, with The Turf beyond. The building which now houses the pub was probably built to accommodate visiting boat crews and their horses, which hauled the barges up to Exeter.

4. Don't go over the lock gates but keep straight on up the canal, passing through a small white gate. This stretch is beautiful, with bulrushes and water lilies lining the banks, and is popular with canoeists. Cyclists are directed along the lane parallel to the canal.

5. Pass through another small white gate, with a parking area below left. The River Exe, beyond the canal, narrows as you walk upstream, and the buildings of Topsham come into view across the water. Reach Topsham Lock (built in 1832) via another white gate.

6. Turn right across the bridge to reach the Topsham ferry slipway. The ferry runs from April to October, but is always dependent on tide and weather. There is also a ferry service that runs from Topsham to The Turf. Hail the ferryman if he's not waiting for you. Cross the river and have a drink at The Passage House Inn and, if you have time, take a look round Topsham.

7. Facing upstream at Topsham Lock turn left, away from the canal, and pass into the Exminster Marshes RSPB Nature Reserve through a gate by a noticeboard. The footpath ahead leads to a lane, which continues towards the railway. Just before the railway turn left and cross the marshes via a series of footbridges, regaining the tow path near The Turf Lock. Turn right and replicate the outward route back to your car. (Note that this route may be impassable after wet weather, if so return to your car via the outward route from Topsham Lock).

Where to eat and drink

The Turf, in a fantastic position between the canal mouth and the River Exe, is a free house with good food. Open all year round, the pub is only accessible on foot, bike or by boat (tel 01392 575200). The Passage House Inn in Topsham specialises in seafood and welcomes families. It's a great place to sit and watch the craft on the river.

What to see

The Exe estuary is a haven for birdlife. From the path near Powderham look out for oystercatchers and all manner of waders exploring the mudflats; Powderham Marshes is the most important site for breeding lapwings in Devon and Cornwall; and Exminster Marshes attracts winter visitors such as curlews and black-tailed godwits, and breeding lapwings and redshanks in spring.

17 STEPS BRIDGE AND THE RIVER TEIGN

DISTANCE/TIME	5.5 miles (8.8km) / 2hrs 45min
ASCENT/GRADIENT	393ft (120m) / ▲▲▲
PATHS	Woodland paths, open fields and country lanes, several stiles
LANDSCAPE	Steeply wooded valleys and undulating farmland
SUGGESTED MAP	OS Explorer OL44 Torquay & Dawlish
START/FINISH	Grid reference: SX803883
DOG FRIENDLINESS	Keep on lead in field
PARKING	Car park (and tourist information board) at Steps Bridge
PUBLIC TOILETS	None on route

In early springtime many people travel out to Steps Bridge (built in 1816) to stroll along the River Teign, enjoying the sight of thousands of tiny wild daffodils crowding the river banks. But there's a better way to explore this valley, which includes a close look at an example of that most characteristic Dartmoor feature, a tor – and a pint at a Teign Valley pub as an added bonus.

Much of the ancient semi-natural woodland and valley meadows around Steps Bridge is a Site of Special Scientific Interest (SSSI), and many acres are owned by the National Trust. Dunsford Wood (on the opposite bank of the Teign from the car park) is managed as a nature reserve by the Devon Wildlife Trust. These woodlands are glorious all year round: there are snowdrops in February, daffodils in early spring, wood anemones and ramsoms; then foxgloves, woodrush and cow-wheat in summer. Look out for the nest of the wood ant by the side of the path, which can be as much as a metre high. If you place your cheek or hand near to a nest you'll get a shock – the ants squirt formic acid from their abdomens in a defensive move, and it stings.

Blackingstone Rock is another outlying tor, 1 mile (1.6km) southwest of Heltor Rock. Turn right rather than left at Point 4 and you will soon be aware of its huge, granite mass rising above the lane on the left. You can get to the top by climbing up an almost vertical flight of steps which were added in the 19th century for that purpose.

While you're in Bridford, part way round the walk, it's well worthwhile going inside the church. The original chapel on this site was dedicated by Bishop Bronescombe in 1259, to the murdered Archbishop Thomas à Becket, who died at Canterbury Cathedral in 1170. This was still a common practice in many West Country churches during the century following his death. The present building dates from the 15th century, and its most famous feature is the superb eight-bay rood screen, thought to date from 1508. The faces of the richly carved and coloured figures were mutilated by Puritan soldiers during the Civil War, but what survives is still impressive. The doors are also unusual in that they are made in one piece rather than being divided in the middle.

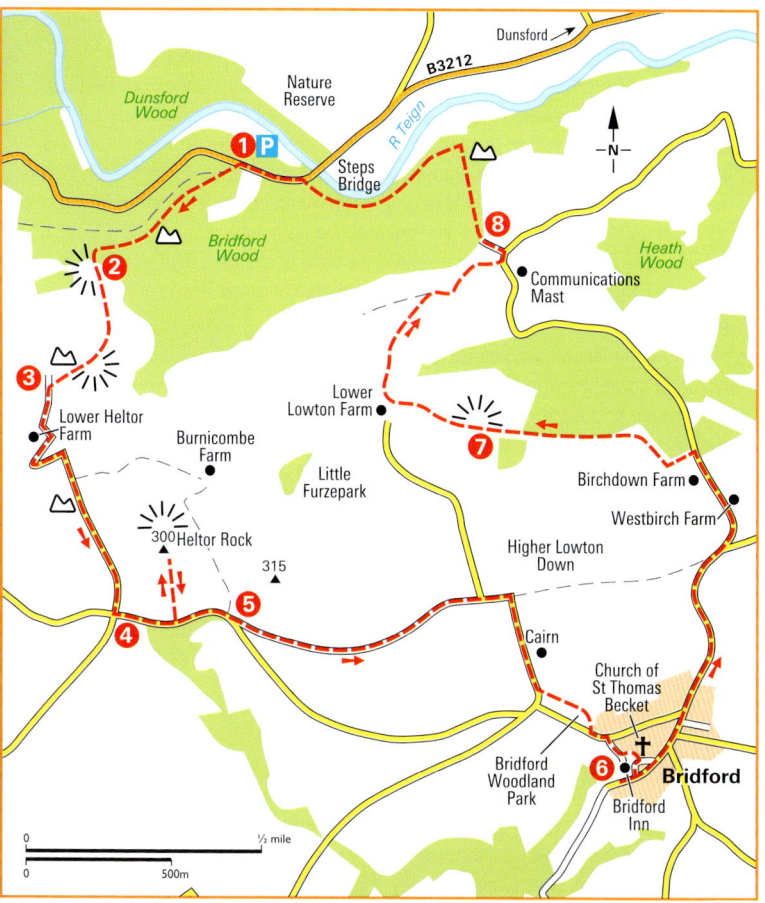

1. From the car park cross the road, and turn right up the concrete track, then left towards the former youth hostel building; the path bears right, and is signed for Heltor Farm. On meeting a track turn left and climb steeply through pretty woodland. At the top follow yellow markers left to pass through an open gateway by a small gate.

2. Follow a fenced path straight up the field and through a small gate. Keep up the left edge of the next field; pass through a gateway and look to the left to see Heltor Rock.

3. At the end of the second field turn left as signed through a wooden gate into a plantation; follow the path to meet a gate onto a lane. Turn left and walk uphill to meet a tarmac lane.

4. Turn left (signs for Bridford). After 200yds (183m) turn left over a stile up the narrow fenced permissive path to Heltor, from where you can enjoy an amazing panorama. Retrace your steps to the road and turn left, soon passing the drive to Burnicombe Farm.

5. Take the next track left (to Lowton). Meet a lane on a bend and keep ahead, following it sharp right; eventually turn left through a gate into Bridford Woodland Park. Follow the permissive path around its edge to reach the lane;

turn left. Turn right down a steep lane signed 'Parish Hall & Church'. Follow the church wall path, down steps and right to find the Bridford Inn.

6. Turn left from the pub and follow the lane through the centre of the village. As the road bends sharp left, take the fourth turning (Neadon Lane) on the right, by a telephone box. Just past where a bridleway joins (from the left) the lane dips to the right, downhill; take the left fork ahead to pass Westbirch Farm on the right, then Birchdown Farm on the left. Keep straight on at the farms; turn left as signed to Lowton Farm on a fenced path, which bears right to a kissing gate; pass through and up the right edge of the next field to a stile in the top corner. Carry straight on through an area of gorse and bracken. Cross a stile by some beech trees.

7. Follow the fenced path along the top of two fields, and down a green lane to reach Lower Lowton Farm. Turn right as signed before the farm on a permissive bridle path, which descends (with a stream, right) then rises to the next signpost; turn right for Steps Bridge down the narrow green lane, passing through a small gate. Continue down the deeply banked green lane until you reach a surfaced lane though a gate.

8. Turn left through the middle gate, signed 'Byway to Steps Bridge'. At the edge of Bridford Wood (by the National Trust sign) turn right following the footpath signposts. The path is fairly narrow and quite steep. On meeting a path go left, then right, keeping down-hill. The path drops down steps to a junction. Turn left, now high above the river to meet the road just above Steps Bridge. Turn left here to return to your car.

Where to eat and drink
The Bridford Inn is a good place for a drink midway through the walk. You'll find benches for picnics in Bridford's Village Garden. In nearby Dunsford try The Royal Oak, open Friday – Sunday at lunchtime and every evening except Sunday and Monday, a good pub with a lovely garden.

While you're there
Go and have a look at the three reservoirs near Hennock, on the ridge between the Teign and Wray valleys – Tottiford, Kennick and Trenchford. Constructed over the period from 1860 to 1907 to service the increasing demand for water from Newton Abbot and Torquay, these beautiful expanses of fresh water, surrounded by coniferous woodland and rhododendron covered slopes offer easy walks and peaceful picnic sites.

TRENCHFORD AND TOTTIFORD RESERVOIRS

DISTANCE/TIME	3.75 miles (6km) / 1hr 30min
ASCENT/GRADIENT	Negligible
PATHS	Raised lakeside paths, some narrow and uneven
LANDSCAPE	Reservoir and woodland
SUGGESTED MAP	OS Explorer OL44 Torquay & Dawlish
START/FINISH	Grid reference: SX804824
DOG FRIENDLINESS	On lead at all times (wildfowl)
PARKING	Trenchford car park (pay-and-display)
PUBLIC TOILETS	Trenchford car park

Anyone exploring the narrow, hedged lanes that thread the ridge between the Teign and Wray valleys on the eastern edge of Dartmoor may be forgiven for expressing surprise when happening upon three linked expanses of open water, fringed by oak, sweet chestnut and rhododendron. These are the Torquay Reservoirs, built between 1861 and 1907. Today, the banks of these tranquil waters provide easy walking routes, linked by a network of tracks and paths that thread the surrounding forest. The walk described here incorporates a number of permissive paths, and can be shortened at Points 3 and 5 if required.

The reservoirs are named Kennick, Tottiford and Trenchford. The dam for Kennick was constructed by Henry Brunel, son of the great 19th-century engineer Isambard Kingdom Brunel, architect of the Great Western Railway and hugely influential in the West Country. The arrival of the railway was the root cause of Torquay's development from a small fishing village into a seaside resort, and as a result the demand for water rose considerably. Tottiford was started in 1861, and soon extended; Kennick was built between 1881 and 1884 to supply the growing populations of both Torquay and Newton Abbot. In 1901 a serious drought led to the building of another dam at Trenchford, started in 1903 and completed in 1907.

At times of low water, parts of old Kennick Farm may be seen in the highest reservoir. To the east lie the remains of Clampitt farmhouse (occupied in the 17th century by one Elias Tuckett, a devout Quaker) and a Quaker burial ground.

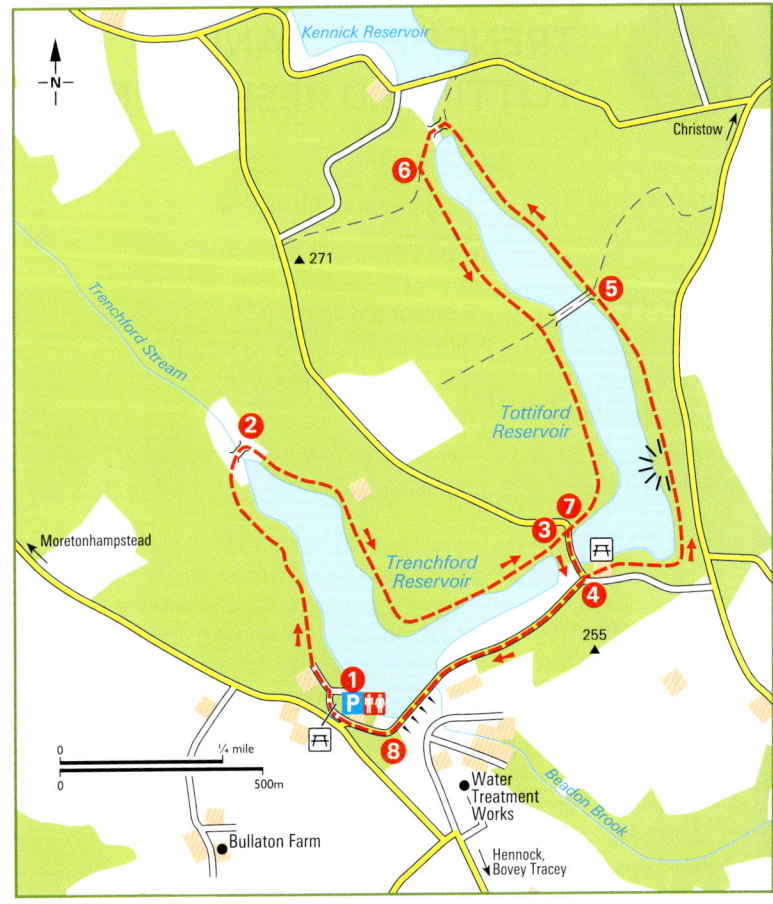

1. Pass the information board and toilet, and follow the path into woodland. Descend towards the reservoir (rooty and muddy in places) and cross a boardwalk, and later another towards the end of the water. Bear right to cross Trenchford stream on a bridge.

2. At the T-junction of paths, turn right and follow the narrow path along the bank. Cross three boardwalks: the dam comes into view ahead. Eventually pass a beautiful stand of beech trees and go through a gate onto the lane.

3. Turn right across the dam of Tottiford Reservoir (to shorten the walk, follow the lane back to the car park), with views right to Trendlebeare Down on Dartmoor. Old Tottiford Mill, situated just below the dam, was demolished in the early 20th century.

4. Where the lane bears right on the other side, turn left on a lane. Opposite a parking area (to your right) bear left past picnic tables and under tall conifers on a permissive footpath. Follow another narrow, raised path along the edge of Tottiford Reservoir, with open views.

5. At a bridge and path junction keep straight on. Eventually the path broadens and becomes grassy, under oak and sweet chestnut trees. On approaching the dam for Kennick Reservoir, duck under rhododendron bushes and bear left past a post with a green arrow. Cross the feeder stream on a footbridge. (Fishing for rainbow trout occurs on Kennick, and the lakeside paths are closed to walkers.)

6. Meet a path on the other side at a post and turn left along the west bank of the reservoir (note occasional forestry operations in this area). Pass a footpath junction at the bridge, and keep ahead past a small wooden shelter. Follow the path back to pass through a gate onto a lane.

7. Turn left across the dam and follow the quiet lane, which bears right and eventually crosses the Trenchford dam – note the impressive banks of rhododendrons. A memorial stone records the start of building on 1 October 1903, and its opening four years later.

8. Just over the dam, turn right through a gate to pass the intake pipe from Fernworthy Reservoir. Pass the picnic area and ascend steps to return to the car park.

Where to eat and drink
In the mid-17th century five men were licensed to sell alcohol in the village of Hennock. Today there's just The Palk Arms, a 16th-century free house serving traditional pub food and with wonderful views east over the Teign Valley towards the Haldon Hills and Haldon Belvedere folly, once owned by the wealthy Palk family.

What to see
The reservoirs are a good place to spot many species of wildfowl, particularly in winter, when visitors include pochard, tufted duck, teal and goosander. Cormorant, heron and coot may be seen all year round.

While you're there
The popular Haldon Forest Park offers walking and cycling routes. Those looking for peace and quiet should visit Haldon Belvedere (Lawrence Castle), a triangular tower built in 1788 by Sir Robert Palk in memory of Major General Stringer Lawrence, founder of the Indian Army. The tower is in private ownership but limited access to the grounds is allowed when functions are not being held.

19 AROUND LUSTLEIGH CLEAVE

DISTANCE/TIME	5.5 miles (8.8km) / 2hrs 30min
ASCENT/GRADIENT	754ft (230m) / ▲▲▲
PATHS	Steep rocky ascents/descents, rough paths and woodland
LANDSCAPE	Deeply wooded river valley and open moorland
SUGGESTED MAP	OS Explorer OL28 Dartmoor
START/FINISH	Grid reference: SX775816
DOG FRIENDLINESS	Keep on lead in fields and Bovey Valley NNR
PARKING	By side of lane at Hammerslake
PUBLIC TOILETS	None on route

Lustleigh is one of those perfect Devon villages that everyone just has to see. The rose-covered cottages and pub cluster tightly around the green and 13th-century Church of St John the Baptist. The quintessentially English cricket field, rushing streams and boulder-strewn hills, all nestling together in a deep wooded valley beneath the eastern fringe of Dartmoor, make this a real magnet. But Lustleigh has a problem (or perhaps an advantage?) – there is no car park, meaning that many people weave their way through the cars parked around the church and drive off again in frustration. But there is another way of getting a feel for the real Lustleigh: drive on through the village, park, and walk back in.

From the ridge approaching Hunter's Tor (after Point 2) you get a superb 360-degree view. To the south you can see the coast at Teignmouth. Following around clockwise you can pick out the familiar outline of Haytor, then Hound Tor (resembling a pack of hounds frozen in flight), Hayne Down and Bowerman's Nose, Manaton church and rocks, Easdon Tor, North Bovey, Bovey Castle, then Moretonhampstead with Mardon Down behind. Continuing round there is the stark outline of Blackingstone Rock then, far beyond on the Haldon Hills, the white tower of Haldon Belvedere, a folly erected in 1788 by Sir Robert Palk.

Lustleigh still holds a traditional May Day ceremony, which takes place on the first Saturday in May. The festival had died out, but was revived in the early years of the 20th century by Cecil Torr who, while living at Wreyland, wrote his famous three-volume work *Small Talk at Wreyland*, a charming record of rural life. The crowning ceremony at that time took place at Long Tor on the outskirts of the village. The May Queen, dressed in white and garlanded with spring flowers leads a procession around the village beneath a canopy of flowers which is held aloft by other Lustleigh children. She is then crowned on the May Day rock in the Town Orchard. A new granite throne was set in place on the rock to celebrate the Millennium, and the names of recent May Queens are carved below.

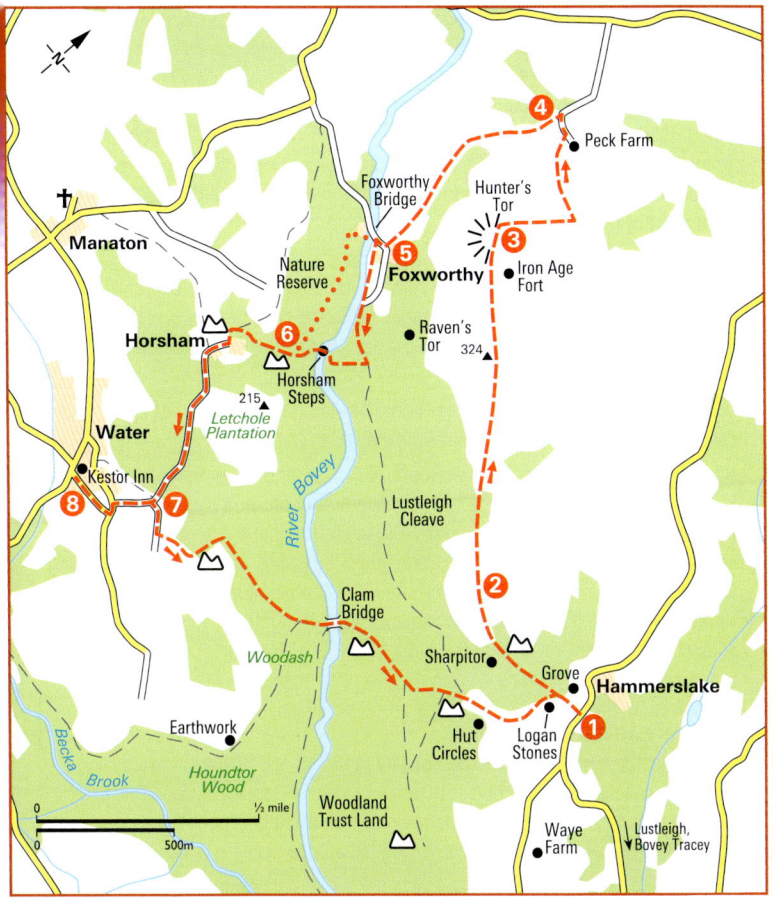

1. Once parked walk north up the lane (away from Lustleigh) and turn left up a narrow rocky path between the houses 'Logan Stones' and 'Grove', following bridleway signs 'Cleave for Water'. At the gate go straight ahead, signed 'Hunters Tor', and climb steeply up to the top, where there are lovely views towards Hound Tor.

2. Walk right through oak woodland; eventually you reach open ground and follow the path straight on over the highest part of the ridge (1,063ft/324m) and across the remains of the Iron Age fort to reach Hunter's Tor.

3. Pass through the gate right of the tor and follow the signed path right downhill to meet another signed path left. Walk downhill through one gate, then immediately right through a gateway and descend towards Peck Farm (often muddy). Go through the gate left of the farm and straight on down the rough drive.

4. Shortly after turn left through a gate signed 'Foxworthy Bridge' and continue along a wooded track to reach the beautiful thatched hamlet at Foxworthy via a gate; turn right.

5. At the path junction go left, signed 'Horsham'. Follow the track into mixed woodland through a gate. After five minutes or so follow signs right for 'Horsham for Manaton & Water', to the River Bovey. Follow the river bank left to the 'crossing' (on huge boulders) at Horsham Steps. (Note: If you are concerned about crossing Horsham Steps, don't turn left for 'Horsham' at Point 5, go right, down the drive, which crosses the river. Take the first footpath left and keep ahead until you rejoin the main route during Point 6; turn right uphill).

6. Cross over, taking care, and follow the path steeply uphill (the path avoiding Horsham Steps comes in from the right) and through a gate. Keep ahead through another gate by pretty cottages (note the tree-branch porch). Keep straight on up the track, following signs for 'Water' through Letchole Plantation.

7. At the crossroads of tracks turn right ('Manaton direct') to meet a T-junction by Water Mill. Turn right to the Kestor Inn.

8. Retrace your steps to the crossroads. Go straight on downhill, signed 'Bovey Valley', to a split in the track. Keep left, eventually passing through a gate, and continue down the steep, stony path. Cross the river at the bridge and proceed steeply uphill to the signpost. Go left, signed 'Lustleigh via Hammerslake', and left again at the next signpost (very steep). At the next junction keep ahead uphill; where the path forks drop right to reach the gate; turn right down the rocky path back to the lane at the start.

Where to eat and drink

The Kestor Inn in Manaton (technically in the village of Water) has a range of bar snacks. The thatched 15th-century Cleave Restaurant and Bar at Lustleigh has a delightful garden and serves excellent food. The Primrose Tea Rooms provide the perfect setting for a Devon cream tea, open in the summer months only.

While you're there

Becky Falls are just south of Manaton on the Bovey Tracey road. This natural waterfall, where the Becka Brook tumbles more than 80ft (24m) over a succession of huge granite boulders, is at its most impressive after heavy rainfall.

THE BOVEY VALLEY AND BOVEY TRACEY

DISTANCE/TIME	4.25 miles (6.8km) / 1hr 30min
ASCENT/GRADIENT	196ft (60m) / ▲
PATHS	Woodland and field paths, some muddy; several stiles
LANDSCAPE	Wooded river valley and parkland
SUGGESTED MAP	OS Explorer OL44 Torquay & Dawlish
START/FINISH	Grid reference: SX814782
DOG FRIENDLINESS	Dogs should be kept under control at all times
PARKING	Station Road car park on the B3344, Bovey Tracey by Riverside Community Centre
PUBLIC TOILETS	At car park and Home Farm Café

The road signs as you approach Bovey Tracey proudly proclaim the town as being the 'Gateway to the Moor', and although this may be debatable (the town is 3 miles/4.8km from the open moor, and gives no impression of Dartmoor proper) it is certainly true that the character of the landscape changes markedly as you leave the town. To the west the road climbs steadily up towards the tourist honeypot of Hay Tor, and the northern route travels past picturesque Lustleigh through the wooded Wray valley to reach Moretonhampstead and the open moorland beyond. The town's other claim to fame is that it is home to the headquarters of the Dartmoor National Park Authority, based at Parke, a splendid house set in spacious parkland just to the west of the town. The River Bovey runs through the National Trust's Parke Estate, and the area provides an excellent range of walking opportunities.

The building housing the National Park's offices at Parke was built around 1826 on the site of a derelict Tudor house, and left to the National Trust by Major Hole in 1974. In 1999 the 11 National Parks of England and Wales celebrated the 50th anniversary of the legislation that established them. Dartmoor National Park, covering 368sq miles (953sq km), was number four (in October 1951), following the Peak District, the Lake District and Snowdonia. Walkers should appreciate the purposes behind the National Parks movement – 'the conservation of the natural beauty, wildlife and cultural heritage of the area, and the promotion of the understanding and enjoyment of its special qualities by the public'. The office at Parke is open for enquiries during normal office hours. Note too that this route can also be started from the Parke Estate car park, passed on Point 7.

The 12-mile (19.3km) Newton Abbot–Moretonhampstead railway line was opened in 1866, and finally closed for passenger traffic in 1959. A group of enthusiasts tried to keep it open as a preserved steam line, but were unsuccessful. The disused section is now known as the Wray Valley Trail, and is a walking and cycling route.

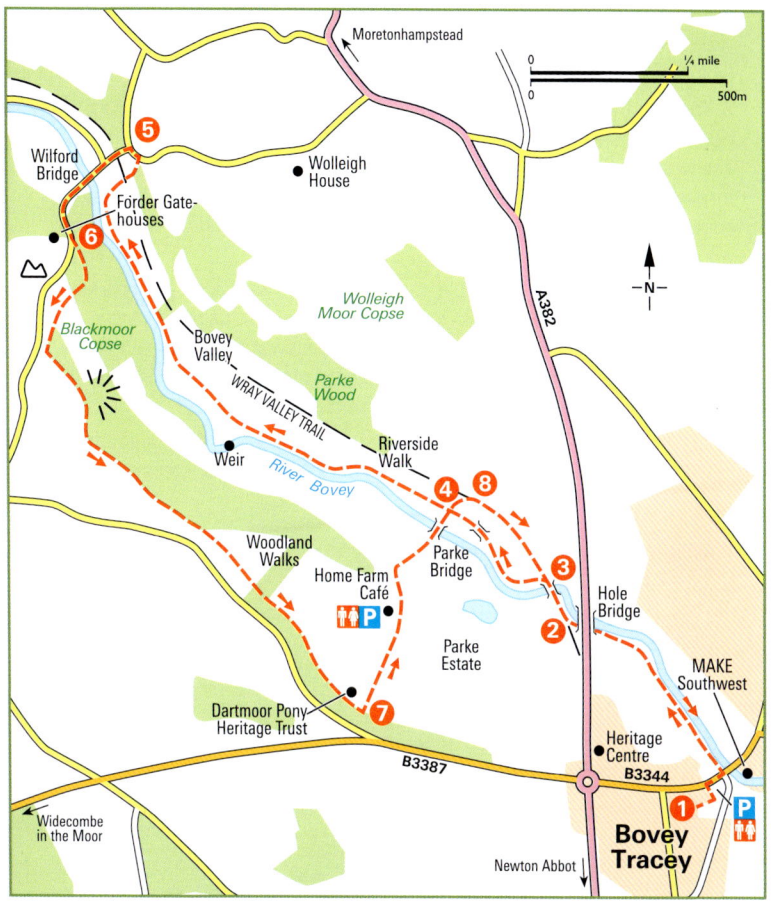

1. Cross the road and turn right, following the signs for 'Town centre shops'. Just before you come to the bridge turn left along a concrete walkway into Mill Marsh Park, past the children's playground and through the arboretum. Keep along the riverbank to pass under the A382 via a walkway.

2. Bear right along the riverbank to join the trackbed of the old Newton Abbot-Moretonhampstead railway line. Follow the path over the Bovey.

3. Turn immediately left down wooden steps and through a kissing gate to follow the river. Cross a stile at the field end and continue on a narrow, rough path, high above the river. Descend wooden steps; cross a footbridge into the next field.

4. Parke is over the bridge to the left, and the old railway line is right, but keep ahead across a pasture into woodland, then go left on a raised wooden walkway to the river. The path winds on, then runs along between woods with fields on the right, then over a footbridge to meet the river at a weir. Keep following the river, eventually passing through two kissing gates. The path bears away from the river through rough ground, then returns to the bank. Keep ahead to pass a footbridge over the river, left. A little later the path bears right to cross the railway track. Turn half left downhill to a lane via a small gate.

5. Turn left (signed 'Manaton') and pass between the old railway bridge piers. Walk across Wilford Bridge, ignoring signs to Lustleigh, right. Continue up the lane to reach Forder Gatehouses.

6. Turn left though a kissing gate and keep ahead for 150yds (137m); turn right up steps into woodland and climb steeply to meet a path. Turn left. The wooded path is narrow, with wooded views over the Bovey Valley. Go through a beech wood and kissing gate into a large field. Keep to the right edge, gradually going downhill, to leave via a kissing gate and down a narrow wooded path parallel to the road.

7. The path ends at a kissing gate; turn sharp left to walk across the parkland and the drive to Parke car park (turn left for Home Farm Café and toilets, beyond the car park). Walk downhill to cross the lower drive, then left below the house, ending at a five-bar gate. Go through and turn right to cross the river at Parke Bridge, then ahead to join the old railway track.

8. Turn right and follow the track until it crosses the Bovey, then bear left to pass under the A382 and enter Mill Marsh Park. Retrace your steps to your car.

Where to eat and drink
Home Farm Café, signed from the car park passed at Point 7, is a great place to stop for a bite to eat – sit indoors or outside. Bovey Tracey has a number of pubs and cafés. The Terrace Café, at The Devon Guild of Craftsmen, near the walk start, has a lovely rooftop seating area.

What to see
Look out for the charismatic dipper as you stroll along the river bank. This usually solitary little bird can often be seen bobbing about the rocks in the river. It has a white throat and breast and chestnut underparts, and a characteristic peculiar to the species – it can walk and swim underwater in fast-flowing streams, searching for food.

While you're there
The Parke Estate is home to the Dartmoor Pony Heritage Trust, established in 2004 in response to concern about the long-term survival of the traditional type Dartmoor pony on the moor. You can see their ponies in fields by the car park. The Devon Guild of Craftsmen, found by the bridge in Bovey Tracey, is also worth a visit for viewing the work of Devon's top craftspeople.

DARTINGTON HALL ESTATE

DISTANCE/TIME	6.5 miles (10.4km) / 3hrs
ASCENT/GRADIENT	164ft (50m) / ▲
PATHS	Fields, woodland tracks and country lanes
LANDSCAPE	River meadows, parkland and mixed woodland
SUGGESTED MAP	OS Explorer OL44 Torquay & Dawlish
START/FINISH	Grid reference: SX799628
DOG FRIENDLINESS	Keep on lead; dogs (except guide dogs) not allowed within Dartington Hall grounds
PARKING	Opposite entrance to Dartington Hall and Gardens
PUBLIC TOILETS	Outside entrance to Dartington Hall
NOTES	Larger organised groups require permission from the Property Administrator (01803 847000) in advance

You could be forgiven for thinking that Dartington is really nothing more than what you see as you cross the roundabout on the A382 leading south from the A38 to Totnes – just somewhere you pass en route to the South Hams. But there's so much more to Dartington than that, and the story behind 'the vision' of Leonard and Dorothy Elmhirst, who bought the estate in 1925, is a fascinating one. This walk circles the estate and you should allow time at the end to visit its central buildings.

Dartington Hall was described by Nikolaus Pevsner in his classic book on the buildings of Devon as 'the most spectacular medieval mansion' in Devon. The great hall and main courtyard were built for John Holand, Duke of Exeter, at the end of the 14th century, and although all the buildings have since been carefully restored, to walk through the gateway into the courtyard today, with the superb Great Hall with its hammerbeam roof opposite, is to step back in time. Arthur Champernowne came to own the manor in 1554, and made various alterations, and the estate stayed in the hands of the Champernowne family until 1925. Further restoration work was carried out in Georgian times, but by the time the Elmhirsts came on the scene the Hall was derelict.

The Dartington Hall Trust, a registered charity, was set up in 1932, and evolved from the vision of Leonard Elmhirst and his American wife Dorothy Whitney Straight, who bought the derelict hall and 1,000 acres (405ha) of the estate and set about making their dream a reality. He was interested in farming and forestry, and in increasing rural employment opportunities. She believed passionately in the arts as a way of promoting personal and social improvement. Their joint aim was to provide a foundation where both dreams could be realised, and the Dartington Estate, today a venue for all manner of creative events and initiatives, provides the perfect setting. The beautiful Grade II* listed gardens are open to the public all year and a Christmas craft fair is held in the Great Hall in December.

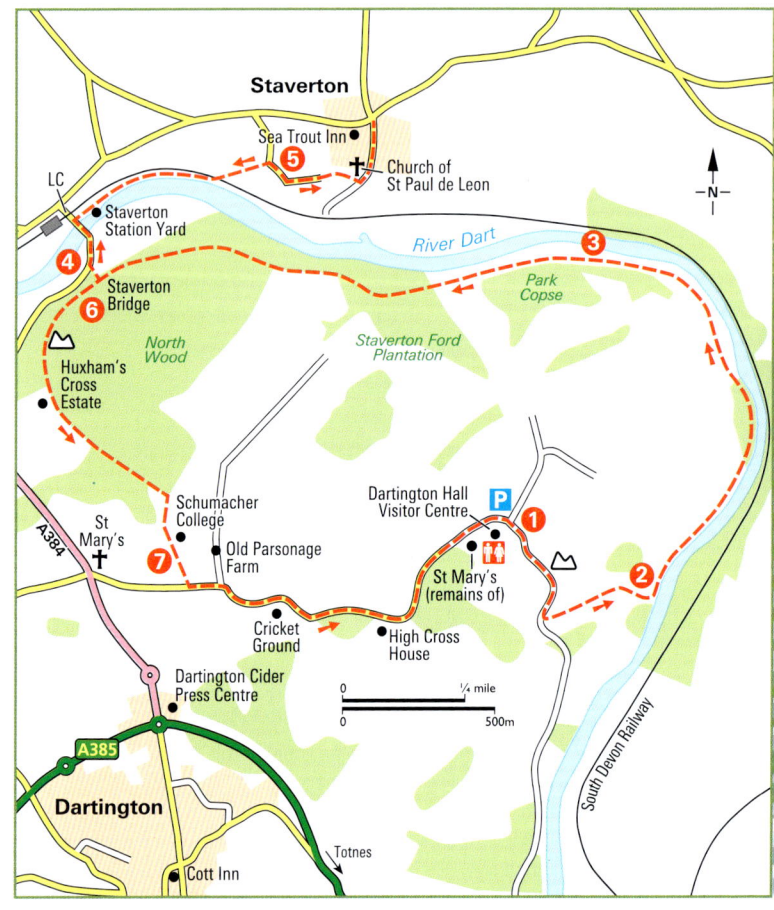

1. From the car park turn left downhill to where the road bends sharp left. Turn left through a gate and walk down the field; keep ahead through a gate to reach the River Dart.

2. Turn left and follow the river upstream through woodland. The Dart here is broad, tree-lined and slow moving. Continue through riverside meadows, and eventually pass through an open gateway in a high wall on to a wooded track.

3. Walk along the river edge of the next field (Park Copse left). At the end of that field a gate leads into Staverton Ford Plantation. Bear right to follow a narrow path back towards the river. This path, stepped in places, runs parallel with the Dart, leading into a broad woodland track through North Wood. When you see buildings nearby through the trees on the right, turn right at a crossroads and walk downhill to a metal gate and a lane.

4. Turn right to cross Staverton Bridge. At the level crossing turn right to pass through Staverton Station Yard into a park-like area between the railway and river. Follow the path across the single-track railway and walk on to meet a lane by Sweet William Cottage.

5. Turn right and follow the lane to its end. Go straight ahead on a small path to pass into the churchyard of the Church of St Paul de Leon, a 9th-century travelling preacher. Turn left at the lane, and left at the junction to visit the Sea Trout Inn. After your break retrace your steps to the metal gate past Staverton Bridge.

6. Turn immediately right to rejoin the track. Follow this until it runs downhill and bends left. Turn right towards a gate, then left on a narrow concrete path. The houses of Huxham's Cross can be seen, right. Eventually the concrete path leaves the woodland to run between wire fences to meet a concrete drive at the Schumacher College. Follow the drive to meet the road.

7. Turn left to pass Old Parsonage Farm. Keep on the road back to Dartington Hall, passing the gardens and ruins of the original church (right), until you see the car park on the left.

Where to eat and drink
Within the grounds of Dartington Hall The White Hart pub and The Green Table Café both serve great food. At Dartington Cider Press there is Bayards Kitchen and a great food shop. Outside the estate the thatched and beamed Cott Inn (established in 1320) is in the heart of the village and has a pretty garden, and the 15th-century Sea Trout Inn at Staverton offers very good food.

What to see
The South Devon Railway runs from Buckfastleigh to Totnes. Staverton Station has featured in many television programmes and films, such as *The Railway Children*. The station at Buckfastleigh has old locomotives and rolling stock on display, a museum and café, riverside walks and a picnic area. Nearby is Dartmoor Otters & Buckfast Butterflies.

While you're there
Visit Dartington Cider Press Centre, a wonderful place to browse and shop. Open seven days a week, free parking. On the last leg of the walk you'll pass an interesting 1930s building, High Cross House, now in the care of the National Trust (open Wednesday to Sunday).

ALONG THE DART VALLEY TRAIL

DISTANCE/TIME	6 miles (9.7km) / 2hrs 30min
ASCENT/GRADIENT	328ft (100m) / ▲
PATHS	Easy field paths and country lanes, several stiles
LANDSCAPE	Gentle river valley, rolling fields and woodland
SUGGESTED MAP	OS Explorer OL20 South Devon
START/FINISH	Grid reference: SX807600
DOG FRIENDLINESS	Dogs should be kept under control at all times
PARKING	Long stay car park at Steamer Quay
PUBLIC TOILETS	Steamer Quay

Once through Baltic Wharf, early on in the walk, look back at Totnes. You get a great view of the impressive Norman motte-and-bailey castle, and the 15th-century red sandstone church just down the High Street. The castle dominates the town, and from the motte you get a clear impression of the structure of the town, the original parts of which were walled in the 12th century. Much of the town walls remain today. There is evidence that there was a Saxon burh at Totnes in the 10th century, when coins were minted here. The town celebrates its heritage in many ways, including an Elizabethan market (Tuesdays, May–September), very appropriate for a town that has so many 15th- and 16th-century buildings. Much of the town's centre, including the historic East Gate, was badly damaged by fire in September 1990, but the sympathetic reconstruction is very successful.

It's worth having a better look at the castle, one of the most complete surviving examples of a Norman motte-and-bailey construction in Britain. Built near the north gate of the town, the late 11th-century motte rises 55ft (16.8m) from the bailey, and from its substantial walls – much of which are still in existence – you can get a clear picture of the historic development of the town below you, aided by English Heritage's effective artwork reconstructions. The castle was built in the heart of the Saxon town, and the great surrounding ditch, part of the original fortification, is today home to characterful cottages and pretty gardens.

Lovely Ashprington is very quiet and well preserved, tucked away in a fold of the hills. It was recorded in the Domesday Book as the Manor of Aisbertona, and until an auction in September 1940 most of the greystone houses, with characteristic latticed windows and barge-boarded gables, belonged to the Sharpham Estate.

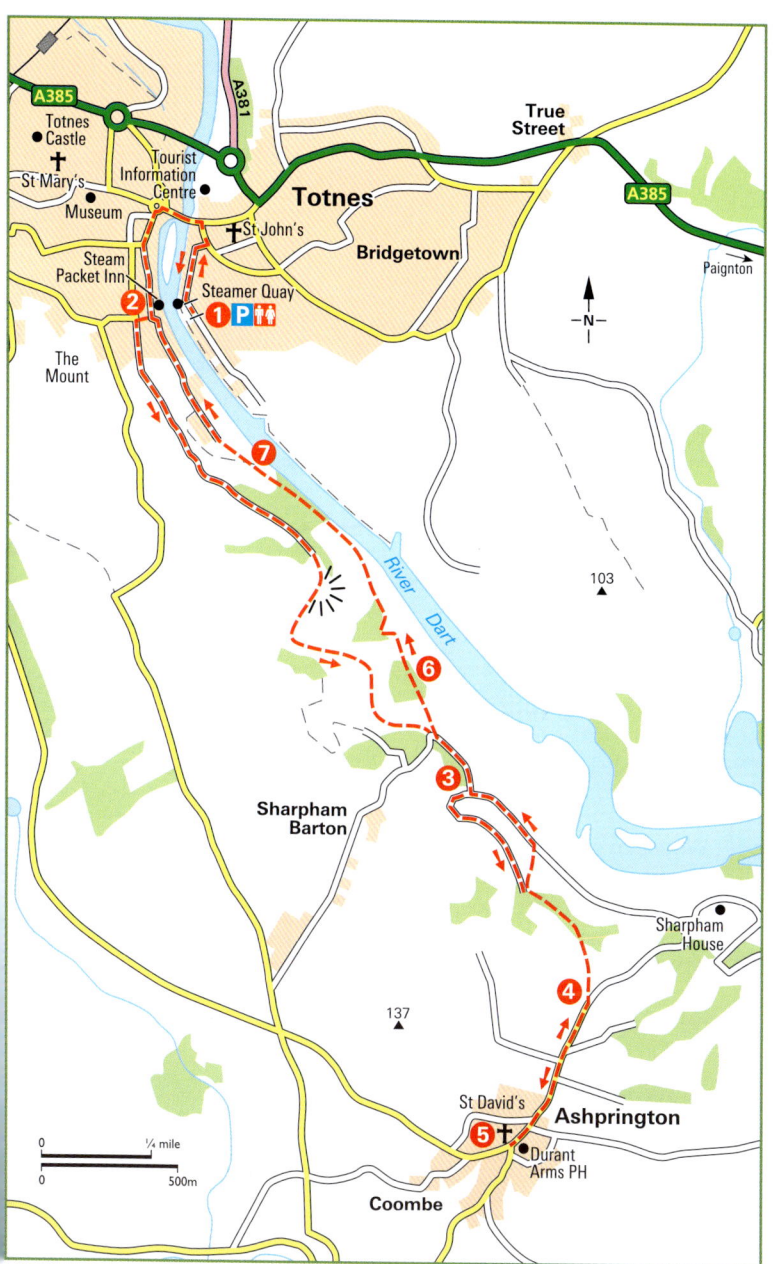

1. From the car park exit turn left along the road, then left into Seymour Road. At the main road turn left opposite Seymour Terrace to cross the late Georgian bridge. At the small roundabout turn left through The Plains, and go straight on along New Walk. Follow the public footpath sign left along the river's edge (pretty at high tide, muddy at low) to rejoin the road to the right of the Steam Packet Inn.

2. Pass St Peter's Terrace and turn right up a steep lane. Turn left to Ashprington (National Cycle Route 28). The surfaced track ascends gently to join a tarmac drive. Pass through a gate by stone pillars and soon emerge into parkland with wonderful views over the River Dart. The next gate, under trees, enters the Sharpham Estate; the next leads back into parkland. The drive undulates across parkland before dropping downhill to pass through a gate with a pond right.

3. Follow the cycle track right around the field edge, soon bearing left and climbing into a former plantation and passing a stile (left). This long, gently ascending path gives way to a pretty hedged track (Leafy Lane), to meet the lane by the entrance to Sharpham House.

4. Cross the lane; turn right on the permissive path, which ascends gently to rejoin the lane for the final descent into Ashprington village, passing 12th-century St David's Church to find the Durant Arms (left).

5. Retrace your steps to the stile passed on Point 3, and turn right down the field to cross another. Turn left on a track between fields. Rejoin the cycle track briefly; where it starts to climb keep ahead along the bottom edge of parkland to a path junction.

6. Keep ahead and through a gate into woodland. Cross a stile into a field; keep along the right edge and over a stile into woods. Cross a stile and boardwalk by an old quarry, then another into a field. A kissing gate leads back into woodland, with the river close by.

7. Ascend to a kissing gate and follow a fenced path past Baltic Wharf. Cross a stile and turn left across a parking area. Meet the lane opposite the Steam Packet Inn and retrace your steps to Steamer Quay.

Where to eat and drink
Totnes has a huge range of cafés and eateries, including many wholefood and/or organic places – you're spoilt for choice. On the walk you pass the Steam Packet Inn by the river, which offers a wide range of food and accommodation to suit all. The Durant Arms (and hotel) in Ashprington has been an inn since 1725. It's a very pretty building, and was renamed in honour of the local Durant family from nearby Sharpham.

What to see
Sharpham House was built between 1770 and 1824 for Captain Philemon Pownall, with prize money from the capture of a Spanish treasure ship. The estate, situated on the south-facing slopes above the Dart, is now home to a working farm producing award-winning cheese and a mindfulness retreat.

While you're there
Take a ride on a preserved steam railway. You can catch the South Devon Railway from Totnes to Buckfastleigh, or for a longer trip take a boat downriver to Kingswear and catch the train back up to Paignton, where buses connect to bring you back to Totnes. The Dartmouth Steam Railway and River Boat Company has an office on Steamer Quay.

COLETON FISHACRE

DISTANCE/TIME	5.5 miles (8.8km) / 3hrs
ASCENT/GRADIENT	525ft (160m) / ▲ ▲ ▲
PATHS	Undulating coast path, tracks and lanes, steep steps; several stiles
LANDSCAPE	Coastal cliff top and deep combes
SUGGESTED MAP	OS Explorer OL20 South Devon
START/FINISH	Grid reference: SX910512
DOG FRIENDLINESS	Dogs should be kept under control at all times
PARKING	National Trust car park at Coleton Camp
PUBLIC TOILETS	None on route

This is a walk that's full of surprises. Starting near the lovely National Trust house and gardens at Coleton Fishacre, it runs along a particularly beautiful piece of the South West Coast Path (much of which was purchased by the National Trust in 1982), dropping down into Pudcombe Cove and along the lower edge of the gardens before climbing steeply up the other side of the valley and back on to the open cliff. Shetland ponies have been kept here in the past to encourage regeneration of the indigenous vegetation. Further on along the path you will find all sorts of strange concrete structures scattered about the cliffs, causing you to wonder what on earth it is you've stumbled across. The scenery changes again as the walk takes you inland along the eastern side of the Dart estuary, with fine views of the 15th-century Dartmouth and Kingswear castles. For sheer variety and constantly changing themes, this walk is very hard to beat.

Given to the National Trust in 1982 by Roland Smith, Coleton Fishacre enjoys a spectacular setting in this very quiet corner of South Devon – it's very much off the beaten track. The house, reflecting the Arts and Crafts tradition, was designed and built in 1925–26 for Rupert and Lady Dorothy D'Oyley Carte, of Gilbert and Sullivan fame. It is sited at the head of a deep, sheltered combe, providing the perfect environment for its 15-acre (6ha) sub-tropical garden, based around a succession of streams and water features that fall gently down the narrow combe towards the sea at Pudcombe Cove.

The remains of Kingswear Castle (1491–1502) lie near to Point 7. Similar in shape to the square tower at Dartmouth Castle on the opposite shore, it was abandoned soon after 1643, outclassed by the range of guns available at its counterpart, and today belongs to the Landmark Trust and is available as holiday accommodation. The official title of the group of buildings encountered on the coast path south of Kingswear is the Inner Froward Point Coast Defence Battery, dating from World War II and almost complete, apart from the guns. There are the remains of all kinds of wartime constructions here, apart from the lookout just above the sea. The site includes the foundations of several Nissen huts, two shell magazines, two gun positions and a shell incline, and two searchlight emplacements near sea level. It's all a trifle unexpected after the peaceful approach along the coast path but reflects the importance of the river mouth to successive military generations.

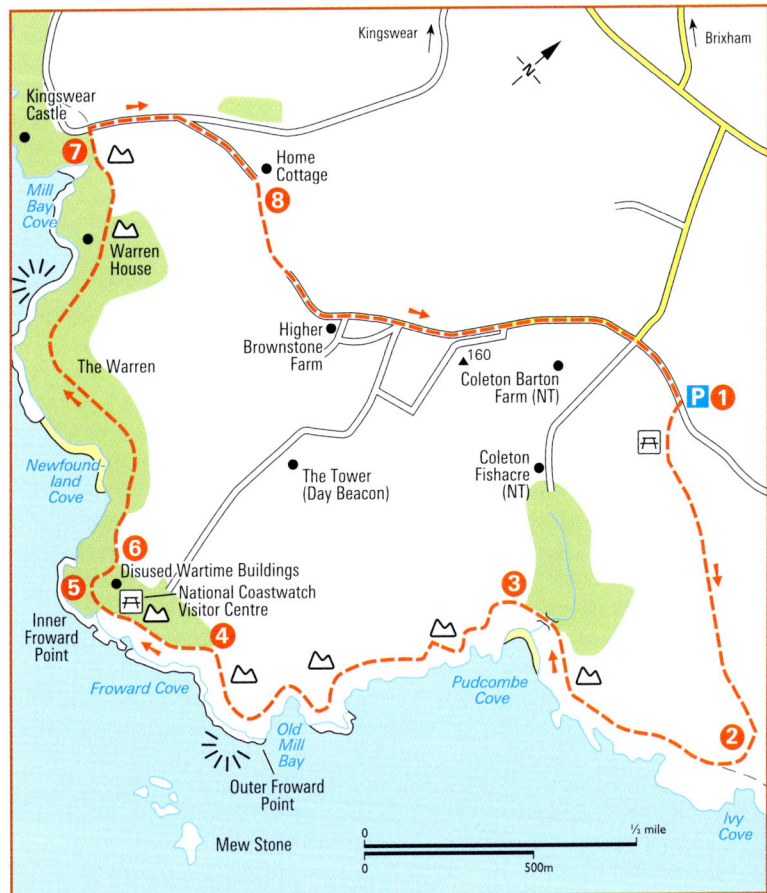

1. Walk through the kissing gate in the top corner of the car park (by the donation box) to take the permissive path towards a metal gate and stile ('link path to Ivy Cove'). Keeping the hedge right, walk downhill to cross another stile, then another, and then another at the bottom of the field. Bear left to another stile. Continue uphill to reach the coast path (signs to Pudcombe Cove, right).

2. Turn right and follow the path along the cliff. Eventually go through a gate and descend steeply and over a footbridge to reach the gate at the bottom of Coleton Fishacre gardens (there is no public right of way into the gardens).

3. Follow the coast path on, then sharp left up steep wooden steps, to leave the estate via a gate and on to Coleton Cliffs. The path drops steeply, then climbs again above Old Mill Bay – with great views of the Mew Stone

– followed by a steep climb up to Outer Froward Point, with views towards Start Point. The path undulates, then climbs steeply to reach the back of Froward Cove. Follow coast path signs left for Kingswear.

4. Pass through a gate, keep ahead, then follow coast path signs left, very steeply downhill through woodland. The path then undulates towards Inner Froward Point.

5. The look-out (once housing a searchlight) is the next landmark, followed by 108 steps up to a gun emplacement. Follow the miniature railway line uphill, then follow the concrete walkway and steps through disused wartime buildings. At the top reach a path junction by the National Coastwatch Visitor Centre.

6. Turn left for Kingswear to walk through woodland behind Newfoundland Cove, through a gate, and down a broad woodland track (estuary on the left). Plod down 84 steps to Mill Bay Cove and turn right down a tarmac way. Turn left through a gate and climb the 89 steps up to a drive, then 63 more steps to a lane.

7. Turn right (signed 'Brownstone'). After 250yds (229m) the lane forks; gratefully take the right fork downhill to Home Farm complex (signed Home Cottage).

8. Follow the footpath signs, right, up a steep, rocky path to a concrete lane, and on to pass Higher Brownstone Farm. Walk on up the lane to pass the National Trust car park, then the gates to Coleton Fishacre, and back to Coleton Camp car park.

Where to eat and drink
Parking in Kingswear is difficult but there is The Ship Inn, by the church, and The Steam Packet Inn on the road to the ferry. There is a National Trust café and restaurant at Coleton Fishacre.

What to see
The Tower (day beacon), set at 475ft (145m) above sea level above Inner and Outer Froward Point, can be seen for many miles. Hollow and built of stone in 1864, it stands 80ft (24m) high. Day beacons, or day marks, are unlit navigational aids, intended to assist those at sea during daylight hours. A path runs towards it from the wooden signpost at Point 5 of the walk, and then on to Brownstone, which you could use to shorten the walk by about 0.75 miles (1.2km) – but you'd miss some superb scenery.

While you're there
Take a ride on the Dartmouth Steam Railway. The station is near the lower ferry slipway in Kingswear. The route passes along the wooded east bank of the Dart, then over the Greenway Viaduct, through Greenway Tunnel, back to the coast at Goodrington Sands and on to Paignton. You can link your trip with a cruise along the Dart.

BLACKSTONE POINT AND DARTMOUTH CASTLE

DISTANCE/TIME	4 miles (6.4km) / 2hrs
ASCENT/GRADIENT	115ft (35m) / ▲▲
PATHS	Uneven coastal footpath and green lanes
LANDSCAPE	Farmland, cliff tops and river estuary
SUGGESTED MAP	OS Explorer OL20 South Devon
START/FINISH	Grid reference: SX874491
DOG FRIENDLINESS	Livestock in some fields; keep on lead at NT Little Dartmouth
PARKING	National Trust car parks at Little Dartmouth
PUBLIC TOILETS	Dartmouth Castle

Dartmouth seems to have everything. The town has a rich and illustrious history and, with its smaller sister Kingswear on the opposite shore, occupies a commanding position on the banks of the Dart. With its sheltered, deep-water harbour it developed as a thriving port and shipbuilding town from the 12th century. By the 14th century it enjoyed a flourishing wine trade, and benefited from the profits of piracy for generations. Today, pleasure craft and the tourist industry have taken over in a big way – the annual Royal Regatta has been a major event since 1822 – but Dartmouth has lost none of its charm. One of its attractions is that there are all sorts of ways of getting there: by bus, using the town's park-and-ride scheme, by river, on a steamer from Totnes, by sea, on a coastal trip from Torbay, by steam train, from Paignton or on foot along the coast path. Now cared for by English Heritage, 15th-century Dartmouth Castle enjoys an exceptionally beautiful position at the mouth of the Dart. Replacing the 1388 fortalice of John Hawley, it was one of the most advanced fortresses of the day and, with Kingswear Castle opposite (of which only the tower remains) was built to protect the homes and warehouses of the town's wealthy merchants. A chain was slung across the river mouth between the two fortifications, and guns fired from ports in the castle walls. Visitors can experience a representation of life in the later Victorian gun battery that was established. A record of 1192 infers that there was a monastic foundation on the site, leading to the establishment of St Petrock's Church.

The cobbled quayside at Bayard's Cove has many attractive 17th- and 18th-century buildings, including the Customs House dating from 1739. The single-storey artillery fort was built before 1534 to protect the harbour. A plaque commemorates the sailing of the Mayflower and Speedwell in 1620.

Dartmouth is crammed with good places to eat: you'll find posh fish and chips at Rockfish Seafood and Chips on the South Embankment and, at The Seahorse, you can have seafood and meat cooked over charcoal.

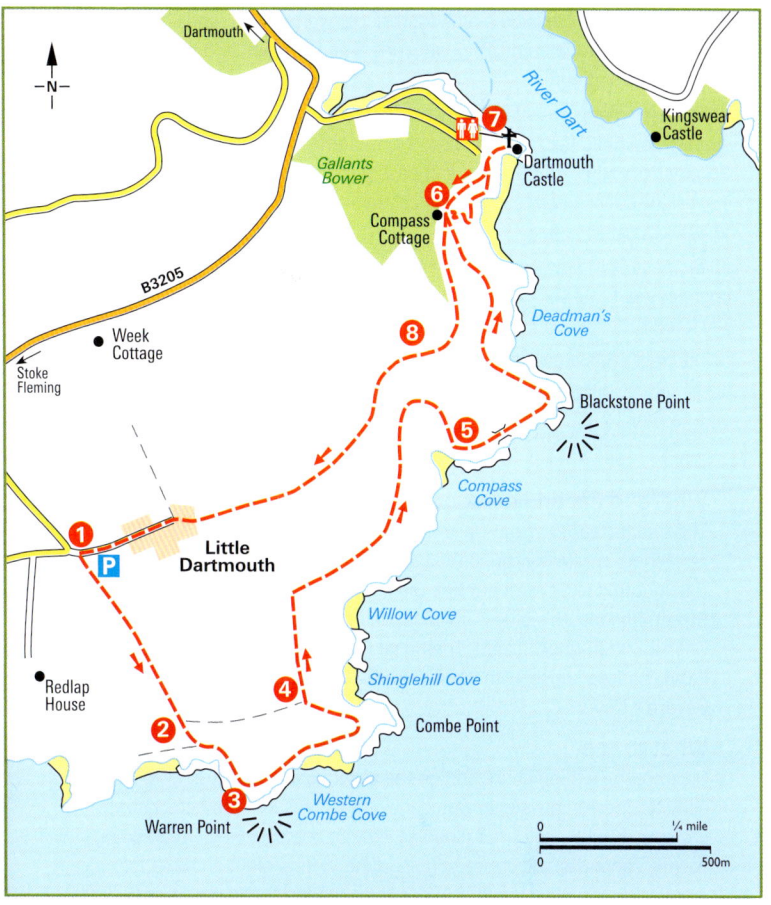

1. From the car park follow the signs 'Coast Path Dartmouth'. Continue through a kissing gate and along a fenced path with a hedge to the right, eventually passing through another kissing gate to reach the coast.

2. Turn left; there are lovely views west to Start Point and east towards the Day Beacon above Kingswear. The coast path runs a little inland from the cliff edge, but you can walk out towards gorse-covered Warren Point (given to the National Trust in 1970).

3. From Warren Point follow the coast to pass above Western Combe Cove (with steps down to the sea) and then Combe Point (take care – it's a long drop to the sea from here).

4. Rejoin the coast path through an open gateway in a wall and follow it above Shinglehill Cove. The path follows a combe inland to pass a pond, then bears right along the back of Willow Cove. Keep along the field edge, then through light woodland, climbing steeply to a gate. Follow the yellow arrow ahead to reach a footpath post, then turn sharp right down the valley, bearing right at the bottom to a stile (Compass Cove right).

5. Turn left, soon crossing a high footbridge over an inlet, and continue towards Blackstone Point. The path runs along the side of the estuary through deciduous woodland.

6. The path meets a surfaced lane opposite Compass Cottage; turn right steeply downhill. Follow coast path signs right to zig-zag steeply down to Sugary Cove, then climb steps and pass picnic tables to reach a turning area. Turn right down steps to reach the castle and café.

7. Retrace your route up the steps, then turn left up the lane to Point 6, keep ahead past Compass Cottage, and continue straight on up the steep lane (signposted 'Little Dartmouth') and through a kissing gate on to National Trust land.

8. The path runs along the top of a field and through a five-bar gate on to a green lane. Go through a gate and the farmyard at Little Dartmouth and ahead on a tarmac lane to the car park.

Where to eat and drink
The Castle Tea Rooms at Dartmouth Castle is ideally placed for refreshment halfway round the walk, and there are masses of options in Dartmouth itself. Check out The Dartmouth Ice Cream Company in Lower Street. Dartmouth's oldest building, dating from c1380, today houses The Cherub Inn (Higher Street). The Royal Castle Hotel overlooking the Boat Float is a free house, with good food, as is the Dartmouth Arms at historic Bayard's Cove.

What to see
Dartmouth, both on shore and on the water, is always buzzing with activity. There's masses to watch including pleasure steamers, private cruisers, brightly coloured dinghies, rowing boats, ferries, ocean-going yachts, canoeists and cruise ships, calling in for a night en route for sunnier climes. Naval craft, ranging from old-fashioned whalers to modern frigates, are connected with the Britannia Royal Naval College, which overlooks the town. You may also hear the whistle of a steam train on the Dartmouth Steam Railway, which runs along the eastern side of the river to terminate at Kingswear Station.

While you're there
Catch the ferry from Stumpy Steps (upriver from the castle) which, within a few minutes, will deposit you in the centre of Dartmouth. You get a fabulous view of all those superb waterside residences that are tantalisingly difficult – if not impossible – to see from the lane above, and the ferry saves you a further 1-mile (1.6km) walk. There's an on-demand shuttle service 10am until 5pm.

ALONG THE COAST TO START POINT

DISTANCE/TIME	6 miles (9.7km) / 3hrs
ASCENT/GRADIENT	328ft (100m) / ▲▲
PATHS	Good coast path
LANDSCAPE	Undulating cliffs and shingle beaches
SUGGESTED MAP	OS Explorer OL20 South Devon
START/FINISH	Grid reference: SX823423
DOG FRIENDLINESS	Keep on lead at all times
PARKING	Long stay car park at Torcross
PUBLIC TOILETS	In Torcross car park and at Beesands

Visit the little village of Torcross, at the southern end of Slapton Ley, south of Dartmouth, on a sunny summer day and it's quite impossible to believe that it could ever be anything but calm and tranquil. The views south to Start Point are particularly wonderful in May, when the point shimmers under a carpet of bluebells. But on 16 January 1917 the fishing village of Hallsands, just to the south, was almost totally destroyed during a huge storm which smashed through the sea walls and washed most of the buildings away.

Perhaps it was the result of extensive dredging work off the coast here between 1897 and 1902, when tons of shingle were removed for Royal Navy building work at Devonport in Plymouth. Around 1,600 tons were dredged up each day, so altering the patterns of coastal erosion. The remaining villages still suffer – Torcross seafront was badly damaged during heavy storms in 1951 and 1979, and the Slapton Sands road washed away for a period in 2001.

This is a versatile walk. You can turn back at Beesands, or Hallsands, or go all the way to the lighthouse at Start Point. From the viewing platform above ruined Hallsands village, you can still see the remains of some of the cottages; there were originally two rows, comprising 37 homes and a range of shops, and a pub, The London Inn. The last resident of Hallsands, Miss Prettijohn, lived there until her death in the mid 1960s. Her cottage, which can be seen from the viewing platform, is now a holiday home.

At Point 5 you'll reach an elegant building (now converted into luxury apartments) that was once home to the Trout sisters. Fisherman's daughters Patience, Ella, Clara and Edith survived the devastation of 1917, and with their mother moved just inland to Bickerton. Ella, using money given to her as reward for rescuing a stricken crewman in the summer of 1917, began (with Patience) to build a new home, Prospect House, on the cliffs above Old Hallsands. This house was opened as a guesthouse – known as 'Trout's' – in 1925. Fifty years later, on the death of the last sister, Edith, the property was sold and converted into holiday flats.

1. From the car park (by the toilets) follow the coast path sign over the road to turn right along the concrete promenade (a sea defence scheme from 1980). At the end, ascend steep steps on to a gravel path, following coast path signs. Here there are great views back along Slapton Ley, the largest natural lake in the West Country.

2. Follow yellow coast path arrows, eventually to go through a gate into a field on the cliff top, then through the next gate and along a path through woodland, which drops down with spectacular views over Widdicombe Ley and Beesands.

3. The path joins a track, which runs behind the beach into the village of Beesands, which has a slightly forgotten feel. Pass the tiny St Andrew's Church and The Cricket Inn (on the right), and continue straight on along the seafront, following signs for Hallsands.

4. The path climbs steeply up the cliff and through a gate onto Tinsey Head. When North Hallsands comes into view, look carefully down to sea level to the ruined village beyond. Go through the next gate and along the lower edge of the field. The beach at North Hallsands is quiet and remote; the houses across the field behind the beach were built to re-house some of the displaced villagers in 1924. Descend through gates and fields to reach the beach.

5. Cross the beach to join the lane behind and keep ahead as signed on the coast path towards Start Point. At new houses ascend wooden steps and keep ahead to pass Prospect House, former home to the indomitable Trout sisters (see Introduction). Walk down to the viewing platform above the old village; there's a real feeling of desolation here.

6. Follow the coast path on towards Start Point. A couple of old apple trees arch over the path, indication of the strength of the winds here. The path leads up to a kissing gate to join the car park for Start Point and Great Mattiscombe Sand, and the gate to the lighthouse (open to the public most days in summer). On the return route enjoy spectacular views along the coast.

Where to eat and drink

The Start Bay Inn opposite the car park welcomes families. The Torcross Boat House offers takeaway fish and chips. The Cricket Inn at Beesands has a great atmosphere and specialises in seafood as does Britannia@the Beach (seafood café and village stores).

What to see

An American Sherman tank is on display in the car park, and is a memorial to American servicemen who perished during Operation Tiger, a training exercise that went tragically wrong in the early hours of 28 April 1944. Nine German torpedo boats intercepted a long convoy of US vessels moving from Portland to Slapton Sands. Two landing craft were destroyed, and two more damaged, leading to the loss of almost 1,000 lives.

While you're there

Slapton Ley is a haven for goldeneye, grey herons, mute swans, tufted ducks, pochards, great crested grebes, mallards, moorhens and coots, and is popular with birders. There's a good information board by the Duckery near the car park.

PRAWLE POINT

DISTANCE/TIME	4.25 miles (6.8km) / 2hrs
ASCENT/GRADIENT	394ft (120m) / ▲▲▲
PATHS	Green lanes, fields and coast path, rocky in places; several stiles
LANDSCAPE	Coastal farmland, rocky coves and level raised beaches
SUGGESTED MAP	OS Explorer OL20 South Devon
START/FINISH	Grid reference: SX780363
DOG FRIENDLINESS	Keep on lead in fields
PARKING	Around green in East Prawle
PUBLIC TOILETS	By green in East Prawle

It seems to take forever to get to East Prawle. The first signpost for the village, seen not far from Chillington, between Stokenham and Kingsbridge in the South Hams, tells you that it's only 4 miles (6.4km) away, and from then on you seem to be constantly turning left or right, along miles of typical banked, flower-filled Devon lanes, and never really getting very far. But then suddenly you're there – by the little green in the middle of the village, with its wonderfully remote yet open feeling. It's completely unspoilt, and very popular with Devon people who want a simple camping holiday without leaving the county. A week under canvas in good weather at Prawle and it's hard to leave. Prawle Point, just below the village, is the most southerly point in Devon. The easiest way to get there is by car, but it's far more satisfying to submit to the sleepy atmosphere and wander down the lanes and along the coast, past some of the most beautiful – and relatively undiscovered – coves in Devon.

The lookout at Prawle Point is today manned on a voluntary basis to keep an eye on this particularly busy part of the coast. Originally a coastguard station, with a 270-degree field of vision, it was used by Lloyds of London to report the arrival of ships from across the Atlantic. In use as a naval signal service station from 1937 to 1940, it shut down as a permanent coastguard station in 1994. Prawle Point means 'lookout hill' in Old English, so this practice could date back to Saxon times.

Prawle Point is home to a great variety of birds and, due to its southerly position, is visited by a wealth of early and rare varieties on spring and autumn migrations. Birders can usually see herring gulls, cormorants, shags, common terns and gannets (and – if lucky – sea mammals such as dolphin and porpoise, as well as grey seals). The rare and localised cirl bunting is also a resident here – there were only 80 pairs in the country in 1989, but successful conservation measures have lead to a considerable increase in numbers.

The volcanic rocks of the coast here are some of Devon's oldest, dating back over 400 million years. Pressure from the earth's movements split the strata and realigned them into parallel bands. The pounding sea then created the split, angular rocks evident today. The raised beach below East Prawle, a distinctive platform 15ft (4.5m) above the present beach, was formed during the last two million years in times of warmer weather conditions and higher sea levels, which altered coastal erosion patterns.

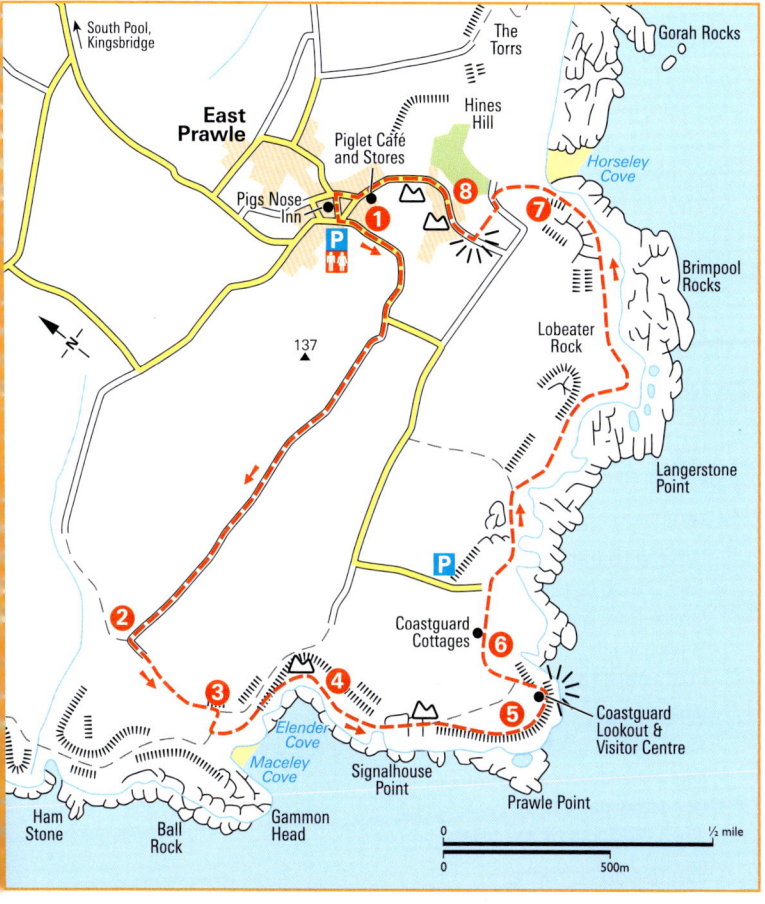

1. Walk down the lane towards the sea, leaving the green to the left and toilets and a phone box right and following a sign 'Prawle Point'. The road bends right and then sharp left, at which point; go straight ahead along a deeply rutted green lane marked 'Public Bridleway'.

2. The green lane ends at a T-junction (metal gates opposite); turn left down a very narrow grassy path between tumbledown, overgrown old walls. There are fine views of the coast ahead. Follow the path through a kissing gate to the footpath post.

3. Turn right downhill to reach the coast path high above secluded Maceley Cove, with Gammon Head to the right. Turn left and walk along the path above Elender Cove. There is steep, scrambly access to both beaches so take care.

4. The path leads through a kissing gate and scrambles on around Signalhouse Point. A steep ascent, partly stepped, is rewarded with fine views ahead to

Prawle Point; look back to see lofty Bolt Head at the mouth of the Salcombe estuary. Follow coast path posts through a gate and across the grassy down, keeping to the right of the coastguard lookout.

5. At the coastguard lookout enjoy superb views east to Lannacombe, Mattiscombe Sand and Start Point. Explore the excellent visitor centre, which will tell you everything you want to know about the area. To continue, follow the grassy path inland, rejoining the coast path, turning right through a kissing gate by the old coastguard cottages.

6. Pass in front of the cottages and along the edge of the level, grassy wave-cut platform which lies just below the original Pleistocene cliffs here. Pass through a gate (note a parking area across the field to the left) and along lovely level meadows above low cliffs. Go through the next kissing gate and round Langerstone Point. Continue along the seaward edge of fields, passing through several gates, with views to Maelcombe House ahead. Eventually pass through two more gates and keep ahead to a path junction.

7. Turn left up the bridleway; soon pass through a gate and keep ahead up the track.

8. Take the first stone stile right to go very steeply up the field. There are good views back to the coast when you stop for a breather. Cross the stone stile at the top and continue right up the narrow rocky track to join the lane; turn right and climb steeply to the village.

Where to eat and drink

East Prawle is home to the quirky Pigs Nose Inn, which welcomes families. You can also get snacks and refreshments at the Piglet Café. The Millbrook Inn at nearby South Pool serves excellent local food and has a lovely waterside location.

What to see

The wreck of the *Demetrios*, a cargo ship that foundered on the rocks below the lookout at Prawle Point in December 1992, is evidence of just how tricky navigation is in these parts. There are 800 recorded shipwrecks along the South Devon coast.

While you're there

Keep an eye out for grey (Atlantic) seals as you wend your away along the coast path. Although it's always exciting to catch sight of one of these wonderfully appealing creatures lounging on the rocks, and feels like a rare treat, there are actually about 85,000 grey seals around Britain (60 per cent of the world population). Naturally curious, they will watch you just as closely as you watch them, if they get the chance. A big bull seal can grow up to 7ft (2.1m) long, and can easily be recognised by his thick, heavy muzzle.

EAST PORTLEMOUTH

DISTANCE/TIME	4.5 miles (7.2km) / 2hrs
ASCENT/GRADIENT	377ft (115m) / ▲▲
PATHS	Rocky coast path, field paths and tracks
LANDSCAPE	River estuary, rugged coast and coves, farmland
SUGGESTED MAP	OS Explorer OL20 South Devon
START/FINISH	Grid reference: SX746386
DOG FRIENDLINESS	Keep on lead near livestock and unfenced cliffs
PARKING	Near phone box in East Portlemouth or in small parking area
PUBLIC TOILETS	At Mill Bay and near The Venus Café

East Portlemouth has a totally different feel to the resort town of Salcombe that lies opposite, over the water. It is small, very quiet and unspoilt, and somewhat belies its rather difficult history. During the 19th century half the population was evicted by the absentee landlord, the Duke of Cleveland, due to their preference for fishing and wrecking over working the land. The 15th-century church is dedicated to St Winwaloe, a 5th-century Celtic saint, and a fascinating gravestone in the churchyard reveals the death by burning at the stake of a girl who poisoned her employer in 1782.

From the tiny hamlet of East Portlemouth is where you get some of the best views of the mass of small boats in the harbour, and the various creeks upriver towards Kingsbridge. Once the haunt of smugglers and pirates, today it has a civilised, prosperous, and because of its sheltered position and deep blue waters, an almost Mediterranean feel. It's extremely popular with the sailing fraternity, with safe waters for novices (at high tide) further up the estuary. This area is a marvellous place for young families, too – at low tide there is a run of white sandy beaches all along the East Portlemouth side.

From this walk it is easy to take the passenger ferry over to Salcombe and pay a worthwhile visit to Overbeck's Gardens, in its a magnificent setting above South Sands. Originally called 'Sharpitor' the house was built in 1913 by Mr and Mrs Vereker, but after they received the devastating news that their son had been killed at Mons in 1914, they offered the house to the Red Cross to be used for convalescent British and allied soldiers. By the time the hospital closed in 1919 over 1,000 men had stayed there and not one death had been recorded. Such was the excellent care, dedication and kindness shown to them by the staff and the Verekers themselves.

In 1928, Otto Overbeck, an inventor and art collector acquired the estate. Probably his most famous invention was the electrical 'Rejuvenator' which he claimed would banish many ailments and defy the ageing process. Through fierce marketing and endless testimonials in newspapers and journals worldwide, the public were persuaded to buy his invention and with the profits

Otto bought the house and grounds. In his will Otto bequeathed the estate to the National Trust and visitors today can spend hours admiring the fantastic collection of rare and sub-tropical plants, thriving in the warm microclimate. The gardens are particularly colourful in spring.

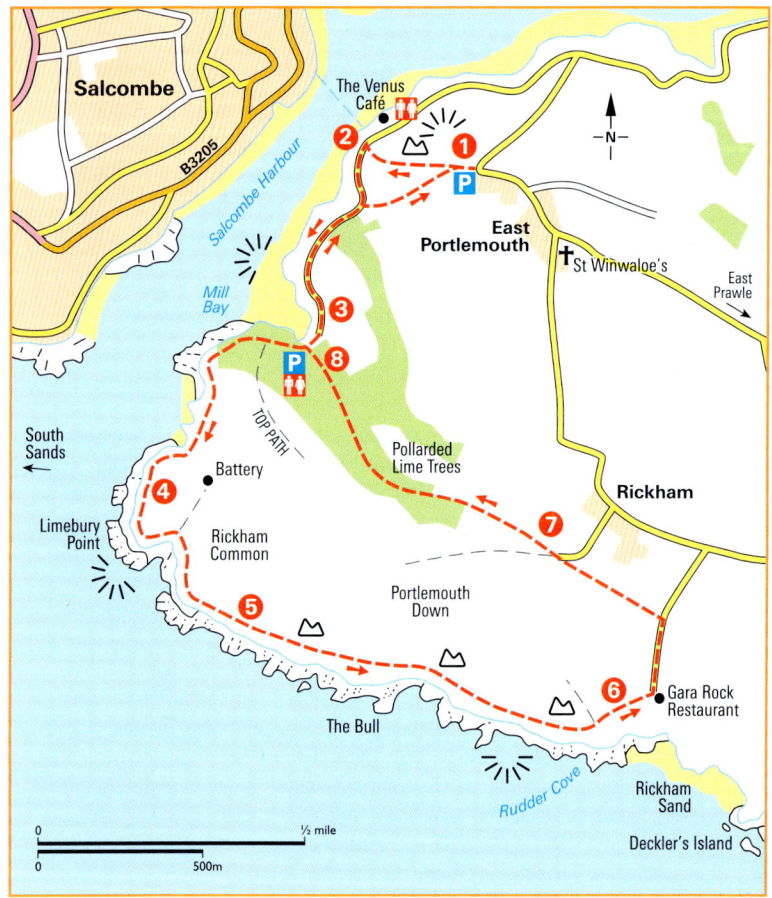

1. Park on the laneside near the phone box (or in the parking area – village hall fund contributions). Walk through the parking area and a gate then go steeply downhill on a narrow tarmac footpath signposted 'Salcombe', which gives way to steep steps.

2. When you reach the lane at the bottom of the steps, turn right if you want to visit The Venus Café and catch the ferry to Salcombe. If you want to get on with the walk, turn left along the lane as it follows the edge of the estuary. This is the official route of the coast path and it passes some very exclusive residences.

3. The lane leads to the pretty, sandy beach at Mill Bay. Carefully follow the acorn coast path signs for Gara Rock through a sycamore wood, with lovely views across the estuary, and glimpses of inviting little coves.

4. At Limebury Point you reach open cliff, from where there are great views to South Sands and Overbeck's opposite and craggy Bolt Head. The coast path now bears eastwards below Portlemouth Down, which was divided into strip fields in the late 19th century.

5. The path along this stretch undulates steeply, and is rocky in places. Keep going until you reach the bench and viewpoint over the beach at Rickham Sand. Just beyond this, as the coast path continues right (there is reasonable access to the beach), take the left fork and climb steeply up below the lookout and through a gate to reach a signpost by the Gara Rock restaurant.

6. Turn left to reach the drive and walk straight on up the lane. After 250yds (229m) turn left through a gate in the hedge signposted 'Mill Bay'. Walk straight ahead through a gate and follow a fenced path to a gate; note Malborough church in the distance. Pass through a woodland strip, then a gate, and cross a farm track. Go through the next gate and down the public bridleway.

7. This runs gradually downhill beneath huge, ancient, pollarded lime trees, with a grassy combe to the right. Walk through the NT car park to reach Mill Bay.

8. Turn right along the lane. If you want to avoid the steps, look out for a footpath sign pointing right, up a narrow, steep, path to regain East Portlemouth and your car; if not, continue along the lane and retrace your route up the steps.

Where to eat and drink
Salcombe has a mass of pubs, cafes and restaurants, but if you want to stay on the East Portlemouth side try The Venus Café (one of a chain of extremely 'green' beach cafés). It's in a glorious position by the ferry slipway, with a pretty garden looking across the water. The café serves great food and drink, and is open every day from Easter to the end of October. The Gara Rock Restaurant perched on the cliff affords spectacular views.

What to see
Many stretches of the coast path are resplendent with wild flowers virtually all the year round, and during the summer months the path below Portlemouth Down is incredible. There are banks of purple wild thyme, heather, gorse, red campion, bladder campion, tiny yellow tormentil and pretty blue scabius. Look out too for the common dodder, a parasitic plant with pretty clusters of pink flowers. It draws the life out of its host plant, often heather or gorse, via suckers.

While you're there
Catch the ferry to the other side and explore the pretty little town of Salcombe. The ferry runs every day, from 8.30am – 6.30pm during the summer and slightly shorter hours in the winter. There's also a lovely river trip by ferry from Salcombe to Kingsbridge.

KINGSBRIDGE AND BOWCOMBE CREEK

DISTANCE/TIME	3 miles (4.8km) / 1hr 30min
ASCENT/GRADIENT	230ft (70m) / ▲▲
PATHS	Fields, green lanes and town lanes, some steep rocky ascents/descents, at times wet underfoot; many stiles
LANDSCAPE	River estuary and rolling farmland
SUGGESTED MAP	OS Explorer OL20 South Devon
START/FINISH	Grid reference: SX735441
DOG FRIENDLINESS	Mostly on lead, and not allowed in churchyard (keep ahead along path)
PARKING	Car park on Kingsbridge Quay (pay-and-display)
PUBLIC TOILETS	At head of quay near car park

The best way to appreciate why the south Devon market town of Kingsbridge has such a long history of seaborne trade – evidenced by a number of fine buildings dating from wealthier times in the 18th and 19th centuries – is to climb high above town. From this walk extensive views over the estuary clearly show this long-established port's commanding position.

Kingsbridge has long been a centre for trade, forming a link between the rural hinterland and the sea. The town flourished thanks to its location at the head of a 5-mile (8km) long navigable estuary at a time when transport inland was difficult and routes frequently impassable. From medieval times – when the town enjoyed healthy trading links with southwest France – until the coming of the railway in 1893, the quays, would have bustled with life. Take a look at the Shambles on Fore Street – a granite-pillared walkway, formerly the site of butchers' stalls in the heart of the medieval town. Later clippers, schooners and barges were built on the banks of the estuary, and packet steamers came to call. The advent of steel ships which could not access the higher reaches of the estuary – coupled with the arrival of the railway – ended the town's life as a port. Kingsbridge is now a popular holiday spot.

Just one of many creeks on the estuary, Bowcombe also has a long history of local trade. Slate from a nearby quarry and cider from the farms was shipped out, and there was at one time a mill at the head of the creek. Today, it's a haven for birds and wildlife.

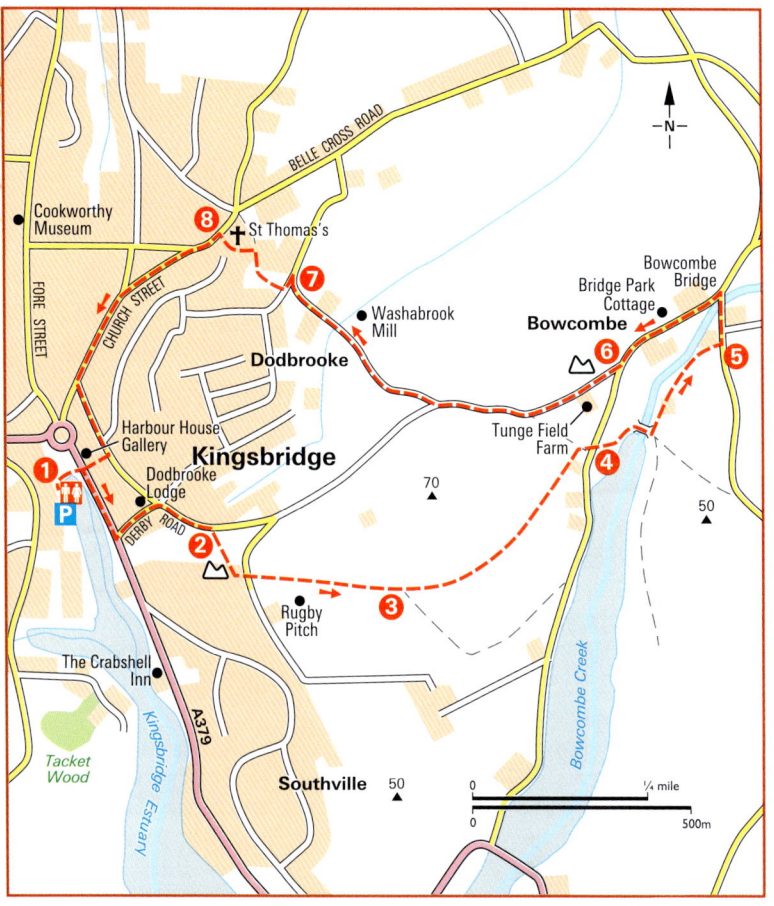

1. From the car park turn right across the head of the river basin and right again down Promenade. Soon turn left up Derby Road, noting Dodbrooke Lodge on your left, once the coach house for Dodbrooke Manor. At the first crossroads turn right down Derby Road, and pass the recreation ground.

2. Where the lane bears left, keep ahead through a gate on a footpath. Ascend a very steep, rough field and go through a gate onto a lane. Cross over and ascend steps on a footpath through the rugby club car park. Cross a stile and continue along the left edge of a field. Cross a stone stile and reach a footpath junction.

3. Follow the top edge of the next field, curving left with the hedge. Cross a stile, and where the hedge bears away, bear right past a fence corner and footpath post. Continue steeply downhill, towards a gate and stile by a derelict building. Pass through and bear right to cross a stile onto a lane.

4. Cross a stile ahead, and follow as the path bears left through a gate in a fence into creekside reed beds. (If you find this stretch too wet return to the lane, turn right, then left at Point 6.) Cross the head of the creek on a bridge, and turn left over a stile into a field. Keep along the bottom edge and go through a gate. Continue along the brook, turning right uphill at field end to a stile onto a lane.

5. Turn left downhill to cross Bowcombe Bridge, then turn left along the lane to pass Bridge Park Cottage.

6. At the entrance to Tunge Field Farm turn right on a deeply banked green lane – this climbs steeply before levelling off. At a byway junction bear right and descend steadily (good spring flowers) to reach Washabrook Mill in a sheltered combe, once a tidal mill for flour and grist. Pass Washabrook Farm and follow the lane uphill to Washabrook Lane.

7. Turn left and follow the road uphill. Around 25yds (23m) after passing a bridlepath on your left, turn right on a tarmac path. At gates turn left into the graveyard of St Thomas's Church, and turn right, then left to pass the church. Round the west end to emerge onto Church Street.

8. Turn left downhill. Where the road eventually kinks right, bear left along Ebrington Street. Where the street broadens, turn right down an alley to find the pedestrian crossing and return to the car park.

Where to eat and drink

There are plenty of eating places near the car park, including The Creeks End Inn, and a vegetarian café and garden at Harbour House Gallery. The Crabshell Inn on the estuary – a crabbing hot spot – specialises in seafood, and has extensive outdoor seating overlooking the water.

What to see

Keep an eye open for wading birds on Bowcombe Creek, once the site of a huge heronry – you may see herons and little egrets. Winter is a particularly good time for spotting redshank, greenshank, oystercatcher and curlew.

While you're there

The old Kingsbridge Grammar School, founded in 1670, now houses the Cookworthy Museum. In 1768 William Cookworthy, who was born in Kingsbridge, patented a method of working with china clay that revolutionised the West Country porcelain industry. The museum focuses on rural Devon life, and includes the original schoolroom and a Victorian kitchen.

BIGBURY-ON-SEA AND BURGH ISLAND

DISTANCE/TIME	4 miles (6.4km) / 2hrs
ASCENT/GRADIENT	246ft (75m) / ▲▲
PATHS	Fields, tracks (muddy in winter) and coast path, several stiles
LANDSCAPE	Rolling farmland and undulating cliff top
SUGGESTED MAP	OS Explorer OL20 South Devon
START/FINISH	Grid reference: SX652442
DOG FRIENDLINESS	Keep on lead near livestock and unfenced cliffs
PARKING	Car park at Bigbury-on-Sea
PUBLIC TOILETS	At car park

The broad, sandy beaches and dunes at Bigbury-on-Sea and Bantham, at the mouth of the River Avon southwest of Kingsbridge, attract hundreds of holidaymakers every summer, drawn by the appeal of sun, sand and sea. There's no doubt that this is a perfect spot for a family day out. Gone are the days of the 16th or 17th centuries when Bigbury was merely famous for its catches of pilchards. But there's something else appealing about this part of the South Devon coast. Just off Bigbury beach, 307yds (282m) from shore, lies craggy Burgh Island, with its famous hotel gazing at the mainland. This extraordinary island is completely surrounded by the sea at high tide but is accessible via the unique, weird and wonderful sea tractor that ploughs its way through the waters.

The island was known as la Burgh in the 15th century, and later Borough Island. There was a chapel dedicated to St Michael on its summit in 1411. The remains of a 'huer's hut' at the top of the island – a fisherman's lookout – is evidence of the times when pilchard fishing was a mainstay of life here, hence the building of the Pilchard Inn, housed in one of the original fisherman's cottages. But it is the island's more recent history that is so fascinating. It was bought in 1929 by wealthy industrialist Archibald Nettlefold, who built the Burgh Island Hotel, much as we see it today. He ran it as a guest house for friends and celebrities, and it became a highly fashionable venue in the 1930s. Noel Coward was among the visitors and it is thought that Edward, Prince of Wales and Wallis Simpson escaped from the limelight here; but the island's most famous connection has to be with Agatha Christie. Two of her books – *Evil Under the Sun* and *And Then There Were None* – were written here, and the influence of the hotel and its location on her writing is clear. By the mid-1980s the hotel had fallen into disrepair, and two London fashion consultants bought the island and restored the hotel to its original art deco glory, complete with the famous Palm Court and authentic Twenties cocktail bar. The hotel has since changed hands again and has undergone further extensive restoration in art deco style.

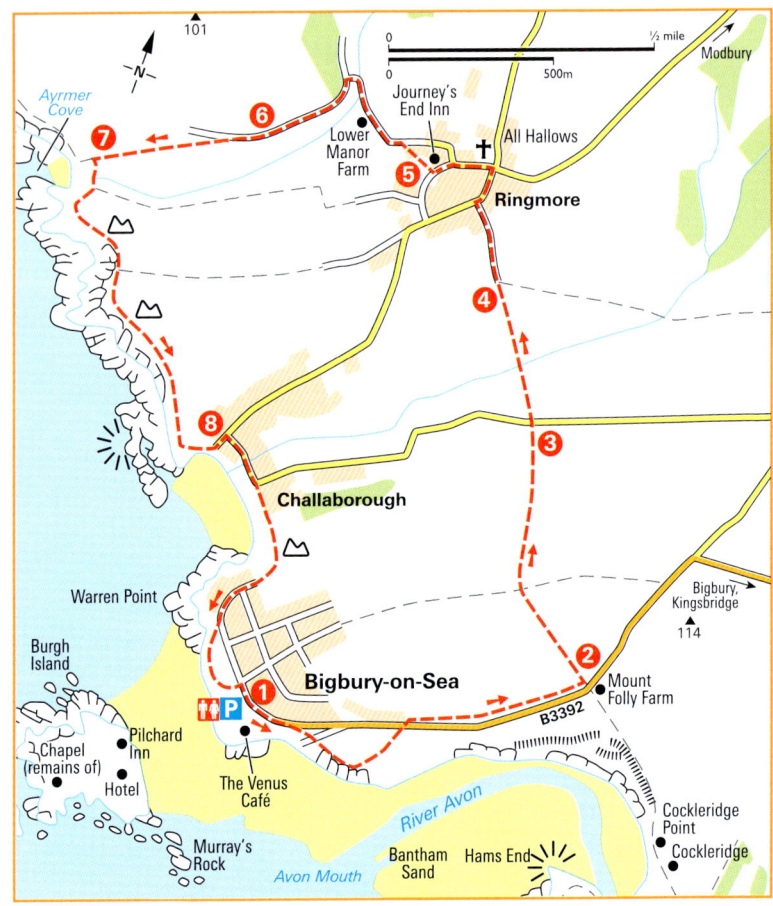

1. From the car park entrance follow coast path signs right, then left towards the road, cross over and continue on South West Coast Path. Go through a kissing gate and turn right uphill, passing through two big gates, to reach a path junction near Mount Folly Farm.

2. Turn left along a gritty track (signed 'Ringmore'). At the field top is a path junction; go through the kissing gate and keep ahead downhill, signed 'Ringmore', with a fence right. Pass through a metal gate, drop past a kissing gate, keep ahead to another on a farm track and walk straight up the next field, crossing a stile on to a lane.

3. Cross over, following signs for Ringmore, through a metal gate. Walk down into the next combe, keeping the hedgebank right. Go through a gate at the bottom and cross the stream on big boulders, then keep straight ahead, uphill, through a plantation and gate on to a narrow path between a fence and hedge.

4. Pass through a kissing gate, bear right then turn immediately left uphill to a path junction; pass through the kissing gate and follow the track to Ringmore. Turn right at the lane, then left at the church to find the Journey's End Inn on the right.

5. From the pub turn right down the narrow lane which gives way to a footpath. It winds round gardens to meet a tarmac lane. Turn left downhill. Walk straight on down the track, eventually passing Lower Manor Farm, and keep going down past the 'National Trust Ayrmer Cove' notice. After a small gate and stream crossing keep straight on at a path junction.

6. Pass through a kissing gate and walk towards the cove on a grassy path above the combe (left). Pass through a gate and cross a stile; a second stile gains the beach.

7. Follow coast path signs ('Challaborough') left over a small footbridge then climb very steeply uphill to the cliff top and great views over Burgh Island. The cliffs are unstable here – take care. The path leads to Challaborough – basically one huge holiday park.

8. Turn right along the beach road and pick up the track uphill along the coast towards Bigbury-on-Sea. Go straight on to meet the tarmac road, then bear right on the coast path to the car park.

Where to eat and drink
The Venus Café at Bigbury has great views over Burgh Island. The Journey's End Inn at Ringmore is atmospheric and has a large garden and there are plenty of refreshment options at Challaborough. Over the river in Bantham try The Sloop Inn, or the Bantham Village Stores and Estuary View Café, up the lane from the pub.

What to see
Explore Ringmore, a pretty village with a mass of thatched cottages dating from the 16th to 18th century. The Journey's End Inn, an old smuggling hostelry, is one of the oldest buildings in Devon (c.1300).

While you're there
Visit Burgh Island, either walk across at low tide or take the lumbering sea tractor. The tractor is great fun and saves getting your feet wet. It runs all year round when the tide is up and can operate in 10ft (3.5m) of seawater and sometimes even in bad weather conditions.

KINGSTON AND THE ERME ESTUARY

DISTANCE/TIME	6 miles (9.7km) / 3hrs
ASCENT/GRADIENT	394ft (120m) / ▲▲▲
PATHS	Fields, tracks and good coast path, several stiles
LANDSCAPE	Farmland, river estuary and roller-coaster cliff top
SUGGESTED MAP	OS Explorer OL20 South Devon
START/FINISH	Grid reference: SX635478
DOG FRIENDLINESS	Keep on lead near livestock and unfenced cliffs
PARKING	By St James the Less Church in Kingston village
PUBLIC TOILETS	None on route

This walk is centred on Kingston and the lovely estuary of the River Erme. Both places are fairly unknown as this part of the South Hams isn't really on the way to anywhere, and it's a fairly long trek along narrow, winding lanes to get there. But it's so worthwhile – you really feel as if you've stumbled on to somewhere special and undiscovered.

When you arrive at the Erme estuary it's easy to believe that nothing much has ever happened here. But the River Erme has a long and interesting history. It rises on Dartmoor, not far south of Nun's Cross, and runs south to leave the moor at Harford, passing through an area of intensive Bronze Age occupation. There is evidence of hut circles, stone rows and cists and, in later medieval times, tin mining activity. Piles Copse in the upper Erme valley is one of the last three remaining areas of ancient oak woodland on the moor. Further downstream old lime kilns can be found; before the estuary silted up, small vessels were able to import coal and limestone here. A river pilot was needed to navigate the waters, and the remains of his cottage can be seen at the back of Wonwell Beach today. The only way across the river is by wading; coast path signs indicate where it's possible to cross at low tide.

The lands on the opposite side of the Erme are within the Flete Estate and were used for much of the filming of Ang Lee's adaptation of Jane Austen's *Sense and Sensibility* (1995), starring Emma Thompson and Kate Winslet. The grand, 19th-century, Grade I listed Flete House has been converted to retirement apartments and many of the original buildings (large and small) are now stunning holiday rentals.

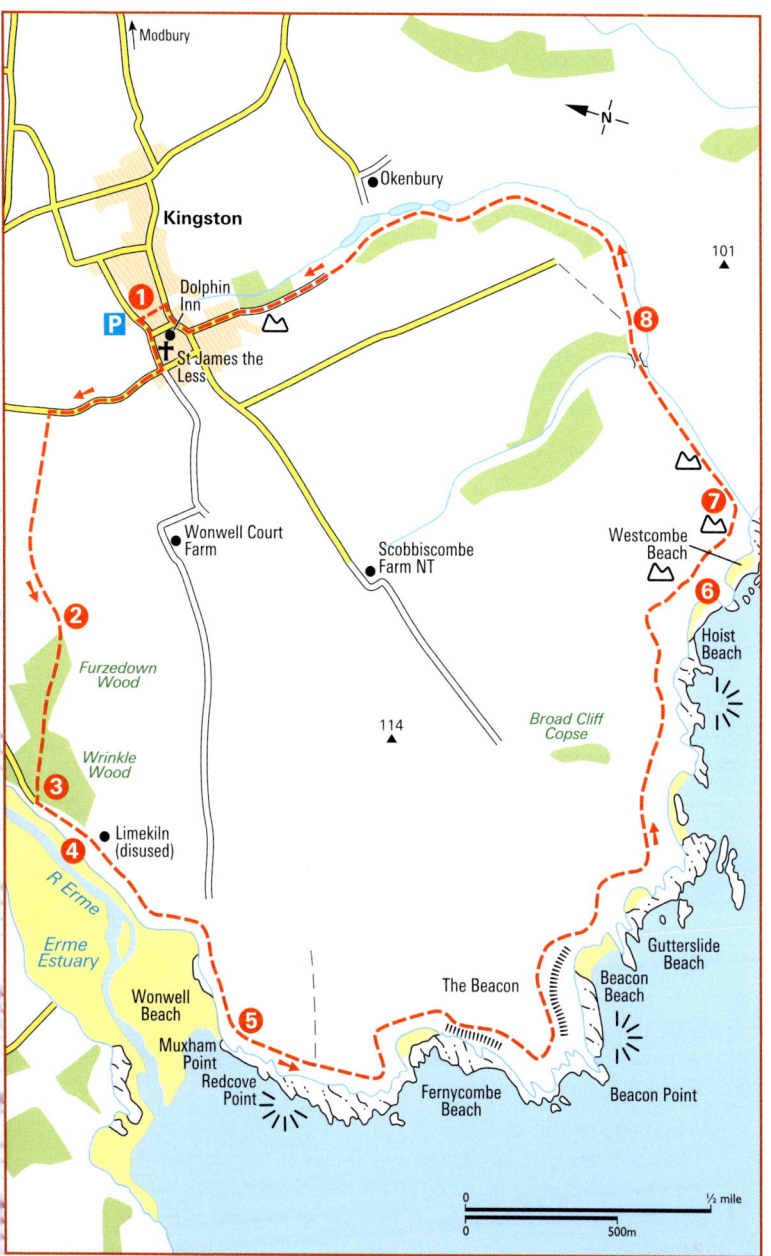

1. With the church to your left, follow the lane up to Wonwell Gate and turn right down the lane signed 'Wonwell Beach'. When it bends sharp right then left, turn left through a gate and straight on, keeping the hedge left. Pass into the next field then keep ahead; follow the sign diagonally right to cross a stile onto a hedged path. Keep along the left edge of the next field and cross a stile. The next stile leads into Furzedown Wood.

2. Descend through delightful woodland (wonderful bluebells in spring), and into Wrinkle Wood, to meet a lane.

3. Turn left; there is limited parking for the beach. Walk down Wonwell Slipway to look at the Erme estuary, an attractive spot.

4. Retrace your steps and follow the coast path signs up steps right signed 'Bigbury-on-Sea'. Follow the narrow wooded path, which leads along the back of Wonwell Beach. Follow the path along the estuary to Muxham Point (with views to Meadowsfoot Beach).

5. Follow the path eastwards to cross a stile (National Trust Scobbiscombe Farm), then sweep across grassland above Fernycombe Beach onto The Beacon, with views to Burgh Island ahead. Walk on through a small gate above Beacon Beach. Follow the cliff top down and up through another gate above Gutterslide Beach. The path drops into a combe before climbing (via a gate) to a bench on Hoist Point.

6. Follow the steep and difficult (often slippery) descent to quiet Westcombe Beach. Take care here.

7. Before the footbridge above the beach turn left, following signs for Kingston. The path runs between a wire fence and a stream; cross a wooden footbridge, right, over the stream and go through a willow plantation. The path twists on through a strip of woodland.

8. Go through a gate at a path junction and straight on up a pleasant, gradually ascending green lane ('bridleway to Kingston'). Continue on to pass ponds, keeping straight ahead at a track crossing, with a stream right (the track is muddy in places). The track runs into a tarmac lane, and uphill into Kingston. At the lane end turn right, then left to the church and your car.

Where to eat and drink
Kingston's 16th-century Dolphin Inn has a pretty beer garden and good food. The next pub, 2 miles (3.2km) to the southeast, is The Journey's End Inn at Ringmore.

What to see
First recorded in 1243, Kingston is a tucked-away village that's a pleasure to explore. There's nothing exceptional, but its isolated yet cosy feel, and the flower-bedecked cottages, soothe away the pressures of modern life. The church dates mainly from the 14th century.

While you're there
If the tide is low enough, wade across the river to Mothecombe. It has a beautiful sandy beach and in the village there's a restaurant, café, bar and takeaway in the old School House; there's a car park and toilets too.

WEMBURY BEACH AND THE RIVER YEALM

DISTANCE/TIME	4 miles (6.4km) / 2hrs
ASCENT/GRADIENT	164ft (50m) / ▲▲
PATHS	Fields, tracks and woodland paths
LANDSCAPE	Farmland, estuary, coast
SUGGESTED MAP	OS Explorer OL20 South Devon
START/FINISH	Grid reference: SX518485
DOG FRIENDLINESS	On lead around livestock
PARKING	National Trust car park, Wembury
PUBLIC TOILETS	Wembury beach

The parish of Wembury has an excellent network of well-maintained rights of way, giving all sorts of circular walk options. This route affords fantastic views over South Devon's most beautiful estuary – the River Yealm, with views up Newton Creek, both popular with sailors – with a return along the Coast Path. Long distance routes feature here too: the Devon Coast to Coast route – a combination of the Two Moors Way (102 miles/164km) and the Erme–Plym Trail (14 miles/22.5km) – meets the south coast at Wembury beach.

The beach here is a great place for rock-pooling and spotting all manner of marine life. Information is available at the Marine Centre by the car park (open from Easter to the end of September, closed Mondays and Tuesday until May, then open from Tuesday–Sunday); entry is free, but donations are welcomed, and a variety of seasonal events take place, such as beach cleans and rockshore rambles. The foreshore at Wembury Point was formed over 400 million years ago, and is part of a European Special Area of Conservation for its flora and fauna. Several unusual species of fish, molluscs, worms and seaweeds have been recorded on the rocky reefs and wave-cut platforms.

The church is situated in magical position above Blackstone Rocks, and it's hardly surprising to learn that the 15th-century tower has been used by sailors as navigation landmark for hundreds of years. It's thought that the present church stands on the site of a Saxon oratory, dating possibly from the 9th century and replaced by a Norman church in the 12th century.

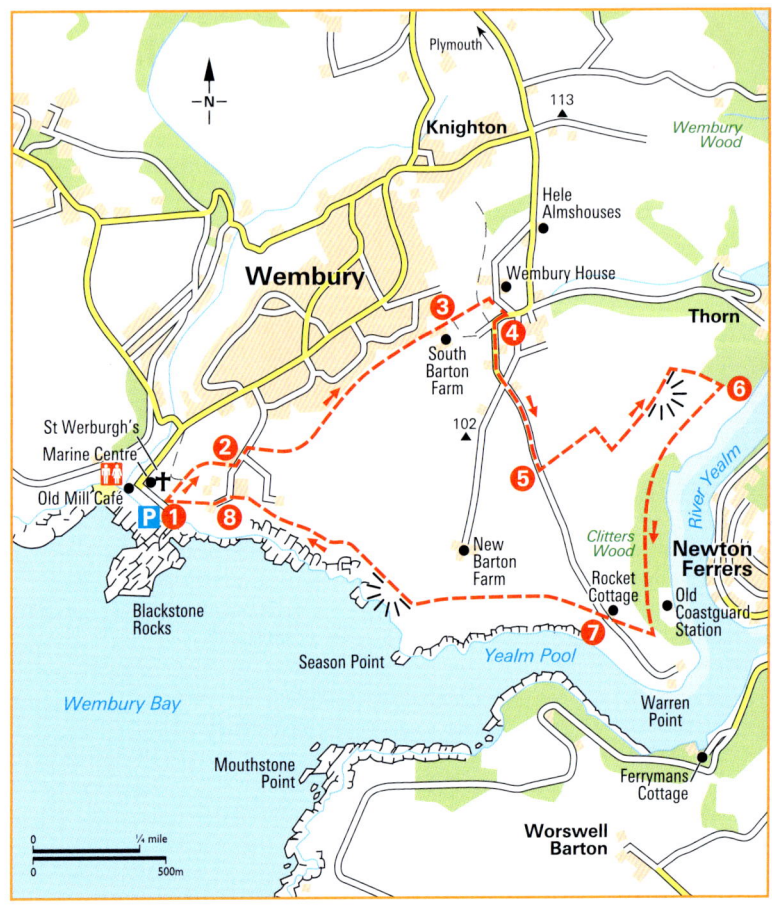

1. Ascend steps near the car park entrance, and at the second Coast Path post, turn left through a kissing gate. Follow the left edge of a meadow (for St Werburgh's Church, turn left through a hedge gap), and go through a kissing gate onto a track.

2. Meet a lane, and turn left and almost immediately right through a kissing gate into a field. Keep ahead and through a kissing gate. Follow the left edge of two fields, then go through a kissing gate onto a fenced path. The next gate meets a footpath T-junction on a green lane (Brownhill Lane).

3. Go straight ahead through a gate. The right of way heads straight across the field, towards the right end of a very high wall (just to left of Wembury House, a late Georgian manor). Turn right alongside the wall, and pass through a kissing gate onto the lane.

4. Turn right along the lane. Where it bears right towards New Barton Farm, keep straight on through a gate onto National Trust land at Warren Point. Follow a stony track, Warren Lane.

5. At a footpath sign turn left through a gate and walk along the top edge of the field. Turn right at the end, then left along a fenced section, and along the top edge of the next field to a footpath post. Turn right downhill towards the River Yealm. Pass through two gates and descend to a footpath junction.

6. Turn right to walk through Clitters Wood (bluebells), eventually passing above the Old Coastguard Station. A few paces on, pass through a gate and turn right up steps. At the next signpost turn right, signed 'Wembury village' (note the Warren Point/ferry is down to the left). This path reaches the Coast Path at a junction by Rocket Cottage.

7. Follow the Coast Path ahead, soon passing through two kissing gates, and later a third (Dartmoor ponies are used to preserve the clifftop maritime grassland here). At a fork keep left, with views to Cellar Beach. Drop across a stream, and views open up to Wembury Point and Rame Head in Cornwall beyond. Pass through another kissing gate. Eventually the path descends through another kissing gate to leave National Trust land.

8. Pass a footpath on the right. Where the track bears right inland, keep ahead on the Coast Path. At the next fork (the path ahead runs into the field by the church) bear left and follow the Coast Path to return to the starting point.

Where to eat and drink
You can sit outside at The Old Mill Café at Wembury Beach every day (from April to end of October and weekends only January to March) in a sheltered area at a millstone table – evidence of a mill on this spot dates from the 13th century. Enjoy breakfast, good coffee, pasties and cakes, and local ice cream; takeaways are also available.

What to see
You'll notice the island of Great Mew Stone off Wembury Point on the last leg of the walk. In 1744 a local man was 'deported' there as punishment for some petty offence. The island was inhabited until 1850; after World War II it was purchased by the War Office, and since 2006 has been owned by the National Trust as a bird colony.

While you're there
Make a day of it and take the ferry to Newton Ferrers or Noss Mayo, two picturesque waterside villages – both with good pubs. The ferry runs daily from late March to the end of September, from Warren Point to the Wide Slip at Noss Mayo, and Yealm Steps at Newton Ferrers.

32 WHERE TAMAR AND TAVY MEET

DISTANCE/TIME	3.5 miles (5.7km) / 2hrs
ASCENT/GRADIENT	180ft (55m) / ▲▲
PATHS	Field tracks and narrow, fenced paths, some muddy after wet weather; several stiles
LANDSCAPE	Farmland and estuary
SUGGESTED MAP	OS Explorer 108 Lower Tamar Valley & Plymouth
START/FINISH	Grid reference: SX459635
DOG FRIENDLINESS	On lead through farmland and along lanes
PARKING	Laneside parking in Bere Ferrers, near harbour
PUBLIC TOILETS	None on route

Two of South Devon's greatest rivers, the Tavy and the Tamar, meet just south of the pretty little peninsula village of Bere Ferrers. This is one of the most picturesque locations in the county, bordered on two sides by the waters of the Tamar estuaries. With just 1.5 miles (2.4km) of land separating the peninsula from the rest of Devon you do feel that you are surrounded by water. The Tamar here forms the Devon–Cornwall boundary.

These rivers have witnessed a huge amount of activity over the generations. Remnants of fords, quays and crossing places can be seen on both the Tamar and Tavy, dating from a time when most movement of people and goods was by water rather than overland.

The area's prosperity came from the many silver and lead mines in the area, which were active from the 13th to 16th centuries, and again in the 19th century. Silver and lead were exported downriver to Plymouth; coal from South Wales and lime came back up again. In the early 19th century more than 1,000 people were employed in local mines, the main ones being South Hooe Mine and South Tamar Consols. Weir Quay, on the west side of the peninsula, was the main quay for the import and export of goods. There are remains of kilns on both rivers, where lime was burned to produce fertiliser.

Another important local product was fruit – the valleys enjoy a particularly balmy climate. There are records of black cherries, pears, strawberries and walnuts being produced and exported in the late 18th century. The coming of the railway greatly assisted the fruit and flower growers, as their produce could reach markets more quickly.

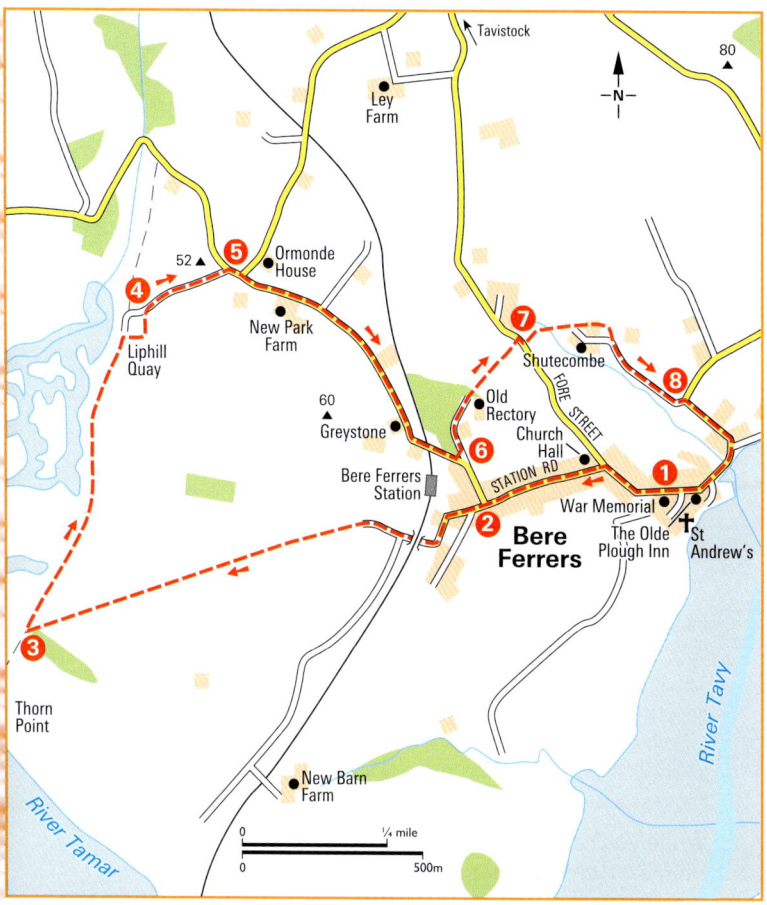

1. From the war memorial and well (dated 1852), walk uphill away from the river. By the Social Club turn left into Station Road, passing the church hall.

2. Where the lane bears right, keep ahead up a lane, still on Station Road and pass under the railway line. Keep ahead up a track, bearing left over a stile by a gate, and cross the field. Pass through a small gate in a larger one and continue, with a fence to your left, eventually descending with glorious views over the River Tamar into Cornwall. Look left to see the Tamar and Royal Albert bridges in Plymouth.

3. Turn right along the bottom of the field, with beautiful oaks to the left and reed beds beyond. Bear right at the end, then left over a V-stile, through a gate and along boardwalks as the path returns to the river. Pass through a gate (access to water, left) and follow the fenced path to a gate. Go through and cross damp ground to reach the slipway at Liphill Quay, a one-time smuggling spot.

4. Turn right, soon ascending a track which rises steeply to meet a lane. Look back for views over the saltmarsh, an important wildlife habitat.

5. Turn right to pass Ormonde House; continue downhill to cross the railway near the station.

6. Just past the station turn left down a drive (footpath sign), soon passing through the left of two gateways (Coach House) into the grounds of the Old Rectory. Follow the drive to the house, then pass to the left of the building (across the garden) and through a gate in the hedge. Now follow a fenced path down across the field, and cross a stile onto a lane. Turn right for a few paces.

7. Turn left over a ladder stile. Head across boggy ground and ascend rough grassland to a footpath post. Turn right here over a stile on a narrow path. Cross a stile and keep along the right edge of the field. Bear right at the end through a field gate and head downhill, passing the entrance to Shutecombe, to meet a lane on a bend.

8. Turn right. The lane meets the Tavy foreshore and bears right past the harbour. Follow Fore Street uphill past The Olde Plough Inn to the start point.

Where to eat and drink
You won't want to leave this magical spot, so look no further than The Olde Plough Inn in Fore Street, where an inn has stood for over 400 years. A beer garden with views to the Tavy, and good home-cooked food – using local suppliers wherever possible, and fresh fish a speciality – add to its appeal.

What to see
With their ancient oak woodlands, saltmarsh and rocky foreshore, the Tamar estuaries form an internationally important wildlife habitat. Huge populations of birds overwinter here or drop in during migration. Look out for common and green sandpipers on the Tavy, and little egrets (like a small, white heron) that roosts in the trees and feed on small fish and crustaceans.

While you're there
The great 16th-century seafarer Sir Francis Drake is said to have lived at Hawcombe (now in ruins) near Ley Farm, north of the village. Later he lived at Buckland Abbey, a few miles away on the east bank of the Tavy which is now in the hands of the National Trust. There's a lot to see here but well worth a visit are The Abbey and the Great Barn built by Cistercian monks in the 13th century.

ALONG THE RIVER PLYM FROM CADOVER BRIDGE

DISTANCE/TIME	3.75 miles (6km) / 2hrs
ASCENT/GRADIENT	180ft (55m) / ▲▲▲
PATHS	Woodland paths, some rocky, several stiles
LANDSCAPE	Oak woodland, steep-sided river valley and open moorland
SUGGESTED MAP	OS Explorer OL28 Dartmoor
START/FINISH	Grid reference: SX554645
DOG FRIENDLINESS	Keep on lead near livestock and birds
PARKING	Car park at Cadover Bridge or NT car park just south of bridge
PUBLIC TOILETS	None on route

This is a popular walk, not only because of its proximity to Plymouth, but also because of the wealth of obvious industrial archaeological interest. The best way to experience this is to start from Cadover Bridge, on the edge of the open moor towards the Lee Moor China Clay Works. You follow the route of the pipeline that carried the china clay in suspension from the works to the drying kilns at Shaugh Bridge (seen in the car park), via settling tanks, the remains of which are passed on the walk.

The area around Shaugh Bridge is a Site of Special Scientific Interest (SSSI), nationally important for plants and wildlife, and there is a constant conservation programme going on here. The bridge itself dates from the late 1820s, and replaces one that was badly damaged in January 1823. Cadover Bridge was named in a charter of 1291 as 'ponta de Cada worth', so its name probably derives from cad, Celtic for 'skirmish'. The Plym is also referred to as Plymma, from the Celtic pilim, 'to roll'.

This is definitely not the place to be on a black winter's night – the Devil (locally known as 'Dewer') has long been associated with the Dewerstone. The Devil's fearsome pack of ghost hounds are said to roam the desolate moors at night, seeking unrepentant sinners, whom they drive over the edge of the crags to the Devil waiting below. One of the more unpleasant legends associated with this distinctive granite formation tells of how an old farmer met the Devil carrying a sack near the rock and, not recognising him, asked if he'd had a good day's hunting. The Devil is said to have laughed, and to have given the farmer the sack. The farmer, delighted, rushed home – only to find that the sack contained the body of his son. And beware, the woods near the Dewerstone are said to be haunted at night by a huge, evil dog with red eyes. Such stories are common in moorland areas, and perhaps date back to a time when wolves still inhabited the more remote parts of the country. Their eventual extinction in Britain was largely due to this process of demonisation.

There are Bronze Age hut circles and cairns on Wigford Down, dating to at least 1000 BC, and Iron Age fortifications protecting the summit of the ridge.

Cadover Cross, near the start/end of the walk, is an ancient restored cross – the modern shaft is made of red granite – set on the line of the Monastic Way between Plympton and Tavistock. It was found lying recumbent in 1873 and re-erected, only to fall and be put up again in 1915, set in a large socket stone. It stands over 7ft 6in (2m) tall.

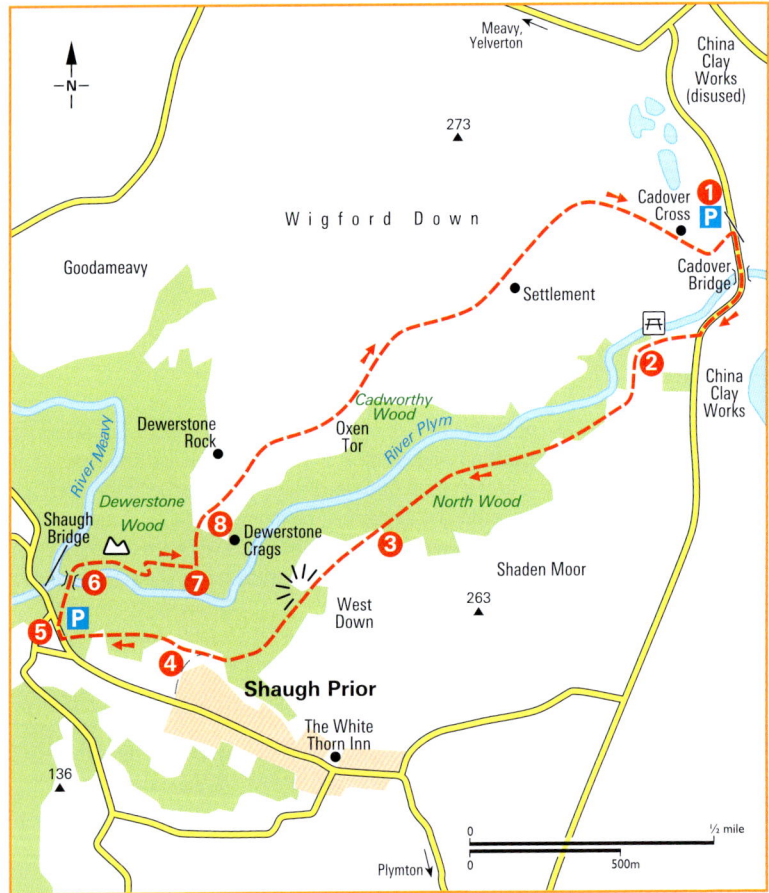

1. From the car park, walk away from Cadover Bridge, with the river on your right. Pass through a kissing gate and through a small group of willows into woodland. The river below is quite delightful, and you'll find masses of great picnic spots along the bank.

2. Two gates lead to a stile and footbridge into North Wood. Keep ahead on the rocky path which follows the course of a large pipe, which appears above ground intermittently.

3. Leave North Wood over a stile. Follow the path through open bracken on West Down; the Plym is below right. Note the dramatic Dewerstone Crags ahead on the other side of the valley. The path leads into silver birch and oak past a settling tank, where it forks. Take the right fork downhill to a path junction and gate.

4. Keep inside the wire fence, following the footpath sign 'Shaugh Bridge'. Stay within the woods as the yellow-waymarked path twists downhill: you can hear the river below to the right. The path leads over a stile to pass settling tanks (right), and eventually meets a road.

5. Bear immediately right and follow the narrow path on and eventually down steps leading into Shaugh Bridge car park. Turn right to walk through the car park towards the river.

6. Cross the river via the railed wooden footbridge to enter Dewerstone Wood (National Trust); look left to see Shaugh Bridge and the confluence of the Plym and Meavy rivers. Follow the path right. It becomes a restored rocky track leading above the river and winds steeply uphill so take your time. After a sharp left bend take the next path right (narrower but still paved). Continue uphill until you are level with the top of granite buttresses (part of Dewerstone Crags) ahead and right, and where the path forks.

7. Bear left and scramble steeply uphill, passing more buttresses (right), eventually to leave the woods and enter open moorland to reach Dewerstone Rock, with glorious views.

8. Turn 90 degrees right at the rock and follow the right-hand grassy path along the edge of the valley to pass Oxen Tor and over Wigford Down, keeping Cadworthy Wood and the Plym Valley on your right. Keep straight on to the boundary wall of the wood, then follow the wall around fields. Eventually the wall bears right and you walk downhill past Cadover Cross with views of the china clay works beyond. Bear left at the cross to head towards the bridge, cross over on the road and walk back to your car.

Where to eat and drink
There's often an ice cream van in the car parks at Cadover Bridge and Shaugh Bridge. The Royal Oak at Meavy, a free house with good food and outdoor seating, is over 500 years old and is set on the village green near the 1,000-year-old tree from which it takes its name. The White Thorn Inn at Shaugh Prior is another traditional hostelry, and welcomes families and dogs.

What to see
The Dewerstone Crags provide the best middle-grade climbing in Dartmoor. The main crag, Devil's Rock, rises 150ft (46m) from the banks of the Plym; to the right lie the isolated Needle and Upper and Lower Raven buttresses. Evocative names for the many routes here include Hagar the Horrible, If I Should Fall and Knucklecracker. In 1960, a climber found a late Bronze Age (c. 1000 BC) drinking vessel here.

While you're there
Buckland Abbey, in the Tavy Valley to the west of Yelverton, has strong associations with Sir Francis Drake. It was originally a small Cistercian monastery, and the house incorporates the remains of the 13th-century abbey church.

PRINCETOWN

DISTANCE/TIME	7.5 miles (12.1km) / 3hrs
ASCENT/GRADIENT	328ft (100m) / ▲
PATHS	Tracks, leat-side paths and rough moorland
LANDSCAPE	Open moorland
SUGGESTED MAP	OS Explorer OL28 Dartmoor
START/FINISH	Grid reference: SX589735
DOG FRIENDLINESS	Keep on lead around livestock and birds
PARKING	Car park behind National Park Visitor Centre
PUBLIC TOILETS	By car park (fee)

Princetown, 1,395ft (425m) above sea level, was founded by Sir Thomas Tyrwhitt in the late 18th century, and named in honour of the Prince Regent, to whom he was both a friend and private secretary.

Tyrwhitt persuaded the government to build a prison here for French prisoners from the Napoleonic wars. Building work started in 1806, and the first prisoners were in situ by 1809, joined by Americans in 1813. At one time 7,000 men were held. Closed in 1813, the prison reopened in 1850 as a civilian establishment, which it remains to this day – a monumental building, best seen from the Two Bridges to Tavistock road, to the north of the town.

There is mention of the ancient landmark of Nun's Cross (or Siward's Cross) as early as 1280, in documents concerning ownership of Buckland Abbey lands. Over 7ft (2.1m) high, it stands on the route of the Abbot's Way – between Buckfast Abbey and Tavistock. The word 'Siward' engraved on its eastern face may refer to the Earl of Northumberland who owned much land in this part of the country in Saxon times, or may indicate some connection to a family named Siward who lived nearby. 'Bocland' on the other face may be a reference to Buckland Abbey. The word 'Nun's' comes from the Celtic nans, meaning combe or valley.

The Devonport Leat is an amazing feat of engineering, carried out between 1793 and 1801 to improve water supplies to Devonport, now part of Plymouth, which at that time was being developed as a naval base. Originally 26.5 miles (43km) long, it carried 2 million gallons (9 million litres) of water a day. Lined with granite slabs and conveying crystal-clear, fast flowing water, today it provides an extremely attractive, level walking route through some otherwise fairly inhospitable terrain. The final part of the walk, back to Princetown, follows the abandoned railway track that Tyrwhitt planned to link Princetown with Plymouth. The line, the first iron railway in the county, opened in 1823. More of a tramway than a railway, the horse-drawn wagons carried coal and lime up from Plymouth, and took stone back. Sixty years later it re-opened as a steam railway but eventually closed in 1956.

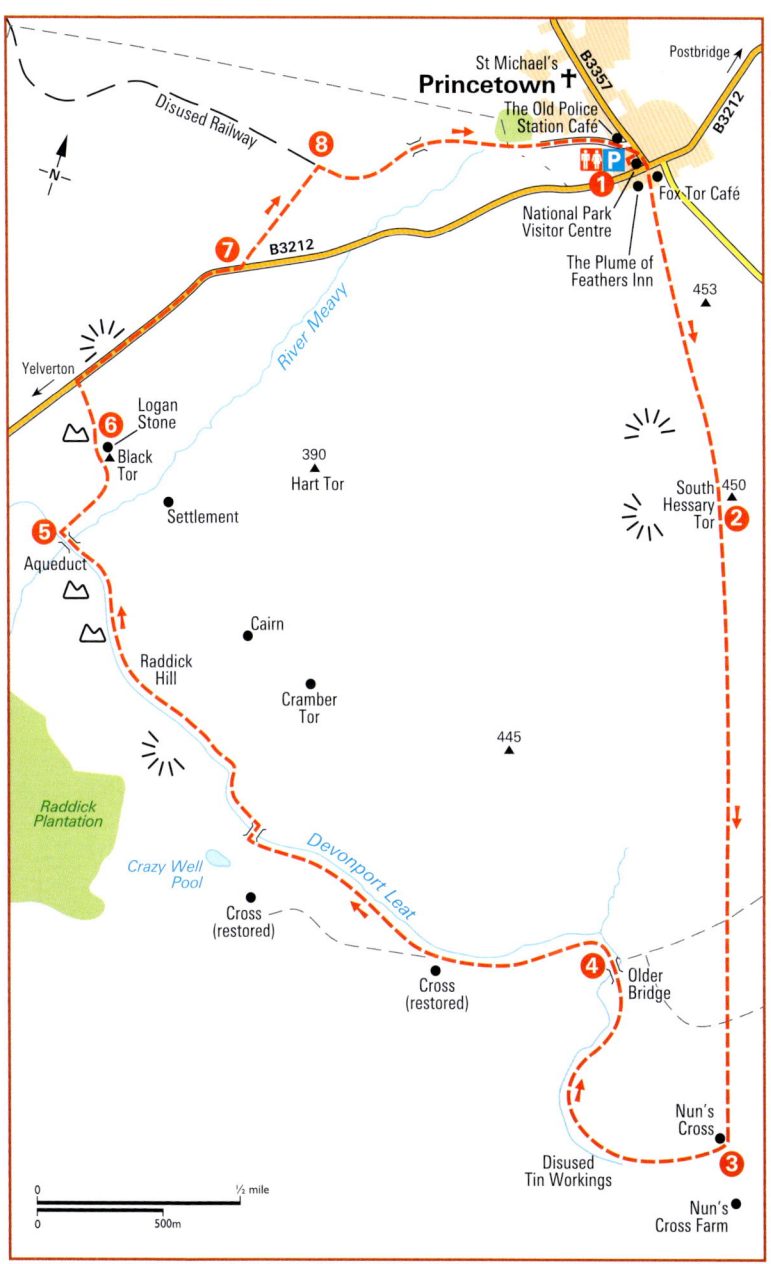

1. Leave the car park past the toilets and turn right to pass the National Park Visitor Centre. Cross the road and follow the lane to the left of the Plume of Feathers Inn. After 100yds (91m) a small gate leads to a broad track which ascends gently to South Hessary Tor, from which there are splendid views to Plymouth Sound, ahead, and of the prison behind.

2. Follow the track as it drops gently, passing boundary stones. It crosses two other tracks (after the first look right to spot the Devonport Leat) before descending to Nun's Cross (2.5 miles/4km from the start). Nun's Cross Farm (originally thatched c.1870) can be seen to the left.

3. Turn 90 degrees right at the cross to pick through old tin workings to find the tunnel where the leat emerges. It's near the ruins of a building under a beech tree. Walk along the right bank of the leat, soon passing a granite cross.

4. Just before a bend meet a track and cross the leat via Older Bridge. Continue along the left bank, with wonderful views of Burrator reservoir to the left. Cross back to the right bank before descending to the valley of the Meavy. One option is a bridge beside blocks of granite as the Burrator reservoir plantations come into view. The descent to the Meavy is steep and rocky.

5. Cross the aqueduct; the leat turns left. Take the grassy path right leading slightly uphill away from the river (there is a wealth of tin working evidence in the valley – worth an exploration). Bear left and climb steeply up to Black Tor on the hilltop.

6. Go straight on past the Logan Stone, one of several on Dartmoor balanced in such a way that they can be rocked on their base, and on across open moorland to the road, with views of Brentor, Swelltor Quarries and the disused railway line ahead. Turn right at the road.

7. Pass a blocked-off parking place and continue along the verge. The road descends past a small parking space; as it rises again bear left by a granite block across rough grassland, aiming to the right of the mast on North Hessary Tor.

8. At the railway track turn right towards the edge of town. Keep left at a fork, eventually passing a small gate to join a road, with Dartmoor Brewery left. Bear right to the car park.

Where to eat and drink
The Plume of Feathers Inn is the oldest building in Princetown, dating from 1785. It has a campsite and camping barn and is a popular stopover. Nearby is the excellent Fox Tor Café, great for walkers. The Old Police Station Café is by the car park.

While you're there
Visit the National Park Visitor Centre (open 10am–4pm April to October, slightly longer in summer months), in the old Duchy Hotel, very near the start. You'll find everything you ever wanted to know about the Dartmoor National Park here. There's an information centre and shop, helpful staff, and audiovisual and 'hands-on' displays.

FROM POSTBRIDGE ONTO THE WILDERNESS OF DARTMOOR

DISTANCE/TIME	4.5 miles (7.2km) / 2hrs 15min
ASCENT/GRADIENT	360ft (110m) / ▲
PATHS	Drift lane and narrow rocky or grassy paths, several stiles
LANDSCAPE	Flat-bottomed river valley and undulating open moorland
SUGGESTED MAP	OS Explorer OL28 Dartmoor
START/FINISH	Grid reference: SX646788
DOG FRIENDLINESS	Keep on lead near birds and livestock
PARKING	Dartmoor National Park car park, Postbridge (pay and display)
PUBLIC TOILETS	At car park

Most visitors to Dartmoor will, at some point, drive right across the moor, and so can't fail to pass through Postbridge. Situated at a natural stopping place halfway across the moor, there has been a ford and clapper bridge (now restored) over the East Dart River here for centuries. The first written reference to the bridge was in 1675, but it was probably built 300 years earlier.

Postbridge developed after the Moretonhampstead to Tavistock toll road was constructed in the late 18th century. The toll house here is recorded as taking £100 per annum in the 1820s, whereas that at Princetown took only £20, emphasising Postbridge's importance on the main east–west route across Dartmoor. There was an inn, the Greyhound, here in the late 18th century, but that had turned into a farm by the end of the 19th century and the Temperance Inn (now the East Dart Hotel) was built to replace it.

Today, Postbridge is one of Dartmoor's hotspots, and the banks of the river near the old clapper bridge are very popular with picnickers. This simple route along the valley of the East Dart River accesses some much quieter picnic spots within an hour's walk.

Prior to the mid-13th century this part of the moor fell within the parish of Lydford, the administrative centre of the ancient Forest of Dartmoor, around 14 miles (22.5km) away on the northwestern edge of the moor. Bodies had to be carried across the moor for burial in consecrated ground in the graveyard at Lydford, along a route that became known as the 'Lych Way'.

Legends and tales of the unexplained are rife on the moor, and that of the 'Hairy Hands' is one of the best known. It is said that around Higher Cherrybrook Bridge, to the southwest of Postbridge, drivers often find their cars forced off the road by some unseen hand... some believe that the 'hands' are all that is left of an Italian who used to work at the old gunpowder factory at Powdermills. On forgetting his tools one day he returned to fetch them, but forgot to take off his hobnail boots. An ensuing spark lead to disaster...

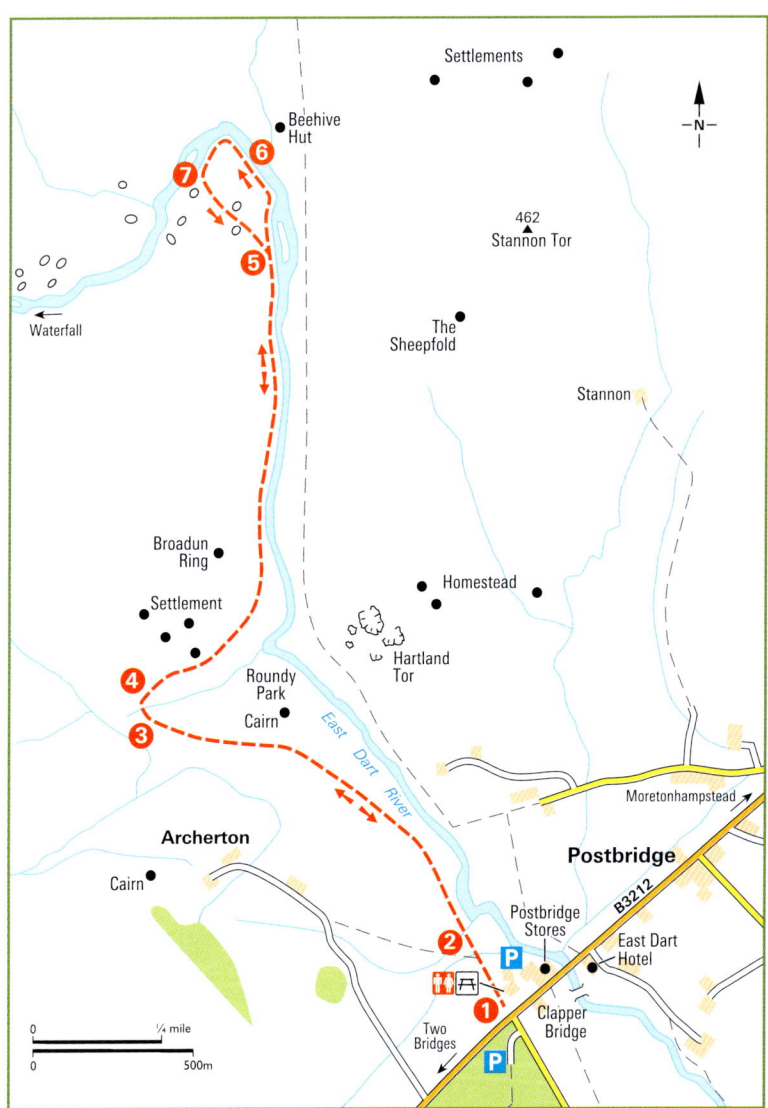

1. Leave the car park by the National Park Information Centre (right), and pass through the bank. Turn right towards the open moor on a path through a broad, marshy area – an old drift lane, used originally for driving livestock up from the farmland to summer pasture on the moor. Many drift lanes are still used at the annual pony drifts each autumn, but this one has been blocked by early 20th-century 'newtake' walls.

2. The path ends at a gate to the right of a line of beech trees in a granite wall. Go through and follow the path uphill to run alongside a wire fence/wall on the right. Just below, towards the river, is the site of Roundy Park, a Bronze Age enclosure with a restored kist (grave), dating from around 4,000 years ago. There are lovely views over the river to Hartland Tor.

3. The path continues to parallel the wall, then descends through boggy ground to cross two converging brooks (Braddon Lake) on well-placed boulders. Skirt a boggy area then bear right, uphill, to a stile in the wall ahead.

4. Cross the stile and follow the path along the course of the disused Powder Mills leat (left), which follows the contours of the hill ahead. The path turns north to run above the East Dart River as the valley becomes narrower, with some glorious views downriver towards Bellever Forest; some wet and rocky patches are encountered on this stretch. Eventually a stile brings you closer to the river, and the path reaches a broad marshy area.

5. Where the leat starts to bear away left drop off the path to the right, pick your way across a rocky stream, and walk along the river bank. Follow the river as it too bears left. Nearby on the opposite bank are the circular remains of a beehive hut, built as a store or shelter.

6. Walk a little further upstream, with the swell of Winney's Down ahead. Pass a deep pool on a left bend and continue upriver as the waters tumble over the rocky bed, to reach a stile. (From here you can go on further upstream to a waterfall 0.75 miles/1.2km, but the path becomes indistinct and difficult.)

7. Turn back at this point and take the path ahead (not by the river) that bears right around the bottom of the slope. This will bring you back to the next stile to retrace your steps back to Postbridge.

Where to eat and drink

The East Dart Hotel is a free house with a good range of food and offering accommodation. There's a beer garden and families are welcome. Postbridge Stores is a well-stocked local shop, with takeaway cream teas on sale. Cream teas are also available at Powdermills Pottery (and gallery), along the road to Two Bridges.

What to see

Moorland walks are frequently accompanied by the warbling song of the skylark in spring and summer. This attractive little brown bird (barely 7in/18cm) rises almost vertically and hovers several hundred feet above the ground, from where you can hear its distincitve song. Nesting in grassy tussocks at ground level, the skylark is Britain's most widely breeding species of bird.

While you're there

Just north of Two Bridges, to the southwest of Postbridge, an easy path runs north up the valley of the West Dart River towards Wistman's Wood, one of Dartmoor's three remaining areas of high-altitude oak woodland. It is said that this is one of the spots where the Devil and his evil hounds are active, driving sinners into the tangled branches from where they never escape.

GRIMSPOUND AND GOLDEN DAGGER MINE

DISTANCE/TIME	6.5 miles (10.4km) / 3hrs 15min
ASCENT/GRADIENT	656ft (200m) / ▲▲
PATHS	Heathery tracks and grassy paths, several stiles
LANDSCAPE	Open moorland; sweeping valleys and ridges
SUGGESTED MAP	OS Explorer OL28 Dartmoor
START/FINISH	Grid reference: SX680816
DOG FRIENDLINESS	Keep on lead around livestock and birds
PARKING	Bennett's Cross car park on B3212
PUBLIC TOILETS	None on route

The area around Vitifer and Birch Tor, near where you park, is a Site of Special Scientific Interest (SSSI), being one of the most spectacular areas of mature heather on Dartmoor, and rich in archaeological remains. Vitifer and Birch Tor mines, with Golden Dagger, were the only three large mines still producing tin in the 1820s, and by the mid-19th century Vitifer employed more than 100 men. It closed in 1870, but reopened in 1900 until 1914. A quantity of iron was also produced from the mines here.

Bennett's Cross is a slanting stone cross marking the line of the ancient track across the moor, followed today by the route of the B3212, which was constructed towards the end of the 18th century. The cross also marks the boundary between the mines at Vitifer and Headland Warren, and between the parishes of Chagford and North Bovey.

The valley between Soussons Down and Challacombe Down has been the scene of industrial activity for more than 800 years, although the name 'Golden Dagger' wasn't recorded until the 1850s. Medieval tinners extracted ore from the stream beds but later workers carried out open-cast mining, creating the deep gullies that are obvious today. Tin was drilled out by hand from underground shafts during the 18th and 19th centuries, and work finally ceased in the early 20th century; Golden Dagger was the last working Dartmoor tin mine. At Point 7 you will see all sorts of evidence on the ground: there's a buddle, used to sort the crushed ore, Dinah's House, last occupied in the 1940s, and Stamp's wheelpit (minus its waterwheel), which was last used in 1916.

When you reach Two Burrows, rest by the old granite wall and enjoy the panorama to the east. The views all along the Hamel Down ridge are breathtaking, and from this particular point you can see (from left to right) Hayne Down, Hound Tor, Honeybag Tor, Chinkwell Tor, and the characteristic outline of Haytor. To the left again you can pick out where the hills drop towards the sea at Teignmouth. There is the most fantastic feeling of peace and freedom up here – it just has to be experienced.

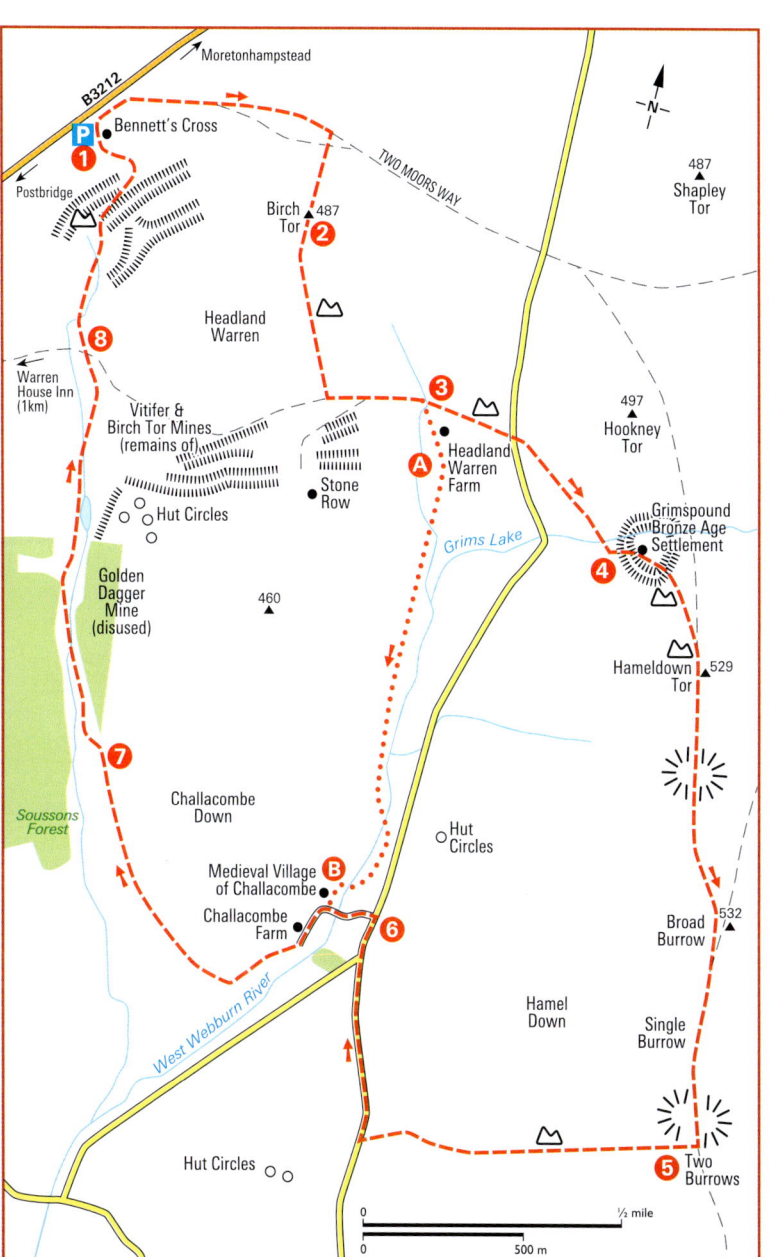

1. Walk to Bennett's Cross; at the cross bear right on a narrow path which bears left uphill. At the hilltop turn right by a cairn and follow a narrow twisting path to reach Birch Tor.

2. A small path leads from the furthest outcrop downhill to meet a stony path at a crossroads. Turn left towards Headland Warren Farm in the valley ahead. Follow a granite wall (right) to a signpost.

3. Go straight on uphill to cross the road. Take the small path leading off right. Cross the stream and follow Grimspound's perimeter wall (left); turn left through the entrance.

4. At the centre of the enclosure turn right and climb steeply uphill to gain Hameldown Tor at 1,735ft (529m). The obvious path on the ridge top leads to Broad Burrow and Two Burrows, where you meet a wall corner.

5. Turn right to follow the wall down the valley side. The wall gives way to a fence, then a line of small beech trees and there are superb views towards Soussons Forest and the Warren House Inn. Cross the stock fence via a stile on a permissive path, and over another stile in the bottom left corner on to the road. Turn right to reach the drive to Challacombe Farm.

6. Turn left down the concrete drive. At the T-junction turn left to pass the farm and barns and through a gate. Take the right-hand of the next two gates (signs to Bennett's Cross) and keep along the field edge.

7. The next gate takes you into the edge of Soussons Forest. After a few paces you reach the fascinating remains of Golden Dagger tin mine. Follow the main track. When it bears left continue ahead on a rough bridleway signed 'Bennett's Cross' and proceed up the valley via a gate through broken ground, evidence of generations of tin-mining activity.

8. When you reach a junction of tracks either turn left over a stream, crossing by a ruined building and ascending to the Warren House Inn, or go straight on, keeping right where the path forks after a few paces. Follow the soon narrow path uphill to a grassy gully. Halfway along bear right to ascend an obvious path which eventually leads to the car park.

Shortening the walk If you don't feel like walking up to Grimspound itself, but consider you can see it well enough from the lower levels, this alternative route cuts out the climb to Hameldown Tor and the walk along Hamel Down to Two Burrows.

At Point 3, turn right at the signpost following the bridleway signs for Challacombe Farm. Pass through a small gate in front of Headland Warren farmhouse and stables, to join the drive via a gate. At Point A bear right through a gate, and then another, and follow the grassy path along the bottom of the valley, keeping the wire fence left. When the cottages before Challacombe Farm come into view stay ahead, keeping the old bank and wall remains right, to pass through a gate and by the cottages, Point B.

The next gate joins the concrete drive to Challacombe Farm at the T-junction just after Point 6. All along this shortcut you have great views of the Bronze Age settlement at Grimspound, which dates from around 1300 BC. The climatic conditions on the moor then were quite different from today, and much of the moor was forested. Neolithic peoples began to clear areas of the moor, and the Bronze Age settlers continued the process. The original enclosure wall (or, possibly, a double wall) was up to 6ft (1.8m) high and about 10ft (3m) wide, surrounding an area of about 4 acres (1.6ha), with two dozen hut circles inside. It was probably used for keeping stock safe, and would have been a pleasant place to live, situated on the slopes by the Grimslake stream, with good grazing.

It is thought by many to be Dartmoor's finest prehistoric monument. The site was extensively examined and partly reconstructed (and its significance fully realised), by the Dartmoor Exploration Committee in 1894. One of the hut circles has been partially rebuilt, including the curved 'porch', protection against the elements.

Where to eat and drink
The Warren House Inn is the tenth highest inn in England, at some 1,400ft (427m). There's a fire in the grate that hasn't gone out since 1845 when embers were carried here from an earlier pub across the road. It is visible for many miles around, particularly from the south, and welcomes walkers.

What to see
The grassy slope below the Warren House Inn is a favourite gathering ground for some of the ponies that roam on Dartmoor. Most of the ponies on the moor are cross-breds, but there are some 'true' Dartmoor Pony herds, including one at Challacombe. Every pony has an owner and they are rounded up each autumn for sale.

While you're there
Look out for the Four Aces, four stone enclosures resembling playing cards on the slopes below Birch Tor near Bennett's Cross. Legend says that Jan Reynolds, a local lad, made a deal with the Devil ensuring him good luck for seven years. In return the Devil could claim one of Jan's possessions. Jan made his fortune playing cards, but seven years later the Devil caught up with him. Before his capture, Jan cast the cards aside. The aces turned to stone, where they remain.

THE TEIGN GORGE TO FINGLE BRIDGE

DISTANCE/TIME	4 miles (6.4km) / 2hrs
ASCENT/GRADIENT	Negligible
PATHS	Riverside paths and tracks, one steep rocky section
LANDSCAPE	Deeply wooded river gorge and meadows
SUGGESTED MAP	OS Explorer OL28 Dartmoor
START/FINISH	Grid reference: SX713894
DOG FRIENDLINESS	Dogs should be kept under control at all times
PARKING	Roadside parking north of Dogmarsh Bridge on A382
PUBLIC TOILETS	On south side of river at Fingle Bridge

Castle Drogo, built in local granite between 1911 and 1930, occupies a spectacular position high above the Teign Gorge near Drewsteignton in northeast Dartmoor. Given to the National Trust by the Drewe family in 1974, it was designed by Sir Edwin Lutyens (on a budget of £60,000) and has the honour of being the 'youngest' castle in the country. Self-made millionaire Julius Drewe established his family seat here due to a romantic notion that his ancestors had connections with the village (he believed that he was descended from Drogo/Dru du Teine, a Norman baron), but he did not live to see his dream fully completed. An elaborate gateway designed by Lutyens, for example, was never built: Julius Drewe had lost heart in the idea after his eldest son Adrian was killed in World War I. Drewe himself died in 1931.

The nearby village of Drewsteignton was once famous for being home to the country's (at that time) oldest and longest-serving landlady. Mabel Mudge (Aunt Mabel) ran The Drewe Arms with her husband Ernest from 1919. After his death she remained in harness until 1994, and during that time the pub remained unchanged; even today this lovely thatched 17th-century building retains the atmosphere of yesteryear. At the time Castle Drogo was built the name of the pub was changed from The Druid Arms to The Drewe Arms.

This walk takes you through the edge of the Drogo Estate along the sparkling upper River Teign and, apart from one rocky section (avoidable so long as the river is low), is fairly easy, although there are some rough underfoot sections. Fingle Bridge and the pub will be buzzing with activity on sunny weekends and during holiday times. The estate is criss-crossed by a network of paths: leaflets on more local walks are available from the National Trust shop at Castle Drogo.

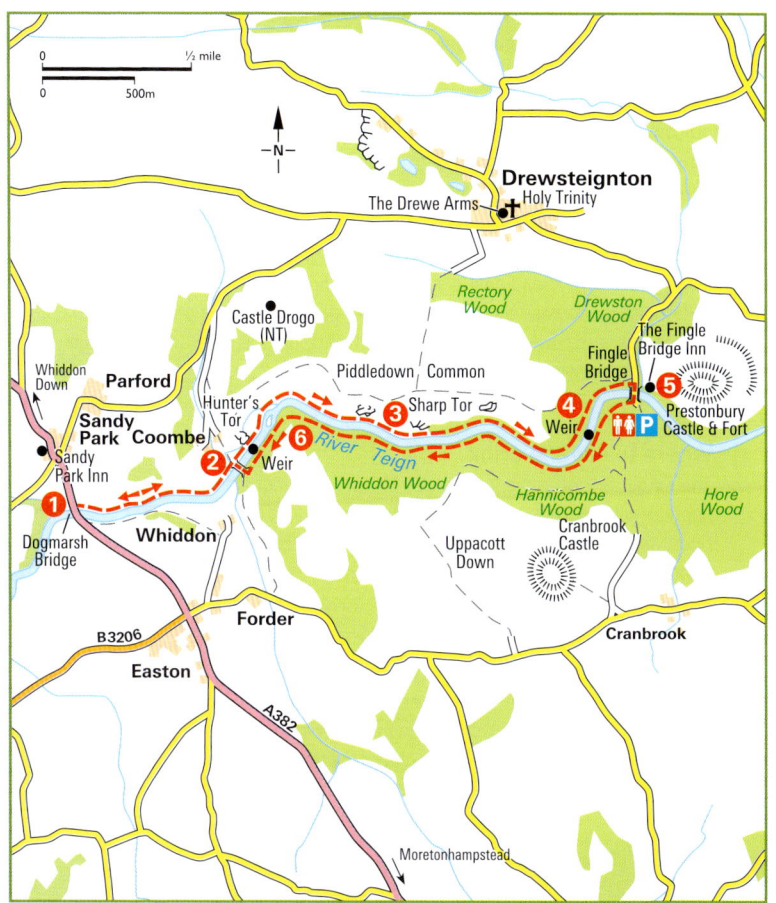

1. Walk back towards the bridge, then left through the kissing gate, following the footpath sign 'Fingle Bridge' (on the route of the Two Moors Way). Walk through riverside meadows, with views of Castle Drogo above left, and the steep-sided Teign Gorge ahead. Pass through a gate into oak woodland, and reach a path junction by a suspension bridge over the river, right (the return route). (The Two Moors Way goes left here.)

2. Follow the Fisherman's Path signs straight on along the left bank to pass a broad pool and weir, from where water is diverted to the renovated turbine house (passed on the return), which provides Castle Drogo with electricity.

3. Eventually the path ascends high, rough granite steps over the base of Sharp Tor, dropping steeply to regain the riverbank (so avoiding a particularly rough stretch which is often underwater). A metal railing provides assistance over the trickiest parts. Once back on level ground continue along the riverbank path.

4. Pass through a small hunting gate and keep ahead to gain a weir, with benches – a great place to picnic. Water was once taken from this point to supply Fingle Bridge Mill, destroyed by fire in 1894.

5. Triple-arched Fingle Bridge and The Fingle Bridge Inn are reached after 2 miles (3.2km). Refreshments have been available at this picturesque spot for years; from 1877 one Jessie Ashplant sold cakes from a basket, 'moving up' to a shed in 1907. Cross the old packhorse bridge and turn right (through Hannicombe Wood) to return on the track which runs parallel to the river. This is fairly level and passes through mixed deciduous then coniferous woodland.

6. Where a small path leads right from the track go and have a look at the pumping station and leat leading from the weir below the castle. Follow the narrow path to the left of the building to rejoin the main track just before a five-bar gate. Keep ahead past a superb 8ft (2.5m) granite wall, then turn right over stone steps to pass down and over the footbridge to the other bank, to rejoin the outward route at Point 2. Turn left through the gate and walk back across the meadows to your car.

Where to eat and drink
The Fingle Bridge Inn, a pub since 1897 at this famous beauty spot, is popular with tourists – and game fishermen – and has tables on the riverbank. It's a free house, is open all year, and is particularly busy on Sunday lunchtimes. The Sandy Park Inn, just north of Dogmarsh Bridge, is a characterful pub with a reputation for good food.

What to see
Look up above Fingle Bridge and you will see the precipitously steep slopes leading up to the site of Prestonbury Castle Iron Age hill fort, facing its counterpart Cranbrook Castle on the other side of the valley. These two impressive sites, built by Celtic peoples to guard the Teign Gorge, provide evidence of relatively sophisticated habitation in the area as long ago as 750 BC – more than 2,000 years before Julius Drewe's dream came to fruition.

While you're there
Take a look at the pretty village of Chagford, a couple of miles west along the River Teign (a lovely walk at all times of the year). One of Dartmoor's most popular settlements, the village has plenty of independent and characterful shops, cafés, pubs, a 15th-century church and an extraordinary general store run by the same family for over 150 years. The octagonal Pepperpot in The Square was the original market house, built in 1862.

BELSTONE CLEAVE AND COSDON HILL

DISTANCE/TIME	4 miles (6.4km) / 2hrs
ASCENT/GRADIENT	394ft (120m) / ▲▲▲
PATHS	Riverside path, rough underfoot with rocks and roots
LANDSCAPE	River valley and open moorland
SUGGESTED MAP	OS Explorer OL28 Dartmoor
START/FINISH	Grid reference: SX619935
DOG FRIENDLINESS	Under control at all times, on lead in nesting season (1 March–15 July)
PARKING	Laneside or car park in Belstone)
PUBLIC TOILETS	None on route

The pretty little village of Belstone – an attractive mix of cob and thatch cottages and granite-built Victorian houses – sits 1,000ft (305m) up on the northern edge of Dartmoor. Much of the parish is open moorland, within which can be found a number of granite tors and archaeological monuments.

On the slopes of Belstone Common, the Nine Maidens stone circle dates from Bronze Age times – though legend has it that it represents a group of maidens turned to stone for dancing on the Sabbath.

The infant Taw is particularly lovely as it rushes through rocky Belstone Cleave. The Henry Williamson Bridge, passed at Point 4, is inscribed with words taken from his famous novel *Tarka the Otter* (1927) which succinctly sum up the character of the river at this point:

'Amid rocks and scree that in falling had smashed the trunks and torn out the roots of willow, thorns and hollies...It wandered away from the moor, a proper river with bridges, brooks, islands and mills.'

A short extension to the walk from Point 5 will take you to the Finch Foundry, now in the hands of the National Trust. A working foundry from 1814 to 1960, it produced around 400 tools for agricultural and mining purposes daily during its heyday. There was a grinding house on the site in the 13th century, powered by water leated from the Taw – you can see a sluice gate and leat at Cleave Mill on the opposite bank around Point 4 of the route – and in the 19th century a smithy was set up by the Finch family. Apart from tools the site also produced serge for army uniforms, made from local wool. There are daily working demonstrations (booking in advance is advisable).

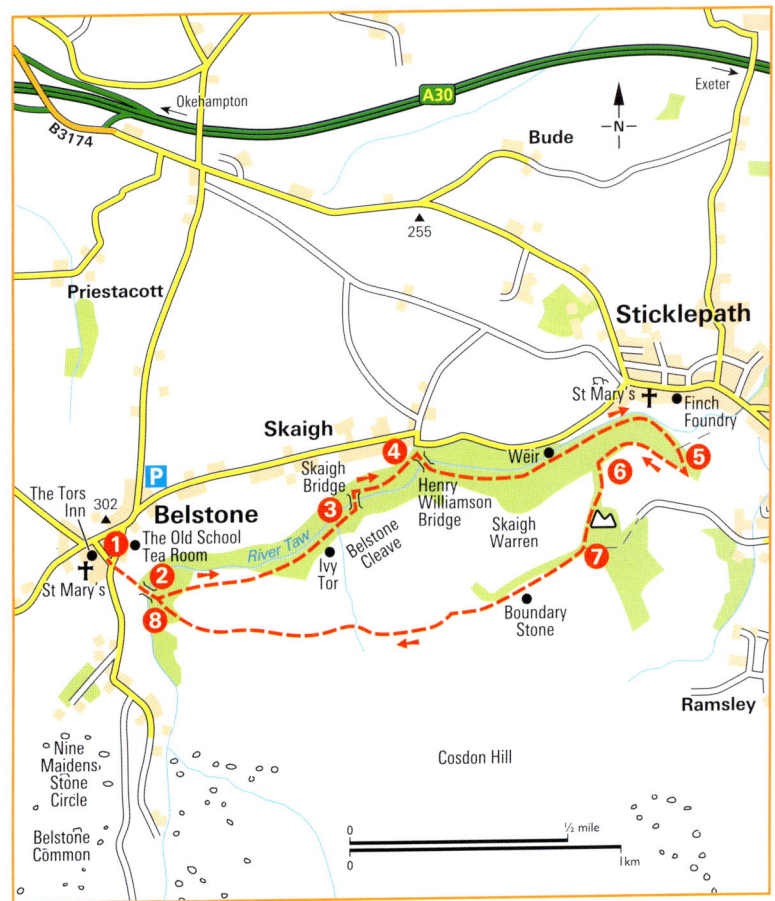

1. The walk starts from The Tors Inn. Pass to the left of the building, and on reaching the Great Green bear left off the lane across the grass, dropping to soon pick up a track that descends to the River Taw. Bear right to cross it via a footbridge.

2. Turn left past the ford, then right away from the river, with a wall to your left. After 100yds (91m) bear left on a narrower path that ascends through gorse; after a few paces, where a wall comes into view ahead right, bear slightly left downhill (straight on also leads to the footbridge at Point 3). The path runs along bracken-covered slopes, eventually dropping steeply, then follows the riverbank (very rough in places). Pass craggy Ivy Tor.

3. Reach a path junction at Skaigh Bridge. Turn left across the river, signed to Skaigh, and climb to a T-junction. Turn right along a woodland path.

4. Take the next obvious path right and pick your way through trees, bearing left towards the river and the Henry Williamson Bridge. Cross over, and continue along the rocky riverside path to pass a weir and gauging station. Continue on more even ground and through a small gate. Cottages come into view on the opposite bank.

5. Reach a footpath junction. (To visit the Finch Foundry turn left here.) On the main walk, turn right on a public bridleway to the moor (also Tarka Trail and Taw–Teign Link) and ascend steeply, soon turning sharp right and climbing through Skaigh Wood. The path levels a little, broadens under oaks, and passes through a gate.

6. Follow the bridlepath left and climb under beeches, with a wall to your left. Follow the wall uphill. Eventually go through a gate on the edge of Cosdon Hill.

7. Turn right on a grassy track, taking the right fork where the wall ends. After 100yds (91m) look left uphill to see a tall Belstone/South Tawton boundary stone; keep ahead to join a broad, grassy path that descends from that stone, and continue gently downhill. The path crosses the Ivy Tor Water and eventually starts to descend, aiming towards the church tower. Meet a walled enclosure, and follow the wall downhill. At the bottom edge, by a gate, bear left on an indistinct and rocky path that descends to the footbridge.

8. Cross the River Taw and retrace your steps up the track, bearing left to cross the lane and return to The Tors Inn.

Where to eat and drink
The Tors Inn at Belstone is a down-to-earth place for a bite to eat. Behind the Methodist Chapel, on the green, lies The Old School Tea Room, open afternoon's only, Friday through to Monday.

What to see
On the return stretch of the walk look for a rough granite wall that crosses the ridge south of Belstone Tor. It's known as the Irishman's Wall, and various stories justify its construction. The most plausible is that it was built in the early 19th century, by Irish workers, as part of a bid to enclose Belstone Common. The men of Belstone and Okehampton, however, were having none of it, and toppled parts of the wall over, rendering it useless.

MELDON RESERVOIR AND HIGHEST TORS

DISTANCE/TIME	6 miles (9.8km) / 3hrs
ASCENT/GRADIENT	1210ft (369m) / ▲▲
PATHS	Grassy tracks and open moorland, some boggy patches
LANDSCAPE	Reservoir, ancient oak woodland and open moorland
SUGGESTED MAP	OS Explorer OL 28 Dartmoor
START/FINISH	Grid reference: SX561917
DOG FRIENDLINESS	Keep on lead near livestock and birds
PARKING	Car park at Meldon Reservoir
PUBLIC TOILETS	At car park

If you want to get a 'quick fix' and to experience examples of almost everything that Dartmoor has to offer, but fairly easily and in a relatively short time – then this is the walk for you. Within 10 minutes of the A30 as it races past Okehampton you can get the lot: a tranquil reservoir, a sparkling river and waterfall tumbling though a beautiful tree-lined valley, wide expanses of open moorland, an area of ancient lichen-encrusted oak woodland and a great view of the highest tors on the moor – and all without expending too much effort. You don't have to tramp for miles over inhospitable moorland or get to grips with a compass to get a real feel of the moor.

Owned by the Duchy of Cornwall, this is one of the best areas of ancient high-altitude oak woodland in Britain, and was established as a National Nature Reserve in 1996. There is a huge variety of mosses and lichens covering the granite boulders from which the stunted oaks emerge. It makes a wonderful focus for the walk. There are two other areas of upland woodland on the moor – at Piles Copse in the Erme Valley and at Wistman's Wood by the side of the West Dart River just north of Two Bridges. In all three places the oaks have remained ungrazed because the clutter of granite boulders beneath has protected them from the local sheep. Black-a-tor Copse feels little visited and remote – the atmosphere is quite magical.

Dartmoor is basically a huge granite intrusion, pushed up through surrounding sedimentary rocks, formed in the same way as Bodmin Moor in Cornwall and the Isles of Scilly. Where it is exposed to the elements this raised granite plateau has been weathered into giant blocks, creating the tors so characteristic of the area. The highest part of the moor lies in the northeast corner just south of the A30, where it rises to 2,037ft (621m) at High Willhays, seen from this walk. The average height of the moor, however, is around 1,200ft (366m).

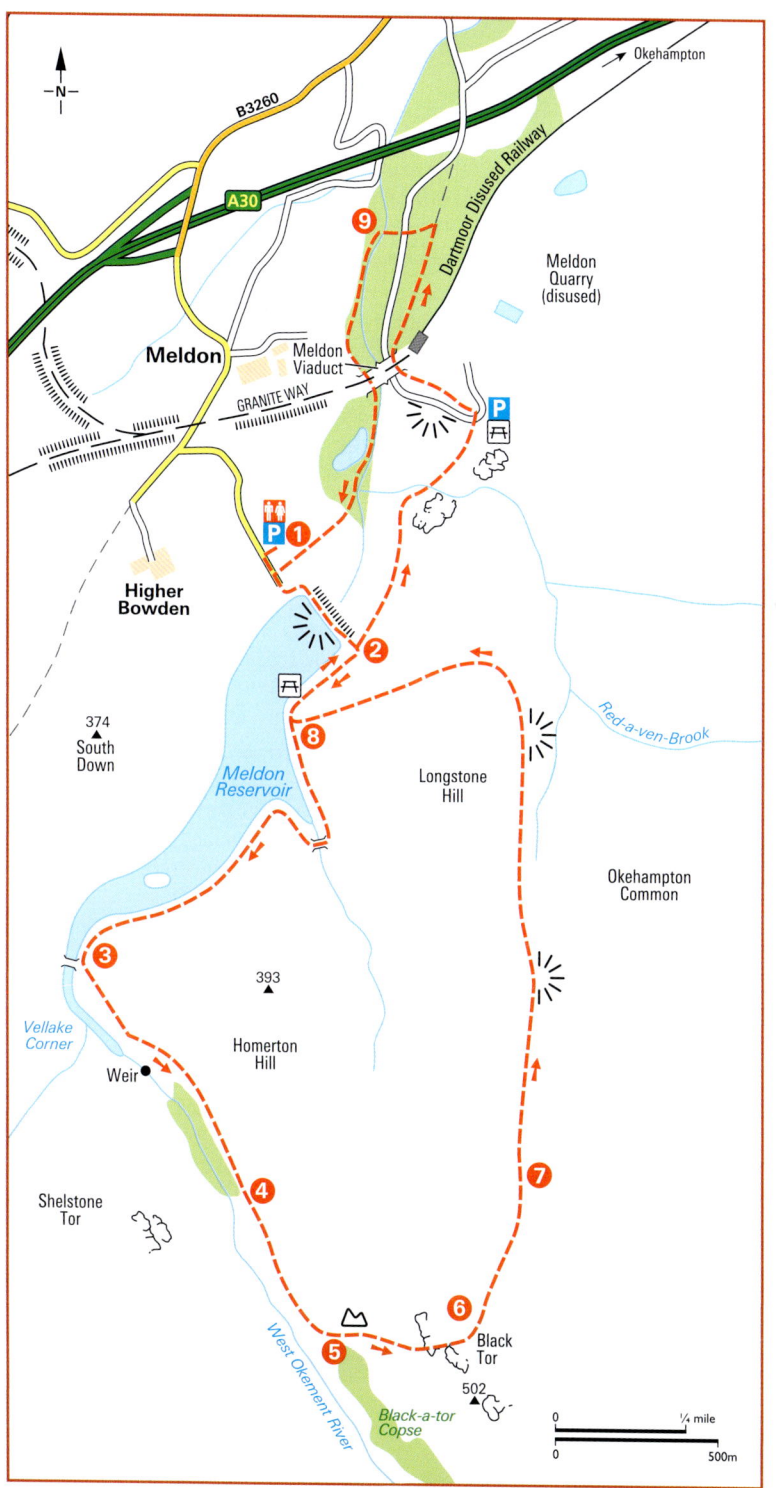

1. Walk up the steps by the toilets, through the gate and go left towards the dam, signposted 'Bridlepath to Moor'. Cross over the dam and go through a gate.

2. Turn right on a stony track alongside a fence. Note a gate (right) leading to a waterside picnic area. Do not go through the gate but keep ahead where the track bears left, following the edge of the reservoir through a side valley and over a small footbridge. The narrow path bears right above the water and runs along the contours before descending into the broad marshy valley of the West Okement River; the swell of Corn Ridge, 1,762ft 537m), lies ahead.

3. Pass the small wooden footbridge and take the narrow path along the left edge of the valley, keeping to the bottom of the steep slope. The path rounds Vellake Corner and passes a water gauging station, then broadens and climbs steadily above the river (right).

4. At the top of the hill the track levels and Black-a-tor Copse can be glimpsed ahead. Follow the river upstream passing left of a granite enclosure, and along the riverbank to enter the copse – a wonderful picnic spot.

5. Retrace your steps out of the trees and bear right around the copse edge, uphill aiming for the left outcrop of Black Tor on the ridge above. Pick your way through the bracken to gain the left edge of the left outcrop. The right outcrop rises to 1,647ft (502m).

6. Climb to the top of the tor if you wish; if not keep ahead in the same direction, aiming for a fairly obvious track visible ahead bearing left across Longstone Hill. To find it go slightly downhill from the tor to cross a small stream, then pass between granite blocks marking the track.

7. The intermittent track runs straight across open moor. Where the Red-a-ven Brook Valley appears below to the right, enjoy the view of (left to right) Row Tor, West Mill Tor and Yes Tor. High Willhays, Dartmoor's highest point, lies just out of sight to the right. The track bears left around the end of the hill, with good views towards the quarry and viaduct, and drops back to the reservoir.

8. Bear right on the track, to walk along side the reservoir and at the dam keep ahead through a small gate. At the fork keep left along the narrow path high above the West Okement River. The path meets a broader one; turn left, downhill, to meander through the former site of the quarry. Cross the Red-a-ven Brook and then a parking area and through a gate to meet a lane. Turn left and after a few paces bear right on a footpath ('Rock Park'). At a fork go left (the right path gives access to the Granite Way, and Meldon Buffet when open), soon turning left again and descending steeply to pass under Meldon viaduct. Follow the path on, now through woodland, and at the second path junction turn left to the lane and cross over and descend to cross the river.

9. Follow the path as it bears left uphill through woodland to meet a broad track via a gate. Turn left, soon walking under the viaduct again. Pass an old lime kiln and flooded limestone quarry. The path ascends through woodland, and into open ground; bear left uphill as signed, then follow the hedge bank back to a gate. Turn right, and right again for the car park.

Where to eat and drink
There are pubs and cafés in Okehampton, and Betty Cottles Inn on the Tavistock Road at Graddons Cross. If you have time, walk along the Granite Way cycle track (passed just before the car park) to have tea in old GWR carriages at the east end of the viaduct and enjoy the amazing views.

What to see
There is clear evidence of the military presence on Dartmoor from this walk. As you admire the view over the Red-a-ven Valley you will notice a line of red and white posts running along the hillside – these mark the boundary of the live firing ranges in this part of the moor. They are used for training on a limited number of days each year (freephone 0800 458 4868), and you can walk within the ranges outside these times – but do not touch any strange objects that you might find.

While you're there
There is a clear view of Meldon Viaduct from the dam. This is a scheduled ancient monument dating from 1874, when the London & South Western Railway line was extended from Exeter to Lydford. Standing 150ft (45.7m) high and 541ft (165m) long, it was originally constructed in wrought iron, and now carries National Cycle Route 27 (Devon Coast to Coast); this section is part of the 'Granite Way' (Okehampton to Southerly Halt).

ACROSS DARTMOOR TO BRENT TOR

DISTANCE/TIME	5 miles (8km) / 2hrs 30min
ASCENT/GRADIENT	425ft (130m) / ▲▲
PATHS	Tracks and green lanes, open fields and lanes
LANDSCAPE	Open moorland and rolling farmland
SUGGESTED MAP	OS Explorer 112 Launceston & Holsworthy
START/FINISH	Grid reference: SX492800
DOG FRIENDLINESS	Keep on lead near livestock and birds
PARKING	Lay-by past cattle grid northwest of Mary Tavy on moorland road to North Brentor village
PUBLIC TOILETS	None on route, but in car park, Brent Tor

Anyone exploring western Dartmoor cannot fail to notice a conical peak, topped with a tower, protruding high above the rolling fields and woodlands towards the Cornish border. This strange natural formation is Brent Tor and, surprisingly, has nothing to do with the granite tors of Dartmoor. It is a remnant of the mass of lava that poured out onto the seabed here more than 300 million years ago, when the area was a shallow sea. The softer rocks around have been eroded away over the millennia, leaving behind this extraordinary landmark 1,100ft (334m) above sea level. The name is thought to derive either from the Anglo-Saxon brene, meaning 'beacon' (to burn) or from the Celtic bryn (hill or mound). Lying just inside the National Park boundary, it provides the perfect focus for a relaxing exploration of this quiet corner of west Devon.

The 13th-century Church of St Michael de Rupe ('of the rock') was originally built by Robert Giffard, Lord of the Manor of Lamerton and Whitchurch, around 1130. Rebuilt towards the end of the 13th century, the 40ft (12.25m) tower was added during the 15th century, and it is the fourth-smallest complete parish church in England. Occasional services are held at this atmospheric spot, and the views from here are quite breathtaking.

It is said that while the church was being built the Devil himself hurled stones from the top of the hill on to the unfortunate parishioners below. Another legend tells of how a wealthy 14th-century merchant vowed to build a church here in gratitude to St Michael for saving one of his cargoes from a storm at sea. The Devil destroyed the building work every night, so the merchant called on St Michael to help again. The saint chased the Devil away and in return the church was dedicated to St Michael.

North Brentor was added to the parish in 1880, and all burials then took place at Christ Church in the village, since the soil on top of Brent Tor was too thin to accommodate a decent grave.

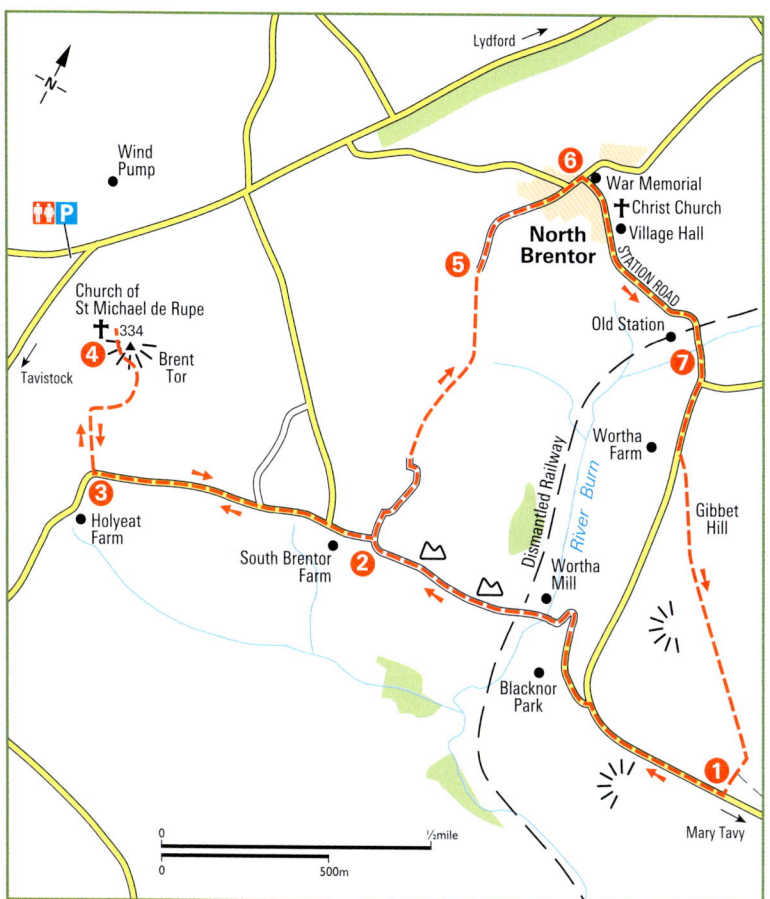

1. Walk straight ahead from your car towards Brent Tor, which positively invites you to visit it. Where the lane bears right turn left along an unfenced lane (dead end sign). Go gently downhill to pass Blacknor Park (left), then a cattle grid. The lane becomes rocky before passing Wortha Mill and crossing the disused railway line and River Burn. The track runs steeply uphill, before levelling off.

2. At the next T-junction of tracks turn left to pass South Brentor Farm and a lane on the right, and keep straight on slightly uphill – under beech trees – to pass 'Hillside' on the left.

3. Pass Brennen Cottage (left); a few paces later the lane bends sharp left. Turn right through a gate and keep ahead up the right edge of the field on a permitted footpath. Turn right through a gate at the top, later bearing left going steeply uphill to reach Brent Tor church.

4. Retrace your steps to Point 2, and turn left. Pass through the gate at the track end and cross the next field. Cross a stile in the top corner, and in the next field go diagonally right to pass through a kissing gate. Cross the next field and through a gateway. Keep the hedgebank on the left and pass through a gate.

5. Follow the hedged track, then keep ahead past houses to meet the lane and then a T-junction. Turn right to reach the war memorial.

6. Turn right slightly downhill to pass the phone box, church and village hall. Follow the lane as it bears right to cross the old railway line. You can see the old station complete with platform canopy below you to the right.

7. Pass over the cattle grid on to the open moor, and up the lane. Where the lane bends right just past the gateway to Wortha Farm, cut left over the edge of Gibbet Hill on an indistinct grassy track. (The lane leads back to the car, but this is a more pleasant route). Once over the crest of the hill you will reach a crossroads of paths; turn right to return to your car.

Where to eat and drink
The unusually named Elephant's Nest at Horndon, a small hamlet just east of Mary Tavy, serves excellent food and drink and has a very pretty garden. The Mary Tavy Inn is found on the A386 at Mary Tavy, and a couple of miles north, the 16th-century Castle Inn at Lydford is worth a visit. There is also a National Trust tearoom at Lydford Gorge.

What to see
Just southwest of Brent Tor is an enclosed area of mounds and depressions, all that remains of a 19th-century manganese mine, a major source of employment from 1815 to 1856. The manganese was used in the production of glass, bleach and steel, and was shipped out down the River Tamar from Morwellham Quay.

While you're there
Visit Lydford, signposted off the A386 to the north. It was a Saxon fortress town with its own mint in the 9th century. Lydford Castle, actually the moor's infamous stannary prison, is worth a visit. Just down the road is the National Trust's Lydford Gorge, where the crashing waterfalls and whirlpools of the River Lyd – the most impressive being the Devil's Cauldron – can be seen from a number of woodland walks. The 98ft (30m) White Lady waterfall is spectacular.

LIFTON TO STOWFORD

DISTANCE/TIME	8 miles (12.9km) / 3hrs
ASCENT/GRADIENT	165ft (50m) / ▲
PATHS	Fields, green lanes and country lanes
LANDSCAPE	Undulating farmland and wooded river valleys
SUGGESTED MAP	OS Explorer 112 Launceston & Holsworthy
START/FINISH	Grid reference: SX387851
DOG FRIENDLINESS	Keep on lead in fields
PARKING	Lay-by on Fore Street (the old A30) opposite Lifton Stores and Post Office
PUBLIC TOILETS	None on route

Lifton, just 4 miles (6.4km) from the Cornish border, suffered for years from heavy traffic on account of its location on the old A30, the main route into Cornwall from Exeter and points east. Since the coming of the new A30 in the 1980s things have definitely looked up. The village has some interesting buildings, including St Mary's Church, dating from the 15th century and built in Perpendicular style, typical of many of West Devon's churches. Lifton also lies on the Two Castles Trail, a waymarked 24-mile (39km) walking route between the Norman castles at Launceston in Cornwall and Okehampton in Devon (both worth a visit). Within minutes of setting off you can lose yourself in the remote and little-visited strip of green, rolling countryside that lies between the new and old A30 routes.

From Points 4 and 7 there are good views of the Gothic mansion of Hayne, rebuilt in 1810, and the seat of the Harris family from the reign of Henry VIII until 1864. There are some splendid 18th-century monuments to members of the family in Stowford's lovely Church of St John the Baptist. Dating from the 14th century, it was sympathetically restored in 1874 by Sir George Gilbert Scott, architect of St Pancras Station, at a cost of £4,000. He was involved in restoration work at Exeter Cathedral at the time. The 19th-century interior woodwork (copied from earlier examples) is said to be some of the finest in England. Look out for the wonderful views towards Cornwall, and the 1770 sundial over the door. Don't miss the inscribed Stowford Stone, found by the entrance to the churchyard, believed to date from the 6th or 7th centuries.

The Wolf river, crossed near the start of the walk, emerges from 730-acre (296ha) Roadford Lake, the largest inland body of water in southwest England, created when the Wolf valley was flooded. This lovely spot lies north of the A30 and has Lakeside Café and gift shop, a sailing centre offering excellent watersport facilities, footpaths and opportunities for birdwatching; there is a Nature Reserve (largely hosting over-wintering birds) on its northwest shore.

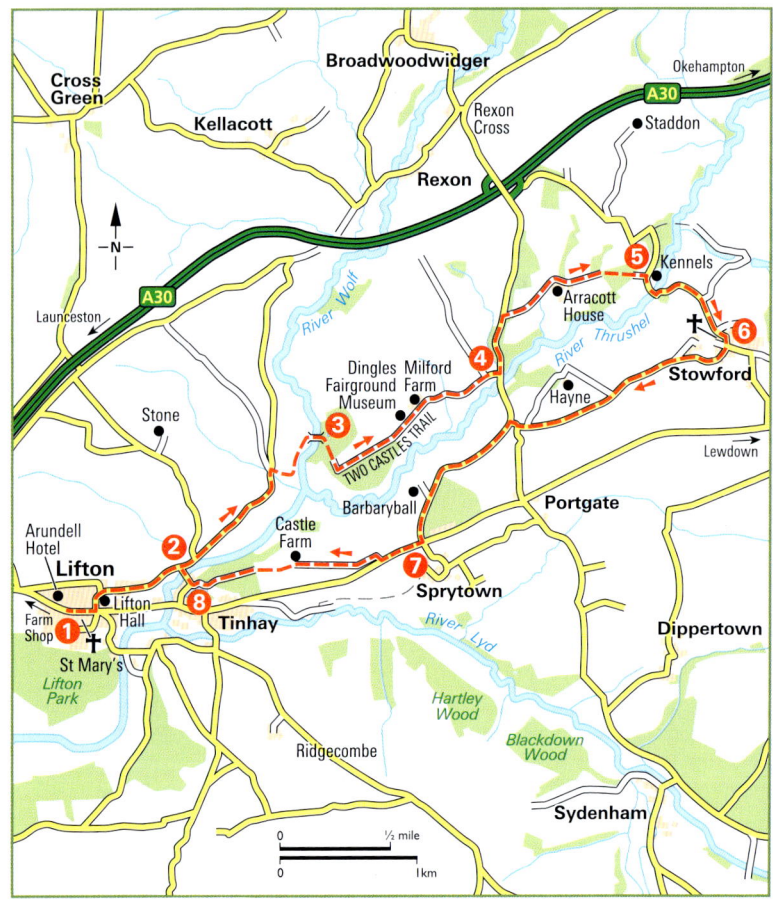

1. Cross over Fore Street and turn right, then left to walk down North Road. Follow the lane past the community academy and out into the country.

2. Before reaching the Tinhay bridge bear left on a lane which soon rises gently, then descends to cross a stream. Immediately turn right through a gate on a public bridleway. Keep along the left field edge; at the end of the hedge continue past a footpath post, then keep in the same direction to cross a bridge over the River Wolf.

3. Pass through a gate and follow the track, through woodland, uphill. It leads into a broad green lane, which bends sharp left and continues slightly uphill then drops to pass the entrance to the car park at Dingles Fairground Museum. Join the tarmac lane to pass the café and buildings of Dingles at Milford Farm (left).

4. The lane ends at a road (Hayne Bridge to the right); turn left. Look out for a gritty track ('Public bridleway') to the right; turn right, eventually passing Arracott House. Go through a gate and along a green lane, which ends at another. Go through a gate immediately ahead and bear right downhill through a plantation, soon bearing left towards the bottom corner to emerge

by a white cottage. Follow the drive to meet the lane opposite Lamerton Hunt Kennels.

5. Turn right to cross the River Thrushel on Stowford Bridge, then climb steeply to find a gate into the churchyard of Stowford's beautiful and secluded church.

6. Leave the churchyard through the main gate and keep ahead to the lane. Turn right, then first right again, signed 'Broadwood'. At the lane end turn right; at the T-junction turn left, signed 'Sprytown'. Follow the road to meet the old A30.

7. Turn right (with care). Look for a bridlepath right (the drive to Castle Farm) and follow it uphill past farm buildings. Two gates lead to a lovely oak avenue. Pass through a gate and keep downhill on a broad banked track, turning right at the bottom (quarry lake left) and through a gate onto a lane.

8. Turn right to cross Tinhay Bridge and follow North Road back to the start point.

Where to eat and drink
Lifton Hall welcomes families, as does the popular award-winning Lifton Strawberry Fields Farm Shop (and restaurant), just up the road from the walk start. The Arundell Hotel in Lifton, an old coaching inn, has been one of county's premier fly-fishing establishments for more than 50 years.

What to see
Stop en route for a visit to Dingles Fairground Museum, a fascinating collection of fairground rides and memorabilia (open Thursday–Sunday, Easter to end October). The café at Dingles is open to passing visitors.

While you're there
Pay a visit to Okehampton Castle at the Devon end of the Two Castles Trail. Once one of the largest castles in the county, and home of the Earls of Devon in medieval times, the substantial ruins include the Norman motte and the remains of the keep, as well as the 14th-century hall. As an added bonus the castle, managed by English Heritage, enjoys a delightful setting with woodland walks and a riverside picnic area.

HATHERLEIGH TO IDDLESLEIGH

DISTANCE/TIME	8.5 miles (13.7km) / 3hrs
ASCENT/GRADIENT	245ft (75m) / ▲
PATHS	Fields and country lanes, several stiles
LANDSCAPE	Rolling farmland and wooded valleys
SUGGESTED MAP	OS Explorer 113 Okehampton
START/FINISH	Grid reference: SS541044
DOG FRIENDLINESS	Keep on lead in fields
PARKING	Car park off Market Way in Hatherleigh
PUBLIC TOILETS	In front of church, Hatherleigh

The name of the Tarka Trail (a long-distance walking and cycling route, much of it off-road) is taken from North Devon author Henry Williamson's classic novel *Tarka the Otter*, published in 1927. It runs for 180 miles (297km) through the peaceful countryside of north and mid-Devon, signed, most appropriately, with an otter paw symbol. The trail covers a huge area, from Okehampton on the northern edge of Dartmoor, across the course of the Taw and Torridge rivers, to Ilfracombe on the north Devon coast, and east to Lynton and Exmoor. It forms a large figure-of-eight, following disused railway lines, various rights of way and permissive paths, and provides excellent opportunities for quiet exploration of the least-visited part of the county.

This route follows a part of the trail that is only open to walkers, and starts in the historic market town of Hatherleigh.

Originally a Saxon settlement, Hatherleigh developed as a staging post on the main route from Bideford to Exeter, and to Plymouth, and has long been an important market town for north and west Devon, although the weekly livestock market has now ceased trading. The town's agricultural heritage is endorsed by the 'Sheep' sculpture by the car park, and the beautiful cow and sheep head figures, in the square, in front of the church, mark the devastating foot and mouth outbreak in 2001.

The town has had its share of disasters over the years: a great fire in 1840 destroyed many of the old buildings, and The George on Market Square (a 15th-century building) was burned to the ground early this century and rebuilt to the original specification, reopening in 2010. The parish church of St John the Baptist had to be extensively restored after the mid-15th century 54ft (16.5m) spire plunged through the roof of the nave in the storms of January 1990.

Hatherleigh is located in a part of Devon that has become known as 'Ruby Country' on account of the dark red-brown Ruby Red beef cattle raised on many local farms. A recent initiative to promote this area for visitors has received a welcome boost via the success of Michael Morpurgo's *War Horse* spin-offs (see While You're There): Parsonage Farm, passed on Point 6, is now home to the War Horse Valley Country Park.

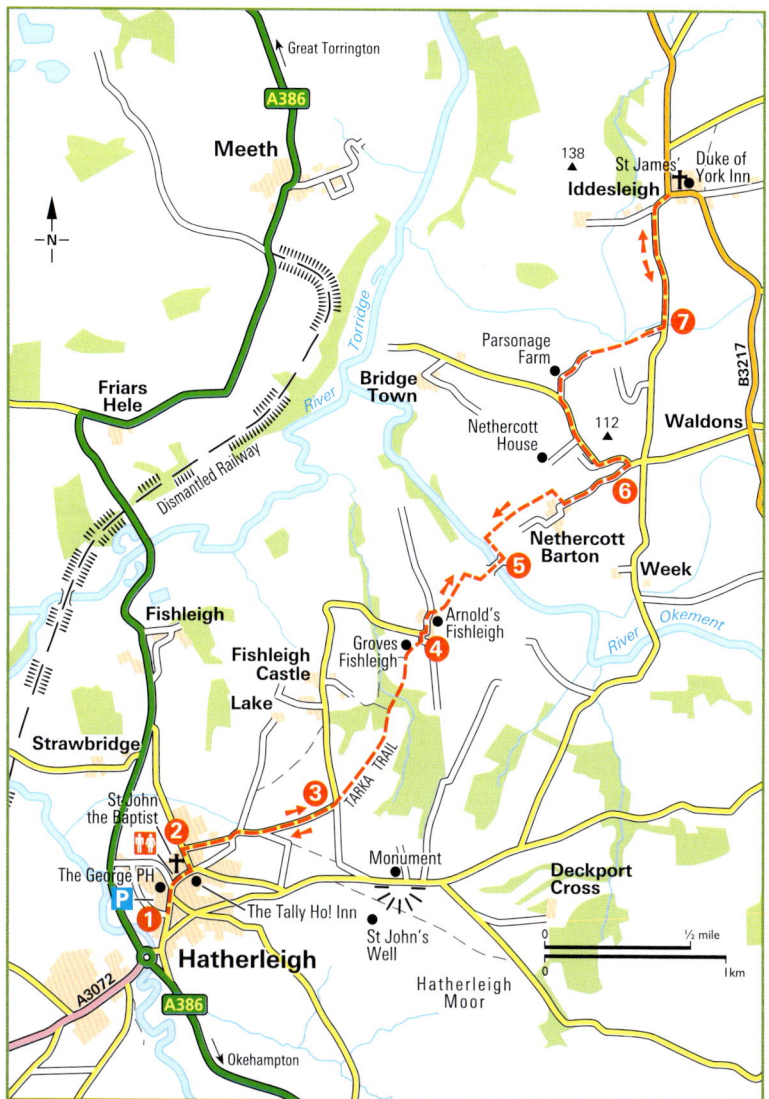

1. Leave the car park past the wonderful 'Sheep' sculpture and turn left up Bridge Street and then Market Street. Pass in front of the parish church, and the Tally Ho! Inn. At the top of the hill follow the road left into Oakfield Road.

2. Turn right up Sanctuary Lane, signed 'to public footpath'. The lane climbs steeply; ignore all footpath signs until you pass Wingates at the hilltop; the lane soon bends sharp left.

3. Go through a gate into a field, signed 'Tarka Trail'. Walk straight across the field, through two gates by an oak tree, then across the next, picking up the fence to the left of four big oaks. Pass through a gate and keep ahead through a conifer plantation, over a footbridge and into a field. Keep ahead over a stile, cross the next field and stile to pass through Groves Fishleigh. Go down the drive and to a T-junction.

4. Turn right towards Arnolds Fishleigh; follow the track left. At farm buildings turn sharp right (footpath) through a gate/stile into an orchard. Keep ahead through a big gate. Bear left; at the field end cross the stile, then right along the edge of the field. Turn right through a gate, left through the next gateway, and follow the field edge downhill to the River Okement.

5. Cross the wooden bridge. Turn left along the river bank, then right at the hedge, keeping the hedge left. Bear left through the next gate, then bear right to a gate on to a green lane, uphill. Follow signs right, through a gate, and along the right field edge to Nethercott Barton. Go through the gate in the corner, turn left uphill.

6. Turn left at the lane, passing the entrance to Nethercott House. Soon bear right down the drive to Parsonage Farm, bearing right at gates to the farmhouse. Pass through a gate and cross the farmyard, then through a gate and along the left field edge. Take the right-hand gate at the end (views to Iddesleigh), and follow the left field edge downhill. A gate leads to a track, which in turn reaches a lane.

7. Turn left uphill at the lane. Go right opposite St James' Church (15th century), then left to the Duke of York Inn. On the return route to Hatherleigh (retracing your outward route) you'll enjoy wonderful, and different, views towards the northern slopes of Dartmoor.

Where to eat and drink
In Hatherleigh try The Tally Ho! on Market Street, or The George on Market Square (the original building dated from 1450). The Duke of York Inn at Iddesleigh dates from the 15th century and is a classic, unspoiled country pub, with good food and a homely atmosphere.

What to see
Although sightings are still rare, there's no doubt that otter numbers in Devon are on the increase. The otter was widespread as recently as the 1950s but, following a sharp decline, conservation schemes were introduced to sustain viable populations. One of Britain's few native carnivores, the otter is characterised by its powerful body (36in/90cm) and strong tail (16in/40cm), and much of its appeal lies in its apparent ability to enjoy life.

While you're there
Nethercott House, passed on Point 6, is home to Michael and Clare Morpurgo's Farms for City Children; you can see calves, chickens, ducks and donkeys from the lane. The inspiration for Michael Morpurgo's novel (and renowned stage show) *War Horse* came from his conversations about days gone by with ageing local farmers at the Duke of York in nearby Iddesleigh.

A COASTAL WALK TO MORWENSTOW

DISTANCE/TIME	6 miles (9.7km) / 3hrs 30min
ASCENT/GRADIENT	328ft (100m) / ▲▲▲
PATHS	Rugged coastal footpath, fields and tracks, many stiles
LANDSCAPE	Deep combes and undulating cliff tops
SUGGESTED MAP	OS Explorer 126 Clovelly & Hartland
START/FINISH	Grid reference: SS213180
DOG FRIENDLINESS	Keep on lead near livestock and unfenced cliffs
PARKING	End of road at Welcombe Mouth
PUBLIC TOILETS	None on route

This walk takes you over the border into Cornwall, along a rugged coastal route – and feels completely Cornish. The colours here are green and grey, and any sense of cosy, comfortable Devon is left far behind as you trudge steadily up and down the switchback coast path south from the stark, remote, rocky beach at Welcombe Mouth. It's a magnificent piece of coastline. Henna Cliff, near point 3, is the highest sheer cliff in England after Beachy Head in Sussex and, in complete contrast, from here you get a clear view of the satellite tracking station on its clifftop position south towards Bude. But it's a real treat to come and explore this part of the coast, where the dramatic scenery and weather conditions constantly remind you of just how insignificant you are compared to the natural elements.

The remote hamlet of Morwenstow, 2 miles (3.2km) from the Devon border, is a fascinating place, best known for its connection with the 19th-century vicar, the Revd Robert Stephen Hawker. This colourful character came here in 1834 and built the pinnacled rectory, to replace the former derelict building, next to the church. He was a drug addict throughout his life, and spent many hours meditating in his hut on the cliff edge, where he also wrote poetry. This eccentric figure is said to have worn a fisherman's jumper and seaman's boots. He is believed to have introduced the harvest festival service, and wrote the famous *Shall Trelawny Die?*, a Cornish ballad. He died in 1875, after converting to Catholicism on his deathbed.

The Church of St Morwenna and St John the Baptist is the most northerly parish church in Cornwall, occupying a striking position just inland from Vicarage Cliff. Its pinnacled tower, visible from the coast path, was a useful landmark. There is a Saxon font, and evidence of the original Norman building in the three arches, with zig-zag moulding, in the north arcade. The church was enlarged and restored in the 16th and 17th centuries, and there is wood carving in the roof, pews and bench endings.

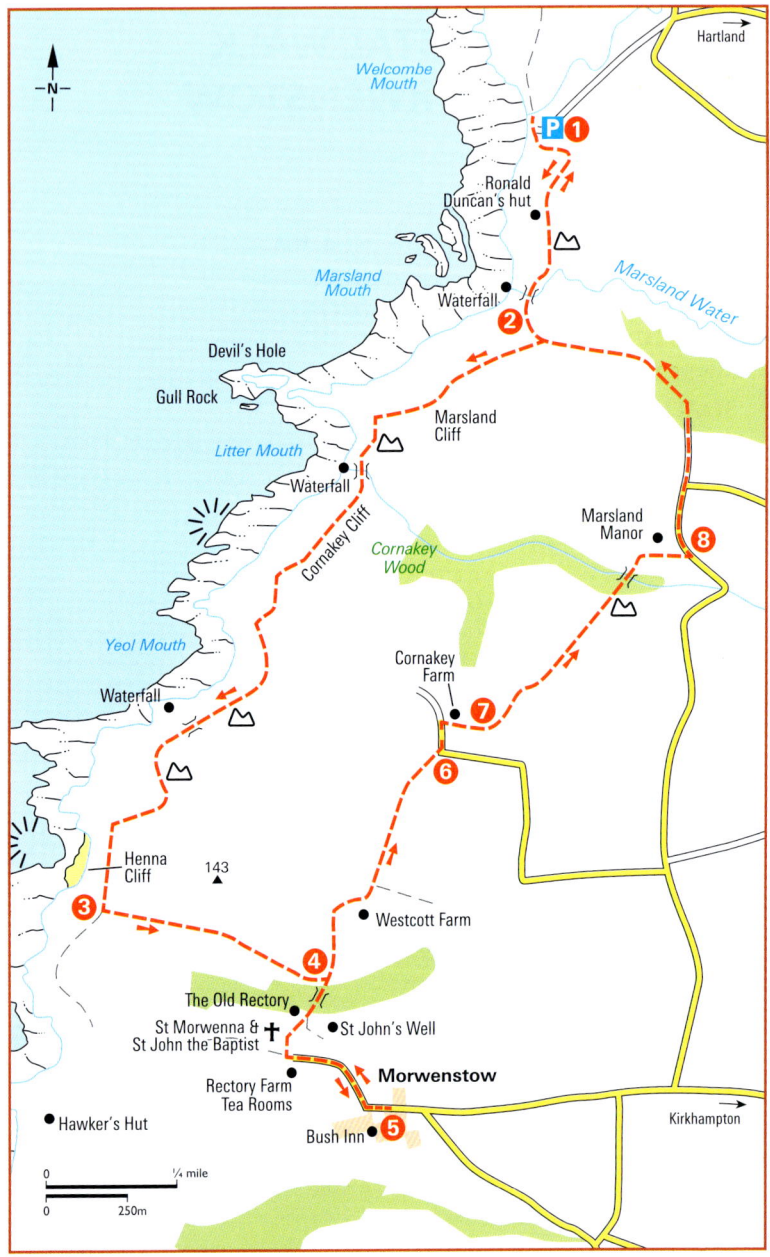

1. Turn left on the coast path and climb to the cliff top; a steep descent leads to a crossing of Marsland Water into Cornwall.

2. Follow the coast path inland, then sharp right on to Marsland Cliff. Pass through a gate above Litter Mouth, then descend steeply into a combe and across a bridge. A steep zig-zag ascent gains Cornakey Cliff. Continue along the cliff edge via four gates, then bear right and descend into a combe.

Cross the footbridge, then climb steeply onto Henna Cliff. Keep ahead to pass through a gate by a metal seat.

3. At the next footpath post turn inland (lovely views to the vicarage and church). Cross a stile in the field corner and keep ahead along the lower edge of the next field to a T-junction of paths.

4. Turn right into woodland and descend to a stile/footbridge. Walk uphill past the vicarage, then cross over a stone stile into the graveyard. Bear right towards the church, then left and left again to exit via the lychgate. Go straight ahead up the lane to find The Bush Inn on the right.

5. Return to Point 4. Go straight on uphill, and through a metal gate. Cross the next bank over wooden steps. Turn immediately right and go through an open gateway at the top right of that field (following yellow arrows) on to a track; keep ahead to meet the farm drive. Turn immediately left through the right-hand of two gates and along the left edge of the field. Climb over a stile, and pass to the left of a small barn. Bear right to a gate and follow the track ahead to meet a tarmac lane on a bend.

6. Turn left towards Cornakey Farm and follow the 'alternative path' right through a gate into a field. Keep ahead then turn left through a gate and down steps. Turn right into a green lane.

7. The track ends at a gate; keep along the right field edge. Pass through the next gate and bear left across the field, downhill. Cross the hedge bank via three stiles and bear half left across the field. Cross a stile into woodland then descend steeply; cross two footbridges and follow the path uphill. Follow arrows (right) through a meadow with Marsland Manor left. Cross a stile on to a lane.

8. Turn left; pass Marsland Manor and keep uphill. As the lane bends right turn left (signed 'Marsland Mouth') on a track. Go through a gate and downhill. At a cottage (right) and information board turn left on a footpath. At a gate keep straight ahead (downhill) to find the coast path. Continue straight on to cross the stream into Devon and retrace your steps back to your car.

Where to eat and drink

Rectory Farm Tea Rooms opposite the church are open daily, 11am–5pm, from the week before Easter to October, and serve a range of snacks, light lunches and excellent cream teas. October opening is reduced. The atmospheric Bush Inn was originally a monks' resthouse. It serves good food and has accommodation.

What to see

On the descent to Marsland Mouth at Point 1, pause at the little stone hut , built by the poet and playwright Ronald Duncan in 1962. If you go straight past the churchyard on your way back to the main route after Point 5, you can follow footpath signs to the coast path. Just to the south (left) you'll find Hawker's Hut (the National Trust's smallest building), a wooden turf-roofed construction, nestling just over the cliff edge, with superb views out to sea as far as Lundy.

AROUND HARTLAND POINT

DISTANCE/TIME	10 miles (16.1km) / 6hrs
ASCENT/GRADIENT	328ft (100m) / ▲▲▲
PATHS	Coast path through fields; country lanes, many stiles
LANDSCAPE	Rugged coastline, farmland and quiet lanes
SUGGESTED MAP	OS Explorer 126 Clovelly & Hartland
START/FINISH	Grid reference: SS259245
DOG FRIENDLINESS	Keep on lead near livestock and unfenced cliffs
PARKING	Car park in centre of Hartland village
PUBLIC TOILETS	Near car park and in Stoke village

Although this walk is a little longer – and more difficult – than all the others in this book, it's a must for anyone who wants to explore all of Devon properly. The section to the east of the A39 Bude to Bideford road is often ignored by tourist guides, and little explored – and that's exactly why it is so wonderful. The village of Hartland was described by a traveller in the 1790s as having 'an air of poverty that depresses it to a level with a Cornish borough' and you do get the impression that life here has been hard.

Devon's north west tip is characterised by an extraordinary change in the nature of the coast. The cliffs along the coast from Clovelly, to the east, although high, are relatively calm and flat-topped, yet turn the corner at Hartland lighthouse and you enter a different world, where the craggy rocks on the seabed run in jagged parallel lines towards the unforgiving cliffs. You can understand why this area is peppered with shipwrecks. The coast path to the south of the point traverses over what is, in effect, a mass of vertical tiltings and contortions, caused by lateral pressure on the earth's crust around 300 million years ago. Hartland means 'stag island', although the area is a peninsula, and the feeling of space and remoteness is made even stronger by the fact that on a clear day there are inviting views of Lundy island, rising majestically out of the sea 10 miles (16.1km) offshore. On stormy days, when the wind is so strong you can barely stand, Lundy mysteriously disappears into a blanket of mist and spray. Lundy island is basically a great lump of flat-topped granite, 52 million years old, 450ft (137m) high, 3 miles (4.8km) long and only 0.5 miles (800m) wide.

Extraordinary Hartland Quay dates back to 1586, when its building was authorised by Act of Parliament. Cargoes of coal, lime and timber were landed here, and in 1616 lead was brought in for repairs to the roof of St Nectan's Church at Stoke. The quay was active until 1893, and once abandoned was soon destroyed by the ravages of the sea. The buildings, including stables for the donkeys that carried goods up the cliff, have now been converted into the Hartland Quay Hotel, museum and shop.

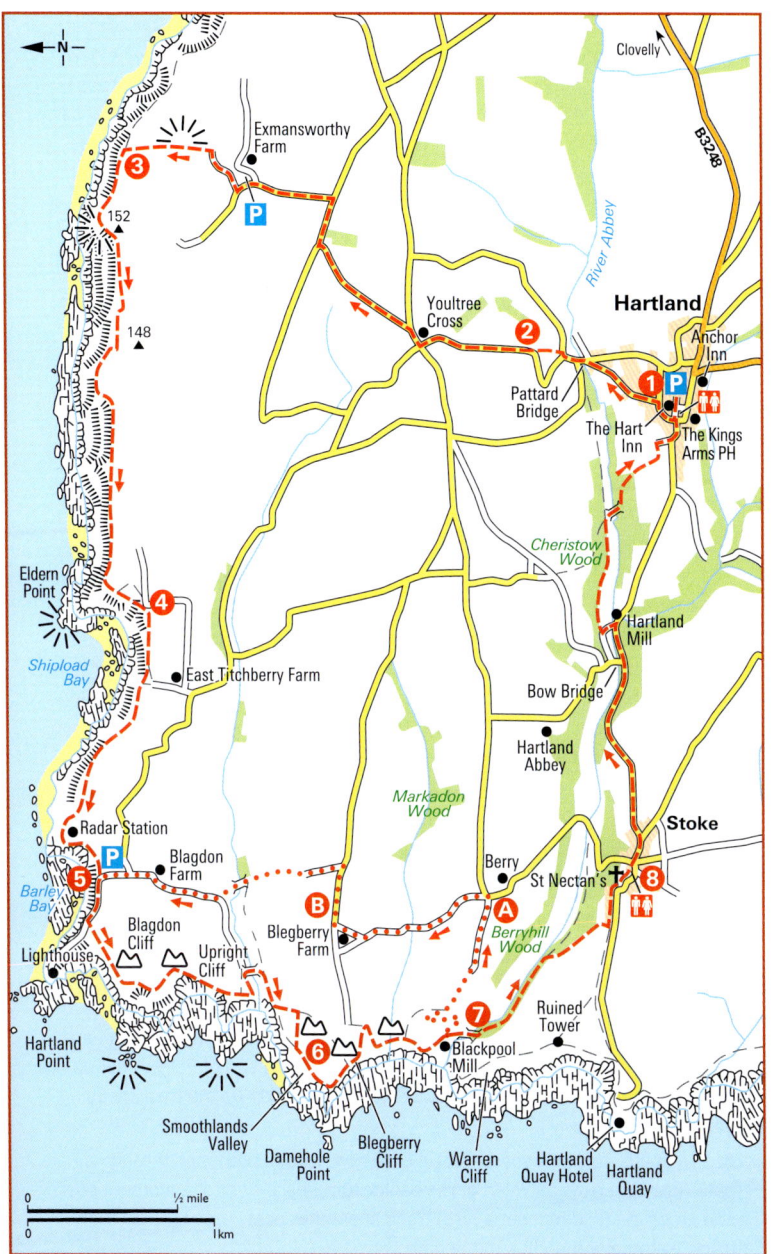

1. Leave the car park past The Hart Inn and turn right down North Street. Turn left down a narrow lane, West Ball Hill, signposted 'Hartland Point'. Cross Pattard Bridge then bear right. Just past a lane to the right, take the footpath right up steps and through a gate/stile. Walk to the top right corner of the field and over the bank to rejoin the lane.

2. Turn right and right again at Youltree Cross. After a few steps turn left at Moor Cross, signposted 'Exmansworthy'. The lane bears right; take the next lane left ('No Through Road'). Pass Exmansworthy Farm; turn right through the car park on to a grassy path, and cross a stile to a green lane. This ends at a stile into open fields. Follow the sign left, then go straight ahead to the coast path.

3. Go left over a stile, soon crossing another, then a footbridge. A run of fields with stiles/gates follows; pass a junction (Exmansworthy left). Continue past Eldern Point and Shipload Bay.

4. Pass a sign to East Titchberry. Follow the coast path on, passing the radar station at Barley Bay.

5. Follow the coast path through the car park (helicopter flights to Lundy) to pass the gates to the lighthouse (closed). Take the steep, narrow, concrete path left, then left again onto Blagdon Cliff, then Upright Cliff. Descend steeply into a combe then cross the stream via a footbridge/gate. Steep steps lead up the other side to a path junction. Follow the coast path right, soon descending into the Smoothlands Valley.

6. Climb steeply on to Blegberry Cliff. Descend carefully into the next combe and cross the stream via a gate, then up the other side and over a stile. Keep uphill through a gate, then descend to the combe at Blackpool Mill.

7. Pass behind the cottage, and cross the stream. (For Hartland Quay Hotel stay on the coast path, then follow the road back to Stoke and Hartland.) To complete the walk turn left, signed 'Stoke', through woodland. Follow the left edge of the field, climbing to a gate. The footpath ahead leads over a stile into St Nectan's churchyard. Leave via the lychgate.

8. Follow the road ahead. Before Hartland Mill turn left on a footpath. At the track turn right; keep ahead, then turn right as signed to cross the river and ascend through woodland. Follow a fenced path to a road. Turn right, then left into Hartland.

Shortening the walk If tackling a walk of 10 miles (16.1km) is not for you, try this shorter route, which still takes in the magnificent coastline south of Hartland Point – but remember – no coast path walks in this part of Devon are easy.

This alternative route starts from the car park (fee payable) at Blagdon Farm. Follow the main walk from Point 5 (Barley Bay) to the end of Point 7, but do not turn right after Blackpool Mill cottage: keep straight on up the track, heading inland (signed 'Berry').

At a footpath sign turn sharp left up a narrow hedged path then through a gate. The path runs between gorse banks; turn sharp right at a footpath post and cross the field to meet a farm track at another post. Turn right up the track, eventually though a metal gate.

As Berry is approached there are wonderful views to the right of the 14th-century church at Stoke. The track meets a lane via a gate on a sharp bend at Point A; turn immediately left through a gate and continue down a green lane. The lane descends into a combe, then climbs to Blegberry Farm. As buildings appear ahead bear right uphill to join a tarmac drive, and up to a T-junction (the farmyard is left). Turn right, Point B; after 350yds (217m) turn left through a gate and down a green lane, signed 'To public bridleway'. This runs steeply downhill to cross a stream on a footbridge, then follows the stream briefly (a vision of beautiful wild flowers in spring).

Pass through a gate and at the footpath post and path junction turn right. Follow the bridleway to Blagdon uphill, through a gate and field, then a gate and track, past the farmyard. Continue up the drive; at the junction keep ahead, soon descending to the car park.

Where to eat and drink
The Hartland Quay Hotel can be reached on foot or by car (toll charge in summer). Hartland has a range of pubs, and sandwiches and pasties are available at The Pop-in stores. You can also get fish and chips.

What to see
Look out for Lundy – best seen from near the lighthouse. You can take a day trip by boat from either Bideford or Ilfracombe (seasonal, depending on tides) or by helicopter from Hartland Point. Every boat trip is tinged with the added edge that changing sea conditions might prevent you from getting there at all – or to get home again.

While you're there
Hartland Abbey, passed on Point 8, dates from 1157 and has been a family home since 1539. The delightful gardens were designed by Gertrude Jekyll and the woodland walk, leading to a spectacular cove, is particularly lovely in spring.

45 CLOVELLY AND THE COAST

DISTANCE/TIME	6 miles (9.7km) / 2hrs 30min
ASCENT/GRADIENT	410ft (125m) / ▲▲▲
PATHS	Grassy coast path, woodland and farm tracks, several stiles
LANDSCAPE	Farmland, wooded coast path and deep combes
SUGGESTED MAP	OS Explorer 126 Clovelly & Hartland
START/FINISH	Grid reference: SS285259
DOG FRIENDLINESS	Keep on lead near livestock and unfenced cliffs
PARKING	National Trust car park at Brownsham
PUBLIC TOILETS	In the visitor centre at the car park in Clovelly

Everyone's heard about Clovelly. It's an extraordinary place – almost a folly itself – best seen very early in the morning, or at the end of the day when most visitors have gone home. Clinging precariously to the wooded cliffs on the long, virtually uninhabited stretch of inhospitable coastline between Bideford and Hartland Point, it has a timeless feel if you see it 'out of office hours', or in midwinter. Once famous as the village where donkeys were used to carry goods – and people – from the quay up the perilously steep cobbled village street (the bed of an old watercourse), today it is best known as a tourist trap. Most people drive to the village and are drawn into the Visitor Centre car park at the top – but it's much more satisfying, and more fitting to Clovelly's situation, to walk in along the coast path from the National Trust lands at Brownsham to the west. The two 17th-century farmhouses of Lower and Higher Brownsham (now holiday accommodation) lie just inland from one of the most unspoiled sections of the coastline. Although the walk is often under trees, you can still hear the pull and drag of the waves on the shingly beach far below.

Charles Kingsley, social reformer and author of *Westward Ho!* and *The Water Babies*, lived in Clovelly as a child when his father was rector of All Saints Church. Clovelly featured heavily in *Westward Ho!*, published in 1855, and the world suddenly became aware of this remote village's existence. Up until then it had been reliant on herring fishing for its main source of income. Charles Dickens also mentioned Clovelly in *A Message from the Sea* (1860).

Clovelly Court dates from around 1740, when the Hamlyns bought the manor from the Carys, but was remodelled in Gothic style in 1790–95. The gardens open daily from 10am to 4pm, and there is a small admission fee. The restored 15th-century All Saints Church has a Norman porch, dating from around 1300, and many monuments to the Cary and Hamlyn families. Sir James Hamlyn, who died in 1829, was responsible for the Hobby Drive, which runs for 3 miles (4.8km) along the cliffs east of Clovelly, and from which you get fantastic views of the harbour below.

1. Follow the footpath from the back of the car park, signed 'Breckland Woods'. Pass through a gate and turn right as signed towards the coast path; soon pass a bench at a path junction. Keep ahead over a stile; walk on to cross another onto the coast path.

2. Go right through a gate (signed 'Mouthmill') into a field on Brownsham Cliff, with good views ahead to Morte Point. Keep along the left edge, through a gate, down steps and along the left edge of the next field. Cross a stile and zigzag downhill through woodland. At the bottom turn left towards the beach, passing a lime kiln.

3. Follow the coast path across the rocky beach. Clamber up a gully to meet a track on a bend; walk uphill (left fork).

4. Eventually follow coast path signs left, then immediately right. Go left up wooden steps to follow a narrow, wooded path steeply uphill towards the open cliff at Gallantry Bower, with a 400ft (122m) drop into the sea. Re-enter woodland and follow the coast path to pass the 'Angel's Wings' folly. Where a path leads straight on to the church, keep left following signs and later via a gate through the edge of Clovelly Court estate. Enter laurel woods via a kissing gate. The path winds down and up past a stone shelter, then through a kissing gate into a field. Keep along the left edge to meet the road at a big gate. Follow coast path signs on to the road ahead that leads to the path to Clovelly village, below the Visitor Centre.

5. Leave the coast path and walk up deep, steep, ancient Wrinkleberry Lane (right of Hobby Drive ahead) to a lane, past the former school building and on to meet the road. Turn right, downhill.

6. Where the road bends right keep ahead on a path parallel to the drive to Clovelly Court. At the church turn left; keep ahead on the lane towards Court Farm, soon passing through the farm. Once past the buildings keep ahead on a track between fields. Pass through a plantation, then bear diagonally right downhill across a field.

7. Go through a gate to the left of the far corner bridlepath. At the end of the next field go through a gate into a plantation, downhill.

8. Turn left on the forest track, following bridleway signs. Turn right as signed to cross the stream and up the long, gradually ascending track to Lower Brownsham Farm. Turn left for the car park.

Where to eat and drink
There are several pubs in Clovelly, including the Red Lion Hotel on the quay.

What to see
Have a look at the charming cove at Buck's Mills, signposted off the A39 at Buck's Cross. There's free parking in the wooded valley just above the village. When herring and mackerel fishing declined in the 19th century local men travelled daily to Lundy to work in the quarry. The popularity of the surname Braund in the village was once thought to result from seven Spanish sailors, wrecked offshore at the time of the Spanish Armada.

While you're there
While in the area take a look at the little working port of Bideford, described thus by Kingsley in *Westward Ho!*: '...pleasantly it has stood there for now, perhaps, 800 years'. Bideford is an unassuming, pleasant place to explore, with an interesting pannier market and ancient 24-arch bridge spanning the Torridge.

NORTHAM BURROWS COUNTRY PARK

DISTANCE/TIME	3.25 miles (5.3km) / 1hr 30min
ASCENT/GRADIENT	Negligible
PATHS	Beach, pathless grassland
LANDSCAPE	Flat coastline
SUGGESTED MAP	OS Explorer 139 Bideford, Ilfracombe & Barnstaple
START/FINISH	Grid reference: SS438305
DOG FRIENDLINESS	Livestock and wildlife, so under control at all times; no dogs on beach 1 May–end September
PARKING	Sandymere car park
PUBLIC TOILETS	The Burrows Centre (when open)

Northam Burrows, a Site of Special Scientific Interest, is an extraordinary and unexpected feature on the more usually rugged north Devon coast: 625 acres (253ha) of level, windswept, grassy coastal plain jutting out into the Taw–Torridge Estuary, fringed by sand dunes, tidal mudflats and saltmarsh, the haunt of sheep, horses and wading birds. It is also used by walkers, and is home to the Royal North Devon Golf Club. The route here follows the Coast Path round the rim of the country park, and returns across the neck of the peninsula, weaving around the golf club greens (fenced off to protect them from livestock).

The Burrows are made up of a number of varied habitats, each supporting different flora and fauna. The dunes behind the pebble ridge run along the northwestern side of the Burrows, and separate the Atlantic from the coastal grassland. On the fixed dunes (behind the mobile windblown ones nearer the shore) you may see signs of badgers and rabbits, and ground-nesting birds such as wheatears and skylarks. The grassland areas are grazed by sheep and horses, and criss-crossed by 15 miles (24km) of drainage ditches. Skern, passed at Point 3, is an area of mudflat colonised by saltmarsh, and serves as a feeding ground for waders and wintering birds such as Brent geese.

The village of Westward Ho! (from where the Pebbleridge car park is accessed) is a strange mix of large Victorian houses, static caravan parks and contemporary apartment blocks. The settlement developed post-1855, following the publication of *Westward Ho!*, a novel by Charles Kingsley (1819–75). Kingsley spent his childhood at Clovelly, a few miles west along the coast.

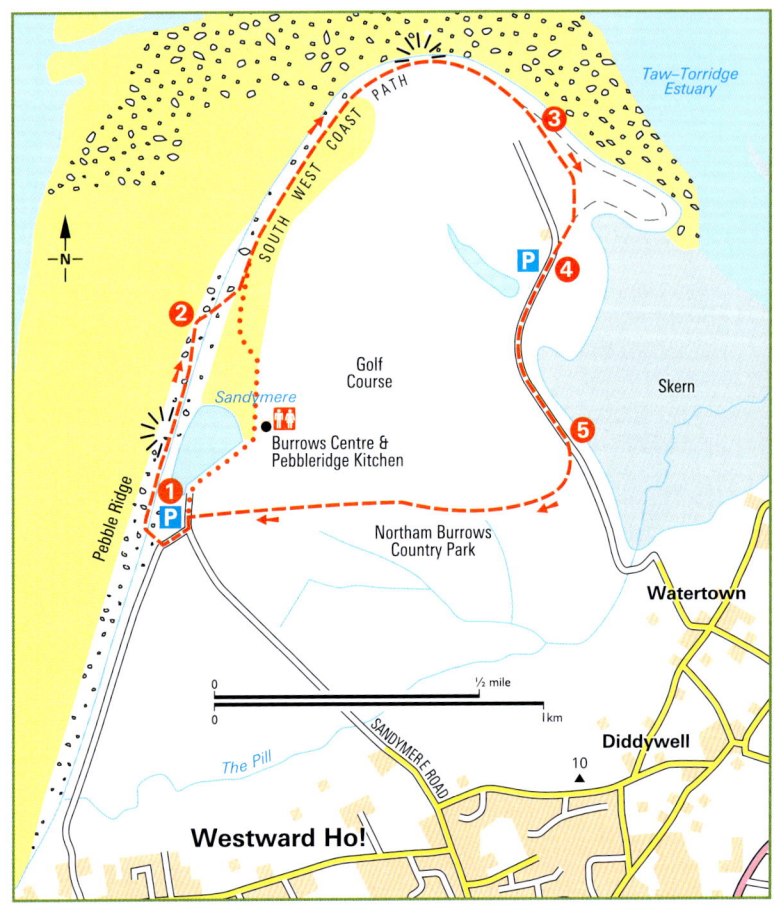

1. From the car park there's a choice of two routes. At low tide cross the walkway over the pebble ridge by the information board, and turn right along the 2-mile (3.2km) long Westward Ho! beach, passing low dunes, with views towards Lundy (left). Past low sandy cliffs the ridge bears right; look for a gap in the dunes, beyond which you may spot a Coast Path post by the 6th hole on the Royal North Devon golf course. Alternatively, follow Coast Path signs along the track past Sandymere (a seasonal pool), then between the dunes and Burrows Centre, to reach the post. (The centre is open from Easter weekend to the end of October.)

2. Pass through the dunes to reach the post, and turn left along the edge of the golf course, following yellow arrows past the 7th and 8th holes of the golf course and along the Taw–Torridge estuary, with views to Braunton Burrows. Cross a level grassy area, with views ahead to Appledore and Instow on the opposite bank of the Torridge.

3. At a Coast Path signpost turn right towards a line of seats overlooking Skern tidal marsh. At the edge of the marsh bear right across level grassland, aiming for a parking area.

4. From the parking area follow the access lane along the edge of Skern, a magnet for birdlife on account of its rich food supply. The best time to spot waders is one to two hours before high tide.

5. At the third 'sleeping policeman' road bump turn right down the grassy bank, keeping to the left of a broad, grassy sward. Initially head for the cliffs to the west of Westward Ho!, then keep ahead along the edge of the golf course, aiming for the car park which will be seen in the distance. You'll cross a fairway as you return to the car park, so watch out for golf balls.

Where to eat and drink
The Pebbleridge Kitchen at the Burrows Centre is in a great location in the heart of the Country Park serving snacks and hot/cold drinks. The friendly and comfortable Village Inn is reputed to be the oldest building in Westward Ho!, dating from 1750 when it was a farm, and serves good home-made food.

What to see
Look across the estuary to the high sand dunes of Braunton Burrows, designated (with the estuary, Northam Burrows and Braunton Marsh) the UK's first UNESCO Biosphere Reserve in 2002 for its unique flora and fauna – over 500 species of flowering plant have been identified. Braunton's Great Field is a rare example of a medieval field system.

While you're there
Explore the village of Appledore – a trading and fishing centre since the 14th century, on the banks of the Torridge. It's a wonderful mix of narrow lanes and drangs (alleyways), old fishermen's cottages, and artists' studios. Long famous for boatbuilding, Appledore's shipyard is still active today. A passenger ferry crosses the Torridge to Instow.

NORTH DEVON COAST CLASSIC

DISTANCE/TIME	8 miles (12.9km) / 4hrs
ASCENT/GRADIENT	426ft (130m) / ▲▲▲
PATHS	Fields, tracks and coast path, many stiles
LANDSCAPE	Rolling farmland, wooded valleys and cliff tops
SUGGESTED MAP	OS Explorer 139 Bideford, Ilfracombe & Barnstaple
START/FINISH	Grid reference: SS457452
DOG FRIENDLINESS	Keep on lead near livestock and unfenced cliffs
PARKING	Mortehoe Station Road car park, Mortehoe
PUBLIC TOILETS	Lee Bay and car park at Mortehoe

This walk is included because it is simply beautiful. Although this part of the North Devon coast is very popular with holidaymakers, you can escape pretty quickly. Just a few minutes' walk from the car park you will see tremendous views of the coast opening up to the left. On a clear day you can see the Gower Peninsula in South Wales, and within half an hour you've left civilisation behind. It's a wonderfully varied route, too. You'll pass the ancient farmstead at Damage Barton to cross a lovely area of unimproved meadowland and penetrate deep down into the wooded Borough Valley to discover the secluded cove at Lee Bay. This is followed by a tough walk along the coast path to the jagged headland of Morte Point, off which the white horses of the strong tidal race rage. It's a walk that shouldn't be rushed – take it gently and revel in the peace and solitude.

Lee Bay is a very special place. The small village, with many cottages dating from the 16th and 17th centuries, lies along a narrow, winding lane running down to an attractive rocky cove. It's one of those places that many people never discover. Its sheltered position has encouraged a wealth of flowers, including hedges of naturalised fuchsia bushes.

Tennyson said of St Mary Magdalene Church in Mortehoe 'that tower of strength which stood four-square to all the winds that blew', and you certainly get a feeling of solidity when you look at the little Norman church, with its tower dating from around 1270. In a sheltered position just inland from Morte Point, it was probably founded in 1170 by Sir William de Tracey, and it may be his tomb that lies in the south transcept. The church is dark, pretty and simple. There is some glorious stained glass, and a superb mosaic chancel arch, completed in 1905.

1. Take the lane opposite the car park signposted to 'Lighthouse & Lee'. Pass North Morte Farm Camping & Caravanning Park to reach the lane end at the private road to Bull Point lighthouse.

2. Follow the footpath to the right of the right-hand gate across Easewell Farm Holiday Park. Continue ahead between buildings as signed (to Lee); pass a pond and through a gate. Bear left uphill across the field to a footpath post, and continue along a track uphill to a gate/stile into a field. Keep the hedge on the left, descend through a gate; keep along the left edge of the next field, and through a gate/stile on to a tarmac drive.

3. Bear left, following signs through Damage Barton Farm, bearing right as signed (Burrough Woods) at the end of the buildings. After a few steps a footpath sign directs you left. Soon after, another sign points right, then left through a gate. Bear right uphill through gorse to reach a footpath post. Go right towards another signpost, fork right, then follow the track through a gate. Head up the field to the next signpost atop a small hill on the left. Turn left through a gate, then bear half right across the field to a lane via a stile.

4. Cross the lane and over a stile into an 'Open Access area'. Follow the footpath across the meadow. Cross over a stile and go steeply downhill into the wooded Borough Valley. At the bottom turn left over a stile.

5. Follow the stream down the valley to the bottom of the wood; turn right over a bridge and stile. Cross the field then a stile and turn right up the lane to The Grampus Inn.

6. Retrace your steps down the path past toilets to the rocky cove at Lee Bay. Turn left steeply uphill and follow the coast path right through a gate. Follow the path down steps to pass the access to Sandy Cove. Continue on to reach a gate/footbridge/gate in a deep combe, then a steep ascent. A gate leads to a descent into another combe and rocky Bennetts Mouth. Cross the footbridge/gate and continue across cliffs above Bull Point, passing to the left of the lighthouse. If the tide's out when you reach Lee Bay, you can make a short diversion to the route to get to Sandy Cove. When you reach Lee Bay, walk across the beach left, near the cliff, and along a deep gully through the rocks – with wonderful rockpools – to reach Sandy Cove. You rejoin the main route by climbing up a steep flight of wooden steps to the coast path.

7. Follow the coast path towards Morte Point. Go through a gate into a small combe – 91 steps ascend the other side. Cross Windy Lag and go through a gate to reach Rockham Bay, where steps lead to the beach. Ascend steps and follow the path on to Morte Point, passing through two gates on the way.

8. Follow the coast path past Windy Cove. Go through a gate, walk past Grunta Beach, then follow signs left, parallel to the road and steeply uphill, to regain the road via a gate by The Old Chapel. Turn left uphill to return to the car park.

Where to eat and drink
The Grampus Inn at Lee Bay was originally a farm; the Fuchsia Tea Garden is found a little further upvalley. In Mortehoe refreshment can be enjoyed in The Chichester Arms or The Ship Aground.

A CIRCUIT INCLUDING HELE BAY AND COMYN

DISTANCE/TIME	3.5 miles (5.7km) / 2hrs
ASCENT/GRADIENT	394ft (120m) / ▲▲
PATHS	Undulating coast path, tracks, quiet lanes; steep and sometimes slippery descent to Hele Bay
LANDSCAPE	Town, coast, wooded valley
SUGGESTED MAP	OS Explorer 139 Bideford, Ilfracombe & Barnstaple
START/FINISH	Grid reference: SS523477
DOG FRIENDLINESS	Lead required on roads
PARKING	Cove car park at Ilfracombe harbour (pay-and-display)
PUBLIC TOILETS	Ilfracombe harbour and Hele Bay

Originally a market town and fishing port, the hilly town of Ilfracombe developed as a holiday resort in the mid-19th century, with a further boost provided by the coming of the London and South Western Railway in 1874. Ilfracombe is a real mix of faded grandeur and contemporary development – epitomised by Damien Hirst's controversial steel and bronze Verity sculpture, which has stood guard over the harbour mouth since 2012, beneath St Nicholas Chapel, a 15th-century votive chapel for fisherman and sailors set on Lantern Hill. This bizarre dichotomy can be enjoyed from Hillsborough, the site of an Iron Age hill fort, on this walk.

The North Devon Voluntary Marine Conservation Area extends for 15 miles (24km) from Hangman Point on the edge of Exmoor in the east to Woolacombe Sand in the west. It includes the section encountered on this walk, from the cliff base out to the 20m-depth contour. The rocky foreshores of this part of the coast, largely inaccessible on foot, are home to some of richest plant and animal communities in the country, thriving at a point where the colder North Atlantic waters meet warmer southern waters. Marine species found here include the wonderfully named snakelocks anenome and edible periwinkle.

The sheltered beach at Hele Bay, today overlooked by holiday caravans, is very much the domain of the bucket-and-spade brigade. But 200 years ago the scene would have been very different, when coal from South Wales was landed on the shore to feed the lime kilns that once sat at the back of the beach to produce fertiliser for local farmers. There are records of three ships still landing coal here from the start of the 20th century right up to World War II.

1. Walk along the right side of the harbour, soon passing through the Marine Drive car park. At the top exit, where the road narrows, bear left downhill on a path (note a small blue Coast Path sign on a lamppost).

2. At a junction of paths, follow Coast Path signs half left on a tarmac way to pass the skate park. Where the path ahead descends to Rapparee Cove, bear right steeply uphill, alongside a hedge. Meet a fence at the top, and bear left through a barrier to ascend through woodland. At the next junction turn right as signed (yellow arrow and acorn).

3. At the next crossroads follow the Coast Path left up steps into Hillsborough Local Nature Reserve. Follow Coast Path signs, climbing steadily (a grassy path running parallel on the left also leads to Point 4), eventually enjoying views over the Hele Valley. The path swings back towards the sea to reach a bench with excellent harbour views.

4. Keep following Coast Path signs, to descend eventually through woodland. Turn sharp right downhill just before a viewpoint above Broadstrand Beach. Zig-zag downhill to reach the promenade at Hele Bay. Turn right, then right again up Beach Road to the A399.

5. Cross over with care, and head along a narrow, wooded footpath to pass through the grounds of The Old Corn Mill and Tea Room. Keep ahead through a gate and go up a narrow track to a lane. Turn right.

6. Where the lane bears right keep straight ahead, signed to Comyn, soon turning left up a lane and climbing steadily. The lane reduces to a track; where it bears left, keep ahead through a gate on a narrow, hedged path – Cat Lane – to emerge through a gate by houses at Comyn. Turn right to reach a path junction.

7. Turn right, signed to Ilfracombe. Pass Chambercombe Manor (open from April to the end of September, and said to be haunted). The lane climbs gently out of this hidden valley to meet a road on a bend among houses. Keep ahead and follow the road downhill to the A399.

8. Cross over and turn left. Turn first right, opposite The Thatched Inn (an unusual building with outside seating), and follow the road to the Marine Drive car park and back to the harbour.

Where to eat and drink
This walk has plenty of opportunities for an ice cream or cup of tea. The Old Corn Mill and Tea Room at Hele Mill (seasonal) is a lovely spot, dating from the 16th century and rescued from dereliction in 1973. The mill is open to the public where you can see wheat being ground. Ye Olde Manor Buttery can be found at Chambercombe Manor (seasonal).

What to see
The tucked-away coves around Ilfracombe were once home to illicit smuggling activity, as evidenced by the names of some: Brandy Cove, just west of Ilfracombe harbour, and Samson's Bay, to the east, where a man called Samson hid smuggled goods in a cave. Contraband may also have been stored at Chambercombe Manor.

While you're there
Visit Combe Martin, said to have the longest village street in England, at the western end of Exmoor National Park. Traces of medieval strip systems can be seen, and silver mining dates back to the late 13th century. The village is famed for its 'Hunting of the Earl of Rone' celebration, which takes place over the Spring Bank Holiday weekend in late May.

HEDDON VALLEY ON EXMOOR

DISTANCE/TIME	6 miles (9.7km) / 3hrs
ASCENT/GRADIENT	787ft (240m) / ▲▲▲
PATHS	Woodland tracks, exposed coast path and quiet lanes
LANDSCAPE	Deep, wooded river valleys and very high cliffs
SUGGESTED MAP	OS Explorer OL9 Exmoor
START/FINISH	Grid reference: SS655481
DOG FRIENDLINESS	Keep on lead near livestock and unfenced cliffs
PARKING	National Trust car park, Heddon Valley
PUBLIC TOILETS	Opposite car park

Within the Exmoor National Park, yet still in Devon, the deeply wooded Heddon Valley, leading to the stark cleft in the coastline at Heddon's Mouth, is a spectacular sight. There is no obvious main route into the valley, which is accessed via narrow lanes from either the A399 (south of Combe Martin) or the A39 between Blackmoor Gate and Lynton/Lynmouth.

While you're in the area take a look around the pretty village of Parracombe. Stop for a while to have a look at Parracombe old church, frozen in time since the late 18th century when a new church was built nearer the village, then follow the course of the Heddon river as it descends through beautiful oak woodland to reach the sea at Heddon's Mouth.

The National Trust owns 2,000 acres (810ha) of land here, much of which is a Site of Special Scientific Interest. The extensive oak woodlands, deep combes, coastal heath and some of the highest coastal hills in England combine to produce one of the most magnificent landscape areas in Devon. The spectacularly steep scree-covered slopes of Heddon's Mouth Cleave – through which the South West Coast Path makes its way – rise to a staggering 820ft (250m), and Great Hangman, the highest coastal hill in southern England at over 1,040ft (318m) lies just beyond Holdstone Down to the west. Exmoor, unlike Dartmoor, runs right up to the coast, and the cliff scenery towards Combe Martin on this walk is superb. There's no access to the sea between Heddon's Mouth and Combe Martin, 5 miles (8km) to the west. The National Trust information centre in the Heddon Valley is open daily from 10.30am to 5pm from April to the end of October.

There is a huge amount of wildlife interest here. The West Exmoor coastline holds one of only two colonies of razorbill, guillemot and kittiwake in north Devon. In the western oakwoods – unique to the west of Britain – you may find green and lesser spotted woodpeckers, pied flycatchers, wood warblers and nuthatches. The Heddon Valley is managed by English Nature to encourage butterflies, in particular the rare high brown fritillary, and dark green and silver washed fritillaries.

1. Walk towards the Hunters Inn. Bear right past the building to walk along a wooded track signed 'Heddon's Mouth'. At the junction keep left, signed 'Heddon's Mouth only'. Where the path splits later keep left, close to the river. Pass a stone bridge over the river and keep ahead.

2. Turn left over a wooden footbridge, then turn right and walk towards the coast to reach the 19th-century lime kiln above the rocky beach. Retrace your steps inland but stay on the west bank (river left) to pick up the coast path to Combe Martin. Pass through a gate, and keep ahead until a sign to Combe Martin directs you right, sharply uphill.

3. A steep zig-zag climb is rewarded with amazing views across the valley and inland. Keep going along the narrow path, which runs parallel to the valley to reach the coast above Heddon's Mouth, then turns left to run towards Peter Rock. The cliffs here are over 650ft (200m) high and sheer, and the path is narrow and exposed – take care. Eventually the path runs inland to meet a wall and a coast path post.

4. Turn right. Follow the coast path west for about 0.75 miles (1.2km), then pass through a gate, turn right, then through another gate to rejoin the cliff edge. Go through a gate above Neck Wood, cross the next field and pass through a gate on to open access land.

5. Keep ahead to reach a path junction; turn left, signed 'County Road'. Head uphill, with the bank left, to reach the rough parking area and lane at Holdstone Down Cross, on the edge of Trentishoe Down.

6. Turn immediately left along the narrow lane, following signs for Trentishoe church (the signpost here misleadingly points back the way you have come). Walk down the lane to find the church above you on the left – this is a good place for a break.

7. Continue downhill below Town Cottage to pass the point where there is a 'To coast path' sign pointing left. Walk straight on down Trentishoe Hill (this lane is unsuitable for vehicles) which runs through wooded Trentishoe Cleave.

8. Turn left at the valley bottom by pretty cottages. Walk along the lane past a footpath sign to the Heddon Valley on the left, pass Harry's Orchard and cross the Blackmoor Water, and then the Heddon river just before the Hunters Inn. Turn right to find your car.

Shortening the walk If the rigours of the coast path get too much for you, you can escape from the cliffs soon after Peter Rock, and take this shorter way to the simple church at Trentishoe.

At Point 4 on the main walk, turn left, signed 'Trentishoe Church'. This lovely, grassy, level path runs inland 720ft (220m) above the valley of the River Heddon, and the views over the deep combes that join the main valley are glorious. It's a very easy walk, and a welcome relief after the coast path.

The path meets the lane at Point A (Point 7 – 'access to coast path' sign). Turn right up the lane and, after 200yds (183m), you will see St Peter's Church above the lane on the right. It's hard to work out why there should be a church here – it's in the middle of nowhere – but 96 people are recorded as living here in 1891. The church is mentioned in the Episcopal Register of 1260. The tiny castellated tower dates from the 15th century, and it is thought that at one time smugglers' contraband was hidden within it. Until alterations were made at the end of the 19th century this was the smallest church in Devon. There's a wonderful musician's gallery, built in 1771, and a lovely piece of information about the first organ, which was introduced in 1861 on condition that 'worthy parishioners are not asked to subscribe as they would expect to be allowed to join in the singing'. The hamlet also featured in R D Blackmore's novel *Clara Vaughan* which was published in 1864 and set in Trentishoe. To rejoin the main route follow Points 7 and 8 from the church back to your car.

Where to eat and drink
The Fox and Goose Inn at Parracombe is an interesting building, with good food. The Hunters Inn, built in 1897 on the site of the original thatched inn is owned by the National Trust, and both the food served and the rooms available to stay in, are of a high standard.

What to see
Exmoor ponies – the closest native breed to a truly wild equine – have been used on these coastal hills (and elsewhere on Exmoor) to encourage regeneration of the heather moorland. Visit The Exmoor Pony Centre near Dulverton to find out more.

While you're there
Have a look at another extraordinary piece of coastal landscape, at the Valley of Rocks just west of Lynton. This craggy dry valley is different from anywhere else on Exmoor, and is characterised by jagged sandstone tors, the result of intense weathering processes over thousands of years. There is a pleasant walk into Lynton on the North Walk along the cliff edge from here. Look out for the feral goats that live among the rocky slopes. Goats were reintroduced here in the 19th century after earlier occupation in the 17th, and are now something of a tourist attraction (though local residents may think differently).

WATERSMEET AND THE LYNMOUTH FLOODS

DISTANCE/TIME	4 miles (6.4km) / 2hrs
ASCENT/GRADIENT	164ft (50m) / ▲
PATHS	Riverside paths, some stony
LANDSCAPE	Deep, narrow, wooded river valleys
SUGGESTED MAP	OS Explorer OL9 Exmoor
START/FINISH	Grid reference: SS740477
DOG FRIENDLINESS	Dogs should be kept under control at all times
PARKING	National Trust car park near Hillsford Bridge
PUBLIC TOILETS	At Watersmeet (National Trust) when café is open

Watersmeet, where the Hoar Oak Water and East Lyn River converge, is a very popular spot for visitors to this part of the Exmoor National Park, and the Watersmeet car park, within a stone's throw of the beauty spot on the A39, is nearly always busy. There is a much more satisfying – and quieter – way of getting there, via an easy and scenic walk that skirts round the busiest paths.

The National Trust owns 4,000 acres (1,600ha) of glorious countryside in West Exmoor – rocky cliffs, steep oak-wooded valleys, open moorland and rushing rivers. Much of the area has been designated as a Site of Special Scientific Interest and there are 70 miles (113km) of footpaths. But in the early 18th century Daniel Defoe described Exmoor as 'a filthie barren waste', in keeping with contemporary views of wilderness areas. Few would agree with that notion today, but the landscape is certainly surprisingly dramatic for southern England – the East Lyn has cut 600ft (200m) into the moorland plateau. Its dramatic incised course is best viewed from the route of the Two Moors Way, which passes through Combe Park before running high above Myrtleberry Cleave on its way to its final destination, Lynmouth. This 102-mile (163km) long-distance walking route links Ivybridge with Lynmouth.

Later in the 18th century popular views of landscape changed. The appeal of the Romantic Movement – promoted by such poets as Wordsworth and Coleridge – meant that landscapes such as Watersmeet and Lynmouth became fashionable and sought after. Revd W S Halliday bought the site in 1829, and built Watersmeet House as a secluded retreat and hunting lodge. Today it provides the perfect setting for a picturesque break.

On 15 August 1952, a 40ft (12m) wall of water surged downriver into Lynmouth. Houses and bridges were swept away by the torrents of water, boulders and debris, and 34 people died. This followed a prolonged spell of exceptionally heavy rainfall, culminating in 9in (228mm) of rain falling on Exmoor's highest ground – The Chains – in 24 hours (one of the heaviest periods of rainfall ever recorded in the British Isles). Over 3 billion gallons (13.6 billion litres) of water fell into the area drained by the two rivers, with disastrous consequences.

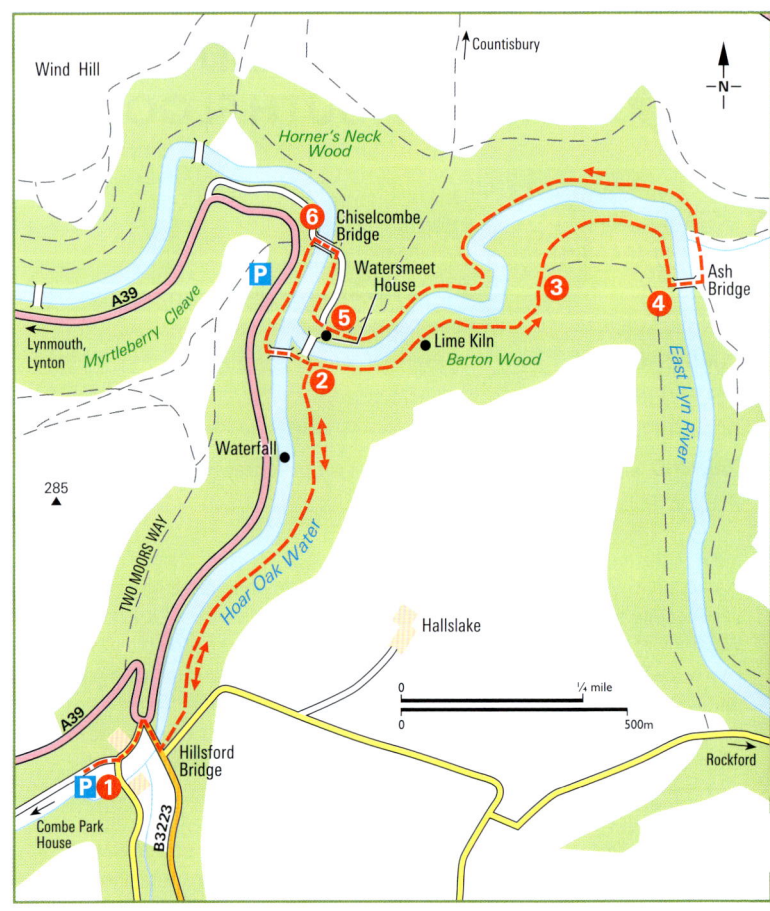

1. Leave the car park and turn left, then right to cross Hillsford Bridge. Turn immediately left through a gate to follow the right bank of the Hoar Oak Water, slightly downhill (signed 'Watersmeet'). The river along this stretch is particularly spectacular after heavy rainfall. Pass a waterfall and viewing point, and soon reach steps (left) leading to Watersmeet.

2. Ignore the steps and follow the path, bearing right, up the right bank of the East Lyn River, passing another path to Watersmeet. Soon pass an old lime kiln, once used to burn limestone brought to the coast by boat from South Wales. Here, Countisbury Common rises to 1,125ft (343m) above the steep-sided river valley. Continue along the path, which winds its way through beautiful hanging oak woodland to reach a junction.

3. Take the 'footpath to Rockford' ahead through Barton Wood, descending through a beech glade to regain the river bank. When Ash Bridge is reached, cross to the opposite bank.

4. Turn left, signed 'Watersmeet', soon passing a path that climbs up to Countisbury. Lovely Crook Pool is passed at a bend in the river; continue along the narrow, undulating path, which climbs quite high above the water before the final descent to Watersmeet House.

5. Follow the river bank past the house, bearing right around the garden fence. Continue along the track down the East Lyn, then turn left over high-arched Chiselcombe Bridge, which was funded by public subscription after the former bridge was destroyed in the famous flood.

6. Once over the bridge turn left, and walk back up the river bank, and up steps. Bear left downhill to cross over the Hoar Oak Water on a wooden footbridge just above the meeting point of the two rivers. Ascend the steps right, following signs 'Hillsford Bridge', then turn right again and retrace your steps upriver to the bridge and back to Combe Park.

Where to eat and drink
The National Trust café at Watersmeet House is open from early March to early November (and February school half term holiday), and the garden provides a wonderful setting for tea. There is a large range of cafés, pubs and fish-and-chip establishments just down the road at Lynmouth and Lynton, but both can become extremely crowded during the holiday season.

What to see
Both red and roe deer can be spotted in the woodlands around Watersmeet and the nearby moors. The red deer is Britain's largest native land animal, and its main stronghold lies in the Highlands of Scotland. The smaller roe deer are extremely shy, and most likely to be seen at dawn or dusk. The bucks have small antlers, with short branches, and the species is characterised by a white patch on the rump, easily visible when the deer is startled and runs off.

While you're there
Take a ride on the Lynton & Lynmouth Cliff Railway, the only water powered railway in the country. The short trip on the railway saves a steep zigzag climb of around 450ft (152m).

Explore the UK at RatedTrips.com

AA